The Big Lie

The Big Lie

The Big Lie

Hale Boggs, Lucille May Grace, and Leander Perez in 1951

By Garry Boulard

PELICAN PUBLISHING COMPANY
Gretna 2001

Library of Congress Cataloging-in-Publication Data

Boulard, Garry
    The big lie: Hale Boggs, Lucille May Grace, and Leander Perez
in 1951/Garry Boulard.
    p. cm.
    Includes index.
    ISBN 1-56554-868-X (pbk.)
    1. Boggs, Hale, 1914-1972. 2. Grace, Lucille May. 3. Perez
Leander 1891-1969. 4. Anti-communist movements—Louisiana—
History. 5. Louisiana—Politics and government—1951-6. Politi-
cians—Louisiana—Biography. 7. Louisiana—Race relations. 8.
Anti-communist movements—United States—History. I. Title.

F376.B68 2001
976.3'063—dc21

2001036330

Printed in Canada
Published by Pelican Publishing Company, Inc.
1000 Burmaster Street, Gretna, Louisiana 70053

*In honor of good cheer and the men and women
of the Esquivel Club*

Contents

Acknowledgments

The story of the 1951-52 Louisiana gubernatorial election and how a faraway ideology—Communism—was used to divide and destroy men on our own state's shores required the help of a large number of people whose memories form the soul of this book.

In alphabetical order, I thank the following people for being so generous with their time and help: Avery Alexander, Archie Boggs, Lindy Boggs, George Brown, Joe Cangiamilla, Maurice Clark, Reese Cleghorn, James Coleman, Walter Cowan, Helene de la Houssaye, Fred Dent, Jr., Laurence Eustis, James Fitzmorris, Norman Francis, James Gillis, Camille Gravel, John Hainkel, Rosemary James, Jess Johnson, Jr., Irvin Joseph, Abe Kupperman, Trudy Wenzel Lash, Stephen Lescher, Naomi Marshall, Robert Maloney, Joseph C. Meyers, Jr., Stuart McClendon, Ellen Bryan Moore, Claire Boggs Morrison, William Nunguesser, Revius Ortique, Trey Ourso, Edgar Poe, Ory Poret, Floyd Newlin, Barbara Rathe, Henry Sevier, Jr., Howard K. Smith, Bill Smolkin, Carlos Spaht, Moises Steeg, Ben Toledano, and Tom Wicker.

I owe, of course, a special debt to the helpful staffs of the three archives I used the most: the Special Collections Department of the Howard-Tilton Memorial Library at Tulane University, which contains all of Congressmen Hale Boggs and F. Edward Hebert's papers, as well as a good deal of material concerning far left and Socialist activism in 1930s New Orleans; the Louisiana Collection of the New Orleans Public

Library, which holds the papers of New Orleans mayors Robert Maestri and deLesseps S. Morrison, as well as several boxes of correspondence relating to Leander Perez, specifically his anti-civil rights work; and the Lower Mississippi Valley Collection of the Hill Memorial Library at Louisiana State University, which contains the valuable scrapbook collection maintained by Lucille May Grace covering the early 1930s to her 1951 gubernatorial run.

For more information on Perez's anti-civil rights activities, I also consulted with the Catholic Council on Human Relations Papers at the Amistad Collection. In tracing Hale Boggs' early days, I turned to the Biloxi Public Library in Biloxi, Mississippi, as well as the Mississippi Department of History and Archives in Jackson.

The Iberville Parish Library staff helped me with information on the Grace family; while the Washingtoniana Collection at the District of Columbia Central Library, with their very useful collection of articles from the old *Washington Star*, proved to be an informative guide for tracing Boggs' congressional career.

The staff of the clerk's office with the 19th Judicial District Court, Parish of East Baton Rouge, dug into their archives to find a transcript copy of the suit filed against Boggs by Leander Perez and Lucille May Grace.

I thank Jack Epstein, whose scholarship on Congressman Hebert spirits this work; Michael Enright, who helped obtain for me valuable congressional papers on Boggs and Perez; and David Ross for his contributions to the dust jacket design.

I also thank the following friends who listened to endless stories from me about this book, and, at least to my face, did so without complaint: Apo Aydin, Denice Bizot, June Galloway, John Lawrence, Charmaigne Padua, Susan Roberts, David Ross, John Tottenham, and Aaron Walker.

The Big Lie

The Louisiana State Capitol: Leander Perez's home away from home. (Courtesy the Louisiana Office of Tourism).

CHAPTER ONE

A Most Important Matter

A damp grayness hung over the Louisiana state capitol on the morning of October 19, 1951, as Leander Henry Perez glided down the marble corridors of a modernistic building that seemed somehow more Latin American than American. Already the hallways were thick with people, but Perez, a nimble man in a smartly cut tailored suit with a white silk handkerchief peeking out from behind his breast pocket, easily saw his way through to a pair of mammoth, twin-paneled doors that opened onto the busy House chamber.

Inside, all was chaos.

Precinct and ward heelers, reporters, lawyers, reformers, and Old Regulars fought for air in an atmosphere thick with smoke as they maneuvered their way through a snake's nest of cables and wires.

Microphones bearing the insignias of the radio stations that owned them prominently decorated a long wooden table soon to be occupied by a young, darkly handsome do-gooder from the big city: Hale Boggs, a loud 37 years old, who arrived to a fantastic clamor of support with his wife, Lindy, serenely vivacious, and their children, Barbara, 12, Tommy, 11, and Corinne, already known to everyone as "Cokie," age 7.

By any measure, this was a quintessentially American family; successful, determined, bouyant, instinctively patriotic and devotedly church-going. "They were just charming and delightful people," said Helene de la Houssaye, the daughter of prominent New Orleans attorney Arthur de la Houssaye, "and they had made a lot of friends."[1]

The de la Houssayes were most certainly Hale and Lindy's friends. That's why they made the morning drive from New Orleans to Baton Rouge that day, to appear in the House chamber with dozens, if not hundreds, of other Boggs devotees, gathering in small, agitated groups or sitting in stunned silence as they anticipated the beginning of the proceedings.

Altogether there were hundreds of people trying to pack into the House chamber—people who were summoned on a moment's notice from every corner of the state—and seats were at a premium.

Powerful and polished members of Congress who had served with Representative Boggs over the previous decade came out. So, too, did the big money crowd from Uptown New Orleans, people who had worked with him as he fought against a city choked with corruption.

Even Boggs' former classmates from Tulane University were there, girls and boys somewhat older now and more the worldwise who had engaged him in passionate debates of wide-ranging idealogical persuasions that were then the rage on campuses everywhere.

It was an irony lost on few that in the span of the fifteen years or so since they had sat under Tulane's shady trees and dreamed of storming barricades, they had become the very establishment they once railed so compellingly against. There was a judiciously healthy sprinkling of lawyers, doctors, and leaders of commerce and industry now shining in their ranks.

Photographers from the local papers, meanwhile, were ecstatic; everywhere they looked sat another Louisiana legend. Suddenly Earl Long, the current governor and a man of excessive appetites who was wearing a colorful tie with the image of a hand-painted, bright-red Confederate flag, galloped into the chamber.

Most of the people who saw him clapped. Some whooped and cheered. And still others—even people who instinctively disdained Uncle Earl—could not help but somehow laugh.

Long smiled widely, shook hands all around, took a drag on a cigarette, and searched for a place to sit. He took a quick swig from a small bottle he kept stuffed inside his suit jacket.

From the House floor, in the midst of the surrounding carnival, silver-haired Capt. William Bisso, an ever-present rose decorating his lapel, unsuccessfully tried to stifle a smile.[2]

Bisso was a tough man, the owner of a thriving tugboat company based in New Orleans and one of the last warhorses of the Old Regulars, the fading political machine of the city that still stubbornly held sway with some voters.

In his nearly fifty years in politics, Bisso had known them all: the powerful and the petty. He had fought and made peace with Huey Long, a national folk hero who rose out of the red clay of Louisiana's north country, and had followed that with a similar romance with Huey's younger brother Earl.

In between, Bisso patiently endured the administrations of a series of well-intended but mostly inept reform governors who now and then sought to rescue the state from the excesses of Longism. Inevitably, after four years of water, the state put a Long back in office, thirsty again for whiskey.

Now Bisso, observing the massive crowd around him and quickly grasping that once again he was in the middle of history, a place where men and dreams are broken, exhibited the discretion that had made him one of the state's wiliest politicos. Whatever he thought of the unfolding carnival before him, Bisso discreetly kept to himself.

Here, too, was the wiry and diminutive Dudley LeBlanc, Acadiana's answer to P.T. Barnum, slaping backs and lighting cigars in the chamber like a man running for office, which he was. LeBlanc had slipped in and out of Louisiana politics for more than two generations now. Sometimes, after he had delivered a poetic, humorous speech about his concerns for the poor, people in Louisiana actually got the idea he was serious about public office.[3]

But LeBlanc was much too energetic and exciteable, and far too much of a showman to settle for politics alone. Across America, nearly anyone who had a radio in the 1930s and

1940s could tell you who Huey Long was. And certain of the lonesome cowboy songs of Jimmie Davis, who would eventually succeed Long, were also famous.

But mention the word "Hadacol" and suddenly, almost violently, Dudley LeBlanc's name sprung to life, the creation of one of the greatest advertising campaigns in American history. No one could precisely say what Hadacol was, but LeBlanc, through his endless promotions, had convinced a fantastically large number of people across the country—millions of them, in fact—that Hadocol could cure whatever ailed them.

And surely it did not hurt in a country enamored of celebrity that people such as energetic and multi-talented Mickey Rooney, bandleader Tommy Dorsey, and the captivating actress Ava Gardner had all endorsed Hadacol. Even more, they travelled across the country with LeBlanc in a star-studded caravan touting the amazing, elusive benefits of his product.

Happily hailing reporters and politicians—no one could long resist LeBlanc's restless charm—he bounded to the front of the House chamber to greet a woman he had known for decades.

Her name was Lucille May Grace, and this was not one of her better days. Tense, uneasy, alternately smiling—if only briefly—at long-time friends and then staring sadly at the floor, "Miss Lucille," as she was known to virtually everyone, was today the center of rapt attention for reporters, photographers, and onlookers.

People strained to get a better view of her, to see what she wore—Miss Lucille was always classy—and study her face.

For her part, Miss Lucille wished she could be anywhere than the crowded House chamber.

She wished she could simply be back home.

Until now, Grace had enjoyed a brilliant career that defied convention. As the only woman in a smoky world dominated by morally elastic male politicians, Miss Lucille thrived. Her efficient handling of the state land office as its long-time register

On the steps of the state capitol, Miss Lucille endures. (Courtesy John Dominis/TimesPix)

had won her the respect and envy of everyone. She won election after election for twenty years and bouquets from both reformers and the press who admitted she did her job well.

Finally, it looked as though Lucille May Grace was about to become the next governor of the state of Louisiana, and the first woman in charge of things. But then she made a mistake that she would come to regret for the rest of her life; a mistake that, indeed, would eventually contribute to the end of her life.

And now Miss Lucille sat in the House chamber with a saddened sense of futility. She felt like a spectator at her own execution, waiting for a dreaded end she could do nothing to prevent.

Wearing a conservative black suit offset by a bright red blouse, Grace was so lost in thought that she barely recognized LeBlanc when he approached her.[4]

This was not going to be a good day for Lucille May Grace.

There were cheers and applause when Boggs and his young family appeared, and laughs and hoots when Earl Long waved his big ten-gallon hat.

But no one hooted or laughed at Leander Perez, known to those who both feared and revered him as the Judge.

Surveying through delicate rimless glasses the chaos and confusion around him, Perez looked pleased, an expensive cigar defiant in the corner of his mouth, a shock of iron-grey hair swept to a pompadour on his head.

"Hello, Judge! Hello, Judge!" Perez's earnest admirers yelled out. Perez thinly smiled in return and sat confidently at one of the small wooden desks normally reserved for legislators. A man—there was always someone around Perez, handing him things, lighting his cigar, opening pesky doors—presented him with a huge stack of papers.[5]

Forever meticulous—not for the Judge the sweat-soaked, rumpled shirts and withered ties of the classic Southern politician—the Judge first made certain that the desk he sat at was clean before stacking the documents before him.

He is a napkin flapper, one journalist observed of Perez, a "brusher of imaginary crumbs and tobacco ashes from the table cloth. And whenever there is the slightest hiatus in the conversation, he gives the table top a smart slap."[6] New Orleans reporter Rosemary James was one among many who did not particularly like the Judge, but found herself succumbing nevertheless to his charms. "He was very intelligent," James, who interviewed Perez, would later recall. "He could be funny when he wanted to be. But he could also be mean."[7]

Perez, for his part, viewed himself as a tolerant man of abundantly good humor, and he freely explained what made him so: "One easy way to relax, you know, is to always have a joke at somebody's expense, maybe, and have a good belly laugh," Perez explained in a low voice that seemed to drip with honey. "That's the best way to relax."[8]

Perez also enjoyed nothing more than a good quip: "I smoke a given number of cigars," the Judge dead-panned, "usually as many as are given to me."[9]

Raucous laughter followed, mostly from Perez.

By 1951 Leander Perez was a millionaire. He had not always been rich. In fact, he was born almost poor, the son of a rice and sugarcane planter who was always just a step ahead of his bills. But Leander Perez was rich now, immensely rich, perhaps even a billionaire, and like so many self-made men whose empires stretched across the boundaries of imagination, Leander Perez always got what he wanted.

Now, sitting at the table, his guards, secretaries, and assistants offering him subservient attention, Perez knew what he wanted.

He wanted to destroy the young man sitting at the table in front of him. He wanted to destroy the likeable, attractive, man-with-a-future who had only recently been voted by a pool of gushing secretaries as the most charming congressman in Washington.

Leander Perez wanted to destroy Hale Boggs—not just best

Leander Perez, the King of Plaquemines Parish, crowns the Queen of the Orange Festival. (Courtesy Special Collections Division, Tulane University)

him in a political election or outmaneuver him in a court of law. He wanted to decimate Boggs in a way that would make any future in politics almost impossible for the young reformer, to finish him off completely as a public man.

And in 1951 there was no better way of doing that than by calling someone a Communist.

Actually, there was *one* better way, and that was to prove it.

And the proof, Perez knew, as he lovingly surveyed the papers before him, was here in irrefutable black and white. "Look at these *Hullabaloos*," Perez had said, referring to the student newspaper at Tulane University that Boggs had written for years ago when he was fired with the far-left passions of a young man. "We're going to tie him up so that he won't be able to move," Perez proclaimed.[10]

Hale Boggs was a Communist, Perez insisted. But even worse, Hale Boggs was also a candidate for governor, with a very good chance of getting elected. Therefore, Perez concluded, he was doing Louisiana a favor by saving it from its first Red leader.

There were one hundred members of the Democratic State Central Committee who had now filed into the chamber. Perez needed to convince only fifty-one of them of the charges against Boggs, requiring them to then drop Boggs' name from the gubernatorial ballot. And if they did that, everyone agreed, Boggs' career would be over. Whether or not he really was a Communist wouldn't matter; if the DSCC pushed Boggs out of the race it would at least *seem* to everyone that Boggs must have done something wrong. And that would be damaging enough.

A terrific din filled the chamber as the DSCC members tried to find their chairs. There were now several hundred people milling about, and empty seats were at a premium. DSCC chairman Henry Sevier, a long-time Perez ally, in a handsome double-breasted suit, looked around the huge room with dismay as he reached his perch near the front of the chamber.

Meanwhile, sitting next to wife Lindy, Hale Boggs began to

contemplate where things had gone wrong. Up until now, he had admittedly led a charmed life. A Tulane graduate with honors, Boggs was elected to Congress on a reform wave at the age of 26, the recipient of very deep Uptown New Orleans pockets who helped him finance his winning campaign. Young, but intelligent, Boggs had a way of prompting people with more power or money than he to like him.

"He was a very impressive person," Joseph C. Myers, Jr., who graduated from Tulane with Boggs, would remember, "the kind of person that people automatically felt, as we used to say back then, was 'going to amount to something.'"[11]

"Hale was truly and genuinely interested in life and problems," Boggs' sister, Claire Boggs Morrison, would later recall. "And I don't think he was just listening to people's problems to listen to them—he really wanted to help. That was the kind of person he was."[12]

Hale Boggs was a crusader. A reformer, "a joiner and a bleeding heart," two cynical reporters would label him.[13]

He was also an intellectual. "I had scads of dates, and while I was maneuvering my late date so the early date wouldn't find out, there was Hale writing editorials about Social Security," remembered Lindy, who fell in love with him when they were both students, eventually declaring: "I believed in him so much that I would have been working for him if I hadn't been married to him."[14]

Above all, Hale Boggs was a young man with an irresistible attraction to utopian dreams, visions of how things could be, how the course of fortune and fate could change men and nations, and what he could someday do to make the world better.

When he first ran for office, he frequently displayed his interests in things far away, talking about poverty in China or the pound in Britain or the power of Russia. It often confused precinct captains in the blue-collar bars of New Orleans' Irish Channel.

Lindy, meanwhile, her feet firmly on the ground, ran his

campaign and office, writing lovely notes to friends and voters and introducing her husband—who rarely had a dime in his pocket during the Great Depression—to blood that flowed very blue in the salons of Uptown New Orleans.

Once elected to Congress, Hale, with Lindy by his side, was surprisingly successful in Washington for such a young man with no previous congressional connections. Sam Rayburn, the powerful but lonesome bachelor Speaker of the House, took a liking to both Hale and Lindy, and even invited Boggs to his "Board of Education" sessions. There he and Lyndon Johnson and Harry Truman and any number of other Southern and border-state powerbrokers wiled away the late afternoons drinking bourbon and branch water and making decisions that would alter the course of the nation.

"I listened in fascination as these powerful men talked of issues and personalities, of the Congress and the presidency," LBJ aide Bobby Baker later said of the small room on the ground floor of the Capitol crowded with a worn sofa and easy chairs where Boggs, Rayburn, and the other men gathered. "They were living examples of the necessity of having in government men with just plain good common sense."[15]

Soon Hale and Lindy had also charmed John F. Kennedy, elected to Congress in 1946, as well as the carousing LBJ and his flowery wife, Lady Bird, who together would become two of Hale and Lindy's closest friends. Even the erudite and stiff Walter Lippmann, the most powerful columnist of his day, a man of great pretentions who regarded even the president— Harry Truman—as a commoner, liked Hale and Lindy, too. It was an affection without precedent, considering that Boggs was, after all, still nothing more than a decidedly junior member of Congress.

And New Orleans, as well, loved Hale and Lindy. They were a team and voters yearned to see them together, particularly with their children, as if their very presence suggested that the old city was younger and more full of promise than it really was.

"To get a photo in the newspaper of Lindy campaigning, par-

ticularly with one of the children, was great stuff for us," said
Laurence Eustis, who was Boggs' official campaign manager in
1940. "They were just so attractive and friendly and young—you
couldn't help but like them."[16]

Although Boggs actually lost in his bid for reelection in
1942—his opponent, crusty old Paul Maloney, whom Boggs
beat in 1940, later admitted that he came back just to teach
his cocky young foe a lesson—Boggs was back to stay in 1946
and won thumping reelection victories in both 1948 and
1950.[17]

"Never in his wildest imagination did he consider running
for governor," Lindy later exclaimed, when wealthy Uptown
reformers first broached the idea of Boggs' taking a stab at
the statehouse. Even a whirlwind tour of the state, in which
Boggs was met with enthusiastic promises of support and
money, failed to sway him. Baton Rouge! He wanted to stay in
Washington, where he was near the center of power, confi-
dante of Rayburn and Kennedy and Johnson, glowing in Lippmann's parched sun.[18]

"Well, Lin, tell me—what do you think?" Boggs asked Lindy
as he steered their sedan to the side of the road on the out-
skirts of New Orleans after their upstate tour, hoping at that
very moment to get back to Washington.[19]

"I hate to tell you this," the wise wife counseled the indecisive
husband. "But I don't think you have any choice. I think you
have to run."[20]

It was obvious that if Boggs did not run for governor, he
would be in more trouble than if he did—even if he lost. The
Uptowners had bankrolled him for years. They were the old
money in the old mansions, and the one thing they would
never forgive was ingratitude.

And besides, the Uptowners were on a roll. In both the
1940 and 1944 state elections a reform candidate backed by
big Uptown money had won the statehouse. And just as exciting, if not improbable, in 1946 they had even elected one of
their own—deLesseps S. Morrison, a diffident attorney with

aristocratic pretentions—as mayor of New Orleans, the last province of the blue collars and Old Regulars.

But, the Uptowners' also knew, voters needed constant supervision. In 1948 they fell back on their old ways and returned Earl Long to the statehouse. His inauguration was an unseemly affair, confirming the Uptowners' worst suspicions: a hillbilly jamboree stocked with Confederate flags, twenty thousand pounds of hotdogs, and one hundred gallons of buttermilk, all of which was voraciously consumed.[21]

Sick stomachs followed.

In his four years as governor, Earl Long seemed to go out of his way to offend the sensibilities of the reformers. He expanded state-run health care and the free textbook program his brother Huey had introduced. The amount and number of state pension checks jumped by more than a quarter. He poured millions of dollars of state money into contracts for new roads and bridges. And the Uptowners, seeing the dollars flow everwhere else, felt very much out of the action.

Perhaps most disturbing of all Long had remained loyal to the National Democratic Party, including President Harry Truman, who was just then advocating civil rights for blacks and free medical care for everyone else.

They clearly needed to regain control of Baton Rouge. And the man who could do it was Hale Boggs. Save the state and you save yourself, the Uptowners essentially told Boggs.

Reluctantly, he agreed.

By the early summer of 1951, Boggs had announced his candidacy. By September he was traveling through a hazy succession of tiny logging and farm towns across northern and central Louisiana, trying to sell a tired state a dream. He gave loud, long speeches from the rugged ends of flatbed trucks in the middle of sparsely populated town squares and on the dusty front steps of boarded-up movie houses in places that time and history had passed by.

He was going to be their next governor! Boggs yelled. Eventually even he came to believe it.

On the floor of the Louisiana House, Hale Boggs (right) formally registers as a candidate for governor. (Courtesy Special Collections Division, Tulane University)

"He made a great effort," judged *Times-Picayune* political columnist James Gillis, who jumped into his sedan and traveled the same routes Boggs did, in and out of little drugstores and bars and gas stations throughout the northern and central swaths of Louisiana where Boggs, as a Catholic from New Orleans, most needed to find votes. "He was beginning to catch on. People said that they liked this young man from the big city. He was very optimistic, and people liked that."[22]

Soon Boggs, far ahead of his competition, had busy campaign offices up and running in every medium-size and large city in the state. Most of the working press was writing about him, calling him the frontrunner, in a field that included conservatives Robert Kennon and James McLemore, not to mention Miss Lucille and Earl Long's entry, Carlos Spaht.

Then, on the evening of October 15, 1951, everything changed.

Boggs was sitting in the French Quarter television studios of WDSU—owned by Edgar Stern, a son in the fabulously wealthy Stern family, who were among Boggs' most important financial supporters. Boggs liked the new medium of television, which would transform in ways the Uptowners could hardly imagine the variety and culture of Louisiana politics.

Suddenly, earthy men like Earl Long could be absurdly reduced in front of a camera in a quiet studio. Uncle Earl always needed a hot crowd.

But Boggs, erudite and contemplative, was enhanced by television. He appeared to viewers as a calm man of principle. He could have sold soap or cars and made a killing. Instead, he was selling himself, and doing nearly as well.

Boggs was at WDSU for another half-hour broadcast. It was only three months until the election, and it looked for certain that Boggs would win the primary, and then, it was assumed, finish off any competitor in the runoff.

Suddenly Boggs was handed a message that had been sent to him by courier from the secretary of the DSCC. The DSCC in 1951 was an important group of people on the front lines of Louisiana politics—assessors, sheriffs, Old Regulars, even a smattering of reformers. And without their approval, no candidate could get his name on the ballot, at least as a Democrat.

And, in 1951, Louisiana's voters rarely voted for anyone else.

Boggs read the message. A brief was being filed that night before the DSCC, the message informed him, arguing that he was not qualified to run for governor, nor was he fit, and could not even be called a Democrat.

The reason, the brief held, was shockingly simple: Hale Boggs was a Communist.

"The big lie!" Boggs derided the claim as soon as he met with reporters outside WDSU's studio. The brief, he noted, was filed under the name of Lucille May Grace. Miss Lucille, the same woman who had a sterling reputation for fair play in Louisiana politics, the same woman who knew both Hale and Lindy socially, had been entertained in their Washington home and had never exchanged an angry word with them.[23]

Now here was Miss Lucille calling Boggs a Communist. Boggs' eyes swept over the papers in his hands. But it was almost as though he did not see Grace's name on them at all.

"This protest is a typical tactic of Leander Perez," Boggs divined. Perez had put Grace up to it, Boggs was certain.[24]

Bravely, Boggs vowed to fight for his name and reputation in front of the DSCC, which would, he also learned, take up his fate in just a short seventy-two hours.

If Boggs lost, it would be the probable end not only of his candidacy but his career as well. This was 1951, a dark era when Communism to most Americans was a dreaded disease that killed and deserved to be killed in return. Any American politician even remotely connected to such an enemy ideology was risking destruction.

But if Perez lost, the Judge's kingdom, that swampy empire he had so lovingly built through the years removed from pesky state noses, might just possibly be threatened by an earnest do-gooder like Hale Boggs. Boggs not only could be one of the few incoming governors not indebted to Perez, but someone who, because of the Grace challenge, would actually have a reason to hate and seek revenge upon the Judge. Somewhere in between was Lucille May Grace, who had imagined for herself such a better campaign. A bumper sticker that fall had said it all. Next to a drawing of a sun bonnet being tossed into the ring were the words: "Lucille May Grace for Governor."[25]

Now her future depended upon the darkness of someone else's past, of the real and imagined things that Hale Boggs had once done, so many years ago, that would prove he was a menace to his state and country.

There wasn't room for one more person in the House chamber. A faintly cool October afternoon was turning ominously thick with the closeness of the crowd.

Hale Boggs, Leander Perez, and Lucille May Grace had the best seats in the house. Earl Long was nervously pacing, his eyes full of mischief, darting across the room.

Suddenly the clamor was pierced by the heavy gavelling of DSCC chairman Sevier who took note of the big audience and remarked: "I realize this is one of the most important meetings that has ever been held by this committee and one of the most important matters ever brought before it."[26]

A quiet fell across the room.

Kazan, criminals, communists, and New Orleans. (Courtesy 20th Century Fox)

CHAPTER TWO

Suddenly a Nightmare

Toward the end of 1946, Tennessee Williams moved into a handsomely furnished apartment on St. Peter Street in the French Quarter. Beneath a skylight the young playwright positioned a table to write on, later observing: "The clouds always seem just overhead . . . fleecy and in continual motion."[1]

Already the author of *The Glass Managerie*, which had been a breakthrough success on Broadway, the young Williams—he was 35 years old in 1946—possessed highly ambivalent feelings about the city he would soon be most often associated with. He admitted to loving New Orleans' food, music, and bonhomie, but once in the city, a later biographer would note, he usually yearned to be someplace else.

Peering out of the window of his apartment, Williams could observe and listen to "that rattletrap old streetcar" as it passed through the Quarter. "Their indiscourageable progress up and down Royal street," Williams said of the streetcars, "struck me as having some symbolic bearing of a broad nature on the life in the Vieux Carre—and everywhere else, for that matter."[2]

Those streetcars had given inspiration to Williams' latest work: a deeply disturbing story of a depleted woman of faded Southen gentility who comes to visit her sister and brother-in-law in their crowded, chaotic French Quarter flat. *A Streetcar Named Desire* was a stunning critical success for Williams on Broadway, beginning in 1947. By 1949 the actual Desire streetcar in New Orleans was out of commission, but Warner Brothers

31

had optioned the play and had scheduled shooting to begin in 1950.

Williams, always fearful that Hollywood would do something imbecillic to his work, turned to Elia Kazan to look out for his interests and direct the film at the same time. He chose wisely. Not only had the dark-haired and intense Kazan directed the stage version of *Streetcar* and so was intimately familiar with the play's power and message, he also knew New Orleans.

In late 1949, Kazan filmed virtually all of his dark thriller *Panic in the Streets* in New Orleans. He was seduced by the feel of a wide-open city.

"We shot on the whorehouse streets, in the low bars, in the wharfs," Kazan later recalled. On another occasion the director remarked: "I ran free all over the city."[3]

The result was a gritty, faced-paced *film noir* that traces the spread of a deadly contagion among the city's low lifes. Working with the enthusiastic help of movie fan Mayor deLesseps Morrison, who was so excited he impulsively appointed a crew of city policemen to daily assist the director and even allowed him to film in the ornate Gallier Hall, the mayor's City Hall home, Kazan freely took advantage of things. He admitted using "the city's people as our extras, and their homes, shops, and streets for scenery," a practice that revealed only one flaw when a city cop, recognizing three of Kazan's extras as bail-jumpers, arrested them.[4]

Obsessive, Kazan also surprised himself by succumbing to what he called the "carny" atmosphere of New Orleans, which resulted in a looser filming schedule and a growing curiosity to explore every dark and dingy corner of the city. In the process, Kazan said, he met a wider and much more diverse circle of locals than normally would have been possible.

This tactile embrace of the city would serve Kazan well when he returned to film the opening sequences to *Streetcar* in the fall of 1950. The images Kazan hoped to capture from New Orleans all naturally centered around streetcars. Repeatedly he filmed one streetcar after another at various locations throughout the city. His most famous shot finally showed a streetcar pushing its way into the old Louisiana and Nashville depot at the foot of Canal Street.

Out of a fog of smoke and confusion emerged Vivien Leigh as Blanche DuBois: "They told me to take a streetcar named Desire, and then transfer to one called Cemeteries and ride six blocks and get off at Elysian Fields," she remarks in the movie's now-legendary opening.[5]

Hampered by a crowd of more than two hundred locals who crowded into the depot hoping for a glimpse of the alluring Miss Leigh, even as shooting continued beyond midnight, Kazan got his movie done. The following year, virtually all of Hollywood was lauding Kazan as a genius, and his two New Orleans movies—*Panic in the Streets* and *A Streetcar Named Desire*—provided powerful visual evidence of that praise.[6]

Yet, as Kazan worked in New Orleans, it wasn't just local movie fans who distracted him. The powerful House UnAmerican Activities Committee (HUAC) was calling, letting him know that they were looking into what they regarded as his suspicious past. Some fifteen years earlier he had belonged to a leftist group that was now listed as a Communist-front operation—and the members of the committee wanted to know if the young director would talk to them.[7]

The problem in "talking" however, was that if one spoke to HUAC, that usually meant naming names, divulging details about other people who, almost always in the distant past, had been involved in one political group or another. Invariably, those groups, nearly uniformly in an entirely different political culture, a decade and a half later were seen as Communist or somehow connected to Communists.

Kazan's dilemma was shared, ironically, by dozens of New Orleanians, perhaps some of the very people he encountered as he made his way along the city's wharves and back streets.

Writers and journalists always liked to make much of how different Louisiana and New Orleans seemed from the rest of the nation. And with its intriguing racial and religious diversity, not to mention its love of good times, Louisiana *was* a different place, as certainly a trainride through Nebraska or Ohio or Virginia or any other state that resembled most of the others would attest.

But in the late 1940s and early 1950s, as the country came under a powerful and menacing spell casually known as "McCarthyism," Louisiana and New Orleans suddenly seemed no different from anywhere else, as common and predictable as Sinclair Lewis' fictional Zenith, Ohio, which was Everywhere, America.

McCarthyism was inspired by one Joseph R. McCarthy of Wisconsin, a ham-fisted first-term Republican senator, who—along with HUAC, which had been doing this sort of thing for most of the previous decade—decided that Communists, on direct orders from higher-ups in the Soviet Union, had wormed their way into every aspect of American life. This had prompted virtually everyone with opinions that were not vividly conservative to fall under suspicion.

To a degree, the Communist hunters were on to something. There *were* Communists in America—even in Louisiana and New Orleans!—tens of thousands of them, many following the Soviet line in everything, and some quite clearly working as spies to infiltrate American life, sinisterly preparing for the day when the Soviet Union somehow took over America.

But how to extract enemy agents without destroying such basic constitutional principles as freedom of opinion and thought vexed the national imagination. President Truman, in an act that prompted civil libertarians to remove his picture from their walls, proposed what he thought was a sensible solution.

In March of 1947 he unveiled a loyalty program that was tailored, he said, to *protect* innocent government employees even as it ripped away the cloak of annonymity from Soviet agents.

"I am not worried about the Communist party taking over the government of the United States," Truman said of his instituted program requiring government employees to mouth an oath of loyalty to the U.S., "but I am against a person whose loyalty is not to the government of the United States, holding a government job."[8]

In a matter of months, Truman noted that some six thousand federal employees had resigned, on top of another 1,200 who were fired as a result of his loyalty program, a program that the president later admitted he proposed primarily to take the wind out of HUAC, which he regarded as dangerously demagogic.[9]

But Truman's effort had the opposite effect: it seemed to confirm that there were indeed Communists everywhere. Why would the president otherwise even need a loyalty oath? The White House itself had provided one more reason why Americans should view one another with suspicion.

II

On August 26, 1948, Sarah Reed—a tired woman wearing a forlorn, flowered hat—uncertainly appeared before the Orleans Parish School Board's downtown office with an unusual plea. The charges levied against her, she maintained, "were not true." She asked the all-male board to disgregard the rumors about her, rumors that said she was a Communist sympathizer, and simply allow her to continue teaching the civics class at Fortier High School that she had conducted for the previous twenty-five years.[10]

Reed, who had, in fact, belonged to at least one far-left political organization in her youth, boldy declared that she loved the United States of America, her community, her school—and her job.

But Reed's impassioned entreaty was not enough for Lionel J. Bourgeois, the superintendent of the board and a man convinced that Communists were somehow infiltrating the parish school system.

A colorful man given to dramatic confrontation, Bourgeois

had once taught school himself at the big Warren Easton High, arriving daily at his classes under a snappy white straw hat. His wooden desk, student Thomas Sancton would later recall, was littered with boxes of pills that the teacher said he needed for digestive problems. But his boys should never worry about their instructor's health. Bourgeois, Sancton decided, was "rugged."[11]

Now Bourgeois ruggedly informed Reed: "Evidence adduced by certain of your students strongly indicates that you are not stressing the American way of life as superior in every respect to Communism and the other 'isms.'" He then quickly proposed that the teacher publicly promise to never again discuss Communism with the children "on school property and during school hours," and that Reed herself would be removed to a smaller school somewhere in the vast parish system where she could do little harm.[12]

On a hot summer's day, the members of the parish school board wrestled with Bourgeois' proposal. They grilled Reed for more than six hours, and she seemed to onlookers like a trapped animal. But the teacher was not without her defenders: more than forty of her students and nearly two dozen faculty members turned out for moral support. One student, 15-year-old Lable Dulitz, frankly told the board: "We spent a lot of time on the Constitution of the United States and in tests Mrs. Reed would base a lot of her questions on the Constitution."[13]

Dulitz then produced a notebook he had kept while a student in Reed's class. Not once, Dulitz concluded after rereading the book, did Reed talk about Communism. Another student, Lamar Hooks, chimed in: "I think that anyone who started all this stupid stuff about Mrs. Reed is crazy."[14]

"It's wonderful the way my boys have come and stood up for me," said an obviously weary Reed as she struggled to hold back tears. "It makes up for a lot a teacher has to take in life."[15]

In the end, the board voted to retain Reed in her current

position. Simultaneously, in case anyone suspected otherwise, they voted to reaffirm their mission to "stamp out" Communism.[16]

For his part, Bourgeois seemed rather less concerned with the damages his charges had made to Reed's reputation, and more with how the school system fared during the controversy. The final decision to retain Reed, Bourgeois happily concluded, "definitely clears the schools of charges which appeared in the local press that Communism as a way of life was being taught in the public schools of New Orleans." [17]

Reed, embraced by a thicket of cheering students and teachers, labled her retention a "great victory for academic freedom in the classroom." But she also knew she was fortunate. She had defenders who rallied publicly to her cause and demanded satisfaction.[18]

Not everyone was so lucky.

Across the city both individuals and institutions were suddenly under attack and suspicion. "I am from Tulane, and to my chagrin there are more Communists who infest that place than Americans," New Orleans Cong. F. Edward Hebert sensationally charged from Washington during a HUAC session in 1948.[19]

This was simply not a serious charge, but one rather out of character for the fun-loving Hebert, who liked nothing more than a good drink, the presence of pretty women, and a boisterous night out on the town.

"Some may wonder how I got reelected if I was always seen out nightclubbing on Bourbon Street," Hebert would one day frankly reveal. "If you know New Orleans and its people, you know that those people who see me when I'm out are votes in the box."[20]

Hebert had begun his career as a newspaper columnist writing about nightclub events and personalities in the 1930s. "Sports, show business, and misfortune (if not tragedy) occupied the attentions of the city's newspapers," Hebert later said as he described his beat.[21]

But by 1948, Hebert—tall, with thick glasses and a beguiling way that both men and women found appealing—was suddenly serious about what he viewed as the coming Communist threat.

"There is every reason to believe that only an infinitesimal part of Communist espionage has been brought to life," Hebert said after HUAC—with fellow member Richard Nixon of California in pursuit—made its case against Alger Hiss, a former top State Department official accused of being a Communist informant. There could be men like Hiss anywhere, Hebert warned. He carted to New Orleans boxes and boxes of a pamphlet entitled "One Hundred Things You Should Know About Communism" that he wanted to see distributed throughout the local school system. "Our boys and girls should know what a threat Communism is to our way of life," Hebert explained.[22]

Superintendent Bourgeois, of course, was only too happy to assist Hebert in his mission. Serious study of the pamphlet, he vowed, would be "required work in all high schools."[23]

As Hebert and Bourgeois went to work on the city's school children, federal and local authorities covered the waterfront. For years the city's business elite had claimed that the New Orleans chapter of the National Maritime Union (NMU) was under the control of Communists. No one knew if the union's business detractors made the claim because they believed it was so or because they were simply and implacably opposed to unions. But by the 1940s they received succor from J. Skelly Wright, U.S. Attorney for New Orleans, who contended that the NMU was, in reality, "nothing more than an arm of the Communist party." He vowed, in return, to destroy what he saw as an intricate local Communist conspiracy.[24]

The New Orleans *Item* at the same time splashingly ran a sensational week-long series on Communist power in the NMU: "This is the story of the struggle for control of a New Orleans maritime union," reporter John Collier wrote in the first sentence of the series. "On the one side are the Communists; on the other, the vast majority of the union rank and file."[25]

In response to outside criticism, the local NMU, beginning in 1947, initiated a painful purging of its ranks, a purging that was given great speed and force by local prosecutors. Charles William McDonald, a long-time and previously obscure NMU member, was branded a "dangerous Communist alien" and deported. Robert Himmaugh, another dockside worker, was sentenced to two years in federal prison for lying when asked about his past Communist affiliations, affiliations Himmaugh had come to renounce. The worker plausibly explained that if he had told the truth he probably would have never gotten his current job as an oiler for the Federal Barge Lines.[26]

"I am a poor man and need my money. . . . I once considered the Communist party a political organization," Himmaugh attempted to explain to federal district judge Herbert W. Christenberry during his trial in the summer of 1949, "but I do not now consider it as such."[27]

From the bench, Christenberry was singularly unmoved. "Your offense was willful and brazen," the judge declared before Himmaugh was ordered to serve his sentence and led away in handcuffs.[28]

At the nearby Kingsley House, a charity for those down on their luck, Emeric Kurtagh, a pudgy man with a trim mustache, was quietly asked to resign as director after rumors about his past Communist ties became known. He, too, had been publicly fingered by HUAC for having once been affiliated with a Communist group. But Kurtagh resisted. He was not now nor had he ever been a Communist, he said. "I have been fighting Communism from way back," he protested. "I challenge anyone to show that I am a Communist or am Communist-inclined."[29]

But no one rushed to Kurtagh's side. One night, several weeks later, Kurtagh was suddenly gone, his tenure as the Kingsley House's director abruptly over. The House would only say, in a press release, that he had, rather quickly as it turned out, decided to accept a "position in New York."[30]

The problem for men such as Himmaugh and Kurtagh and thousands of others like them was that the rules of the game had changed. Before World War II, when they were young men with idealistic and often utopian views of the world, it was common and acceptable to join one or many groups espousing pie-in-the-sky solutions to the Great Depression problems of the day. That some of those groups might have some connection with Communists didn't seem to bother anyone then very much.

The groups provided an outlet for anger and fear for a generation possessing more than its share of both. "You didn't stop to verify every group's credentials," explained Floyd Newlin, who was a student at Tulane University in the late 1930s and greatly enjoyed the spirit of intellectual debate. "You listened and followed if a group came along that had a plan for getting us out of the Depression."[31]

"There was all kinds of activity along those lines," remembered Walter Cowan, also a college student in the 1930s. "People were looking for answers, they were frightened. They never thought what they did in the 1930s would come back to haunt them in the 1950s. Suddenly, it was a nightmare."[32]

For Avery Alexander—intensely interested in Constitutional law, politics, and civil action—meeting and associating with Communists was almost inevitable. Indeed, Alexander, who would one day be a major civil rights voice in Louisiana, took a rather European approach to Communists: if they helped him get what he wanted, they were all right by him.

"In those days you got your friends where you could get them," Alexander later explained, adding that if some group with Communist ties was also pro-civil rights, "that was all most black people cared to know. Keep in mind—we didn't have a whole lot of friends in those days."[33]

But civil rights groups *were* tainted by their Communist connections and lost support among white liberals terrified of any connection with the Reds. A case in point was a group composed of both white and black activists—which was dangerous enough for its day—called the Southern Conference for Human Welfare (SCHW). All the SCHW wanted to do, it said, was relax segregation laws and work for racial equality. By 1947, the group could claim up to six hundred members across Louisiana, with local chapters in Shreveport, Baton Rouge, and New Orleans.

The following year, HUAC confidently concluded that the Southern Conference was thick with Communists. Martha Robinson, a New Orleans liberal, renounced her membership, calling the SCHW a "Communist front group," as did Bill Monroe, who would one day be a correspondent for NBC, fretting about the group's "tolerance of Communism."[34]

The Progressive Party in New Orleans fared even worse. The local chapter for Henry Wallace's bizarre and doomed third-party presidential bid in 1948, the New Orleans Progressives, like their national counterparts, gave shelter to Communists. Arthur Eugene, an agent working undercover, later estimated local Red strength in the chapter at "around a thousand members." The party pretty much died after that.[35]

The recent humiliation of Sarah Reed, meanwhile, was only the first battle between the Communist-hunters and the perceived Communist organizers in Louisiana's schools. Superintendent Bourgeois, still vigilant after the Reed fiasco, instructed the nearly 100,000 students in the parish system to keep their eyes open for any suspicious activity, especially if it concerned teachers. If one expected students who might be nursing a grudge over a bad report card to suddenly pell-mell turn their teachers over to the authorities, they were mistaken.

After the Reed fiasco, no other teachers in the parish system had to worry about proving they weren't Communists. But when prosecutor J. Skelly Wright announced he was certain that Dillard University professor Oakley Johnson was a Communist, the all-black school quickly capitulated by refusing to renew Johnson's contract.[36]

At Tulane a disgruntled former professor named John Keiffer lobbed a terrific charge that made the front pages of the New Orleans press. When *his* contract went unrenewed, he said it was not because he was a Communist, but rather because he was a valiant opponent of the Communists, and that a "powerful group of influential professors" at the school, who he suggested *were* Communists, conspired to throw him over. The school's alumni magazine, the *Tulanian*, offered Keiffer a challenge: "We call upon Dr. Keiffer to announce the names of any communistic professors. Who are they?"[37]

Keiffer never responded. And he didn't have to. The damage from his charges had already been done, perhaps one more reason why, by 1950, virtually every college and university in the state had implemented a loyalty oath that professors were required to sign declaring their fealty to America and their undying opposition to Communism.

Even Loyola University, normally a calm bastion of Jesuit tolerance in the big city, seemed to be doing its part to fan the flames, inviting one notorious Communist-hater after another to its campus, the most prominent of whom was Claire Booth Luce, wife of the powerful Henry Luce, publisher of *Time* and *Life*, who was also a congresswoman in her own right.

Incapable of being a bore, Luce flew into town in the fall of 1948 and immediately angered everyone when she wondered why her Loyola audience was not racially integrated. "If that is the law, of course I shall abide by it," she snapped, "but that doesn't keep me from saying that I think it is a lousy law and un-Christian to boot."[38]

Mrs. Luce, a recent and rather loud convert to Catholicism, quickly adopted the accepted thinking of her church: Communism was unacceptable and must eventually be destroyed. "Communist ideologies and dogma make war seem inevitable," she told her Loyola audience, adding a chilling observation: "The Cold War daily grows hotter."[39]

Other Loyola speakers included Thomas F. Murphy, the tough Irish prosecutor from New York who went after Alger Hiss, and Robert Vogeler, a prominent businessman recently arrested in Communist Hungary on trumped-up charges. "I Was Stalin's Prisoner," Vogeler called his speech in the *Argosy* magazine/Mickey Spillane jargon of the moment. Not to be outdone, Matt Cvetic, who went undercover to report on suspicious Communist doings in the U.S., also made it to Loyola. The title of his lecture: "I Was a Communist for the FBI." [40]

Things were looking shaky down at the Trade Mart too. In the spring of 1949, Trade Mart organizers sponsored a Czechoslovakian art exhibit in the building's downtown New Orleans lobby. One day an active member of the Young Men's Business Association happened by the display and swore he saw suspicious men gathering around, talking in quiet voices, proof that it was a "Communist meeting place," he reported with alarm. The Trade Mart declined to take the story seriously. But by then there were too many other things to worry about.

Superintendent Bourgeois called in an alarming find: a stack of pro-Communist literature he found outside the front doors of McDonough School Number 35. Someone else claimed to have found a similar bundle outside a nearby Louisiana National Guard camp. [41]

Soon it would even come to this: Larry Adler, the harmonica virtuoso, was targeted by the New Orleans chapter of the American Legion just as he was about to go onstage at the Monteleone's elegant Swan Room nightclub in the French Quarter. Adler, the Legion insisted, had once belonged to a Communist group. His harmonica was the instrument of a traitor. The Monteleone promised to pay Adler in full if he would simply leave. Adler refused.

"If I don't go on tonight, my whole future will have been jeopardized, and I will have been done irreparable harm," he protested. The Monteleone, in turn, refused to relent, quickly replacing Adler with the rotund Billy Vine, an aging trouper always ready for a show who really did begin his act with the words: "Ladies and germs . . ." [42]

Several months later the Legion was at it again. The Orpheum Theatre announced it would show *Limelight*, the moody, darkly comic masterpiece starring Charlie Chaplin.

The nightclub act that never was. (Courtesy the *Times-Picayune*)

Charlie Chaplin? Was he not the same man HUAC had labelled as a subversive? Chaplin, Legion spokesman H.J. Thiele declared, possessed a "contemptuous attitude towards American patriotism." After one airing of the film, the Orpheum removed *Limelight* from their bill.[43]

What made things so maddening for local civil libertarians was that the Communist-hunters in Louisiana never seemed to attach any proof to their charges. Their suspicions seemed to be enough. Upbraided by Tulane president Rufus Harris for publicly suggesting that Tulane was harboring Communists, Congressman Hebert was nonplussed: "I cannot believe," he breezily replied, referring to the rumors he had heard about Communist activity at Tulane, "that there isn't some fire where there is so much smoke."[44]

Six weeks later, there was plenty of smoke. Neighbors on Chartres Street in the French Quarter complained about a late night party on their block. When the police arrived, they were shocked to discover white and black students casually socializing, with professors from both Tulane and Dillard universities apparently encouraging the fun. The New Orleans press played it big.

"And Doctor Harris says there is nothing wrong with Tulane's faculty or the teaching at the university," Hebert sarcastically observed.[45]

In a noisy court hearing the following morning, several of the students—at least sixty were arrested for disturbing the peace—broke down and admitted that beyond the offense of black boys dancing with white girls, the party included political activists who were most likely Communists: "Definitely pink and bordering on the red side," one of the students, perhaps an artist, put it.[46]

Although the students, who were found guilty that day of being peace disturbers, would eventually see their convictions thrown out of court, Tulane President Harris had finally had enough. He was convinced that all of the recent talk about Communism on his campus was taking a toll. In an open letter to the *Times-Picayune*, Harris took the unusual step of protesting that "Tulane does not and will not tolerate Communism. We appoint no Communists to the faculty . . . there is no place for Communists here."[47]

Harris' declaration appeared only weeks before two deadly events in 1949 only accelerated local fears: in September Joseph Stalin's Soviet Union, shortly before China—home to 500 million people—fell to the Communists, announced it now had its own atomic bomb. Americans were instantly certain the malevolent Uncle Joe would enjoy nothing more than using it on them.

"One of the first cities destroyed would be New Orleans," a world policy expert, Ely Culbertson, predicted before a terrified Tulane audience. Louisiana Adjutant General Raymond Hufft—who signed the petition to silence Adler's harmonica at the Montelone—was quickly appointed as state head of a national commitee to prepare for attack from the Soviets.[48]

The state's suddenly busy Civil Defense office announced plans to errect hundreds of signs along highways outside Louisiana's medium and large cities with a none-too-reassuring notice: "IN THE EVENT OF ENEMY ATTACK THIS HIGHWAY WILL BE CLOSED EXCEPT TO CIVIL DEFENSE VEHICLES."

In the first issue of the state's "Civil Defense News" in the fall of 1951, the agency also revealed plans to produce more than 100,000 identification tags for school children in New Orleans that could be used to keep track of them in the aftermath of an atomic explosion. In Shreveport civilian defense volunteers, working out the first line of defense for their city, concluded that Shreveport might conceivably survive an attack from an atom bomb, but only if it got help from emergency workers in other cities such as Baton Rouge or Alexandria. That those two cities might be reduced to ashes from the same bomb went perhaps unthought and certainly unsaid.[49]

"We have our program well under way," Louisiana's top fire marshall, Hugh Stewart, confidently declared after visiting

Proof that nothing would be as it was before. (Courtesy the Louisiana Office of Civil Defense)

Lafayette, where the city's firemen went through their paces running from the site of one imagined scene of atomic destruction to another. The director of the civil defense program in Baton Rouge meanwhile declared that a "great number of people would be injured in the event of an atomic attack" of his city. But with the help of at least 20,000 volunteers, thought A. C. Ives, Baton Rouge could recover from a strike by an atom bomb.[50]

In Uptown New Orleans, at the big Sophie B. Wright School, some five hundred young girls one morning giggled as they noisily found their way to the school's civilian defense-approved basement, where they quickly crouched on the floor and buried their pony tails in their hands.

"The girls have learned the safest, quickest way to protect themselves in the case of an atomic attack," Elsie Brupbacher, a reporter for the New Orleans *States*, concluded in a story that was oddly upbeat. Superintendent Bourgeois was ecstatic: the Orleans Parish school system, he now said, was so strong it could even withstand atomic bombs![51]

Mayor Morrison, too, was worked up. How about a vigorous campaign to dig fall-out shelters all across the city? he asked. The mayor even helpfully suggested where the first one could go: in Lafayette Square, directly across from his office. But state Lt. Gov. Bill Dodd proposed instead a series of above-ground shelters—making one wonder by this time what exactly was the point—as he noted, correctly, that most of New Orleans was under water anyway.[52]

III

There were those who perused the day's alarming headlines—"HEBERT SEES WIDE NET OF SPYING," "FBI SCANS ORLEANS REDS," "BATON ROUGE TO BE TARGET FOR 'A-BOMB'"—and wondered, quite rightly, if it was all going too far. It would fall to an authority in the Romance languages, distinguished scholar Henry C. Lancaster of Johns

Hopkins University, to be one of the first voices in Louisiana—he was not of Louisiana, but only visiting—to logically warn the locals about the dangers of too much vigilence. "We must not lock up our citizens in order to keep them free," Lancaster reasoned during an address at Tulane. At a Sunday night banquet with the militantly anti-Communist Knights of Columbus, Bishop Charles Pascal Greco of Alexandria went even further, warning that the dangers of Communism were real, but so was the threat of "Americans who are trying to deprive other citizens of their rights."[53]

And then there was Hale Boggs. By 1950 the young New Orleans congressman—he was only 36 years old—had been happily in the thick of sticky debates over "isms" for most of his adult life. As a student at Tulane in the 1930s, he loved nothing more than discussing and comparing the relative merits of the Democrats versus the Republicans (Boggs loved Franklin D. Roosevelt, and nearly always concluded that his hero saved America). But he also probed the theories of the socialists, the facists, and, finally, the Communists, too. With each theory, based upon a benign absolutism that many during the Great Depression found reassuring, Boggs discovered something wanting.

Fascism, of course, meant Nazism. And from the earliest moments of Hitler's rise in Germany and, later, Franco's similar stairway to the stars in Spain, Boggs knew there was nothing about fascism withs its Germanic emphasis on race that attracted him. He was less certain about socialism and communism, however. Both philosophies talked of utopian visions, of mighty government programs to put in check the ruthless capitalist state that was destroying America. They promised full employment, access to public education, and state-run medical care from cradle to grave.

He found it less easy to discard such notions because, frankly, they were the next step from FDR's New Deal, a series of federal relief programs Boggs repeatedly extolled. But if he was to have a political career of any kind—and by 1937 Boggs had decided he wanted to run for Congress—he needed to turn a blind eye to the temptations of absolutist political visions that were intentionally constructed to be clear and immerse himself in the tempest of traditional American politics, which by its very nature was murky.

As Boggs became a successful politician, he joined with the rest in regularly attacking both Nazism and Communism, the latter of which he described as a "modern, atheistic, godless slavery." And he consistently supported the efforts of HUAC, which he genuinely thought was weeding out Communist subversives across the land, although he oftentimes had second thoughts about the committee's methods.[54]

But sometimes—certainly not often—Boggs displayed an alarming tendency to set off on his own, leaving behind, if only for the moment, the anti-Communist hysteria that was just then drowning Louisiana and the rest of the nation. Twice in the late 1940s, Boggs dared to publicly defend Truman Administration officials accused of being "soft" on Communism. This was a common accusation at the time, smartly avoiding suits of public libel by not saying the person in question *was* a Communist, rather just too indecisive, amorphous, and, well, soft, to effectively engage in its battle.

Then on June 22, 1950, in a general House discussion of the threats Communism posed to America, Boggs offhandedly observed: "In fighting Communism we must not be overwhelmed with fear, nor must we fall for the Communist trick of denouncing and smearing honest and patriotic people."[55]

This was exactly the kind of thinking, thought Leander Henry Perez, fuzzy, dangerous, weak thinking, that got people in trouble.

From his oak- and moss-draped plantation in Plaquemines Parish, Perez was launching what gave the unsettling appearance of being a one-man, last-front battle against the international advance of Communists and Communism. What enraged the Judge, as everyone called him, was simply not that Soviet Communists existed, but rather that so many people in

America did things to offer them support, to pave the way for what seemed like the inevitable day when the God-hating Reds moved en masse into his country and, indeed, Plaquemines Parish itself.

Convinced that virtually everything that came out of Washington was somehow giving comfort to the Communists, Perez by the early 1950s was also certain that most of the country's most important leaders were somehow in collusion with the Soviets. That was why they kept advocating so many big-government programs and seemed obsessed with the race issue, always pushing for the civil rights of Negroes, whom Perez was certain were his inferiors.

Eleanor Roosevelt seemed to attract Perez's greatest enmity. Rarely did he mention her name without also informing his listeners that the popular former First Lady was also a "member of numerous Communist-front organizations."

The red-haired populist dynamo Walter Reuther, president of the United Auto Workers, a union that was emerging as a powerful funding source for civil rights agitation, was similarly a favorite Perez target. So was Harry Truman and his beseiged administration, which, Perez said, faithfully followed the "line of Joseph Stalin" and happily espoused dangerous policies "taken right out of Joe Stalin's book."[56]

Perez's obsession with Communism, however, always had as its focus dangerous, dark events in other places, far away from Louisiana and Plaquemines Parish—in Truman's Washington, for example, or Roosevelt's New York, or Reuther's Detroit. It was always some other place, inevitably in the North, where the trouble took place.

But in early 1951, Perez suddenly trained his anti-Communist attentions on his native state. And he did so with deadly consequence.

CHAPTER THREE

Perez of Plaquemines Parish

The gold-plated dollar signs pressed into the sidewalk cement of the handsome American Bank Building in downtown New Orleans announced to visitors all they needed to know about the goings-on inside.

With a gleaming marble and brass lobby made industrious by the presence of uniformed elevator men greeting their important riders with snappy salutes, the American Bank Building was the essence of a mid-twentieth century Art Deco glow.

It was also a thriving hub of commerce, a place where quiet men in tailored suits made deals that transformed the metropolis.

Dozens of attorneys, physicians, accountants, and architects called the American Bank Building home. On the 12th floor reigned the amiably retired former mayor of New Orleans, Robert S. Maestri, whose net worth from his vast real estate holdings was said to be in the millions. Two floors above stood the corporate offices of the Standard Fruit Company, a plantation enterprise based in Central America with alarming politial muscle at home. The 17th floor, meanwhile, housed the spacious headquarters of Freeport Sulphur, the largest producer of phosphate fertilizer in the South—a multi-million-dollar business in the early 1950s.[1]

But above them all, high in a cloudless sky, was Leander Perez, serene on the 23rd floor, in a lavish office hidden behind frosted-glass front doors with starkly modern furniture that suggested elegant efficiency.

Behind a polished wooden desk, beyond the art-decorated reception room and oak-paneled area of his long-serving secretary, Perez sat in front of windows that looked out over the city as he dictated letters, peered over blue prints and contracts, and played the loud but genial Southern host to any number of lawyers, businessmen, and gallants who grandly bore the title of colonel.

"They tell you Perez is a boss, Perez is a dictator," he groused to one visiting journalist. "The truth is, Perez is just a darn work horse."[2]

And there *was* plenty of work to do.

First, he had the state legislature to worry about, a maleable body of ne'er-do-wells capable of going off in a dozen moronic directions without Perez's helpful guidance. For more than two decades, Perez had attended every single session of the legislature—officially as a mere observer—and always left as the beneficiary of a handful of new laws that would in one way or another contribute to the expansion of his financial and political kingdom.

Then there was the growing, but comically disorganzied States Rights movement—a Southern-white response to civil rights that Perez was now the nominal head of, transforming him into a national figure whose face and name would become familiar to readers of the *New York Times*, *Time*, and *Newsweek*.

Finally, there was Plaquemines Parish, Perez's official home—although he lived with his family, for the most part, in a beautiful mansion in Uptown New Orleans. Because Perez was an efficient man, so was the kingdom he ran in Plaquemines: his dozens of lieutenants took care of the details, who had what parish job, who got what parish scholarship, what zoning law needed to be bent for which businessman friend of Perez.

To outsiders, Perez described the remarkable unity of Plaquemines police jury—the parish's local governing authority—as a metaphor for the tranquil harmony that somehow floated throughout Plaquemines.

"There's hardly ever a dissenting vote," Perez sought to explain, seeming surprised himself. "We work together 100 percent."[3]

But one of New Orleans' two congressmen, F. Edward Hebert—one of the few men brave enough to contradict Perez in private—had a rather different take on how the police jury worked: "Five letters: P-E-R-E-Z," Hebert exclaimed blankly. "And that's it!"[4]

Sixty years of age in the fall of 1951, Leander Perez was remarkably vigorous and virtually impossible to ignore.

"He was a dynamic fellow and he *did* have a presence," recalled Ben C. Toledano, a young New Orleans political activist who was greatly impressed by Perez's style. "Although you could be overwhelmed, you still couldn't help but see that the guy was just extraordinarily dynamic."[5]

And dangerous.

Another conservative activist, William Nunguesser—who would treasure a small Confederate-flag-embossed cigarette lighter Perez gave him that played *Dixie* when opened—one day sat next to Perez at a political rally in the old Tulane University stadium. Somehow Perez bent down and a man accidentally stepped on his hand.

"I then watched his bodyguard beat the guy up," Nunguesser recalled, still shocked years later. "He just beat the guy up."[6]

"When we would go down to the mouth of the river—hunting, fishing, or whatever—there were people that would look after us," Toledano remembers of day-long outings spearheaded by Perez. "They would carry your gun, paddle the pirogue, whatever it was."

Perez never told Toledano exactly who these men were, and Toledano never asked. "All I know is that they were probably employees of the parish," he added with a hint of irony.[7]

Barking out orders, Perez's voice, thought Lester Velie, a journalist, sounded like "an instrument of authority accustomed to be heard." His laugh was a "satisfied belly laugh that only a secure, purposeful, and well-fed man knows how to achieve."[8]

In between all the jokes, Perez liked to goad. "You don't know the facts of life," he grumbled to one visiting interviewer for no particular reason. "You're willing to skim the surface and ride along, just ride along. Take it easy, take it easy."[9]

Informed that the visitor recently resided in Washington, D.C., Perez seemed to perk up. "How long did you live in Washington?" he asked. "Long enough to ruin anybody," he answered quickly for the man. "No wonder you have that attitude."[10]

"What attitude?" the visitor, by now entirely confused, asked.

"I can see by your stance—your attitude," Perez replied, off on a journey. "Sure. No, it's a job you have got to do, that's all."[11]

Even when presumably relaxing, Perez was confrontational. He and his wife, Agnes—dark-haired and said to be one of the few restraining forces in his life—one evening caught the Ted Lewis show at the Roosevelt Hotel's Blue Room. Lewis, an aging vaudevillian whose signature phrase—"Is Everybody Happy?"—had once been a national slogan, was introducing a new dance act called the Caribbeans. The Perezes politely applauded until suddenly seeing who the Caribbeans were: two black male dancers cavorting on stage with a blonde woman in what one reviewer described as a "sexy-dramatic interpretation of 'St. Louis Woman.'"[12]

Perez was furious. "I looked around for a decanter or anything else I could get my hands on," he later explained, recalling that he eventually settled for a large plastic basket of crackers that he threw at the dancers before angrily departing.[13]

Race-mixing. It made Perez shudder.

But Perez could get up a good head of steam over less incendiary provocations as well. One day he and Hebert accepted an invitation to appear on a New York television show called the "Jury of Public Opinion," a program where well-known public officials would argue political points of view before a live audience. Although the topics on the program were weighty, the general atmosphere was one of good-natured banter.

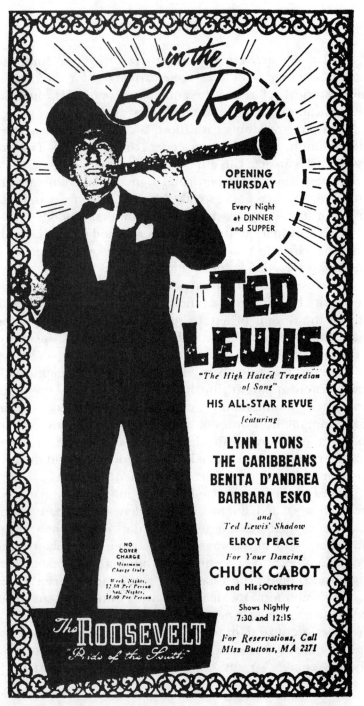

Leander Perez takes a powder. (Courtesy the *Times-Picayune*)

Until Perez arrived. He brought with him an imposing stack of law books, with each one earmarked for the case law and historical references he anticipated wading through for the edification of the television viewers.

"What are you doing with those law books?" Hebert asked with a laugh, trying to save Perez from himself. "This is a show. This is an act. This ain't court!"[14]

Decades laughter, Hebert still laughed when remembering the scene: "He was going to take his time, you know, and refer to this or that. Imagine what a dead show that would be."[15]

It was fortunate that Hebert was so good-natured. As the congressman who also repesented all of Plaquemines, he in many ways served at Perez's whim.

"I enclose a memorandum pointing out some of the evils of this United Nations declaration," Perez informed Hebert in one of the dozens of letters he would write to his congressman, this one complaining about a recent U.N.-sponsored Universal Declaration of Human Rights.[16]

What this had to do with Plaquemines Parish might not be immediately apparent. But Perez discerned that "unlimited, unrestricted immigration" would be the result of the declaration, bringing in "hordes of communists and the forced intermarriage of colored with whites under the penalty of federal law." Perhaps, indeed, these kinds of people were on their way to Plaquemines Parish at the very moment![17]

What Hebert was expected to do about the U.N. matter was never clearly stated. But no one could deny—Perez had spoken.

More explicit was a letter asking the congressman to find out whether or not it was illegal to import Charolaise cattle. Perez wanted to add to his prize-winning herd of bulls and cows and thought the Charolaise from France were the best, "a very fine animal which withstands both heat and insect pests, such as we have in south Louisiana."

Hebert went straight to work, entering into a lengthy correspondence with the secretary of agriculture, which resulted in the government's refusal to allow the cow into the states for fear that the animals might be contaminated. Nothing annnoyed Perez more than if someone would not even try, so Hebert wisely sent him copies of his correspondence with the Agriculture Deparment showing all the work he had done.[18]

Then there was the matter of Walter Washington, the head of the National Association for the Advancement of Colored People, a group Perez detested. Somewhere, Perez wrote, he had heard that Washington said the "only solution to the racial question in America is in the bed." A sensational statement, if true. Could Hebert please confirm it for him, Perez asked.[19]

"Perez has dreamed up another one!" Hebert's secretary, Betty Harter, remarked. It was typical of the bemused resignation a request from the powerful Perez sparked.[20]

"Boy, he was really something," Hebert would someday laugh when reminded of Perez.[21]

But once, when a correspondent said Hebert was a little *too* close to Perez, perhaps nothing more than just one more supplicant, Hebert shot back: "Perez has always been my friend in politics and I hope to always have him on my side."[22]

Hebert genuinely liked Perez. At lavish banquests, where the jokes and drinks flowed, Hebert would inevitably rise—a journey perhaps made smoother by a few gin fizzes. After lavishly praising Perez the Man, Hebert would wind his way up to his expected oratorical pitch. Perez, Hebert intoned, was "the noblest Roman of them all." And then there would be a hail of applause.

"Perez loved it when I said that," Hebert later remembered, chuckling with the memory.[23]

II

Born in 1891 as the seventh of eleven children, Leander Perez had a lineage whose roots, he oftentimes told visitors, reached back to the nobles of Spain. Just as certainly, he denied he was a Mexican.

As farmers, the Perez family had rice, cotton, and sugarcane crops on the Star Plantation some ten miles south of Belle Chasse in Plaquemines. Perez later said his father, Roselius Perez, "got along fine, except when the droughts would hit a year or two running; that was pretty rough."[24]

But Plaquemines Parish was rough.

"About four-fifths of the total area of the parish is swamp and sea marsh," William Harris, Louisiana's secretary of agriculture, observed in 1881. It was also fantastically diverse, with teeming enclaves of Slavs, Spanish-speaking Filipinos, and Italians, who migrated to the parish in large numbers near the turn of the century, becoming a parish economic force with the hundreds of farms they would soon own and operate.[25]

Blacks, too, lived in Plaquemines, first, as slaves, brought in to "work the sugar cane plantations," author James Conaway would later note. By the turn of the century, blacks were no longer in chains, but they also had no real legal or voting rights at their disposal either, cramped into crumbling wooden shacks without electricity and running water for most of the twentieth century.[26]

"A crazed negro of Pointe-a-la-Hache was shot and killed at his home by deputy sheriffs and the Orleans police last week," a front page story in the *Plaquemines Gazette* reported in the spring of 1934, revealing the accepted racial attitudes of the day. "The negro, Euchere Sylve, was known for a long time to be mentally deficient and to be of a troublesome nature."

Proudly, as though they had just successfully ended a hunting trip—which, indeed, they had—the sheriff's deputies posed for a photographer after lobbing a series of tear gas bombs into the man's house and finally finishing him off with a round of shots from rifles fired at close range through a back window.[27]

In 1902 an entry in the *Encyclopedia Brittanica* noted that the "Negro child is on the whole quite as intelligent as those of other human varities, but on arriving at puberty all further progress seems to be arrested." It was a passage that, for

Perez, explained it all; how Negroes could docilely accept their deflated status without protest; how they *should* accept it, because they were incapable of anything more. For decades, Perez would quote that passage, almost verbatim. It was all the proof he needed.[28]

And then there was the question of the Negro's morality—or lack of it. "He is not too far removed from the jungles in his morals," Perez declared. "Make him believe he is the equal of whites, he wants that white woman."[29]

But, Perez protested, he *cared* for the black people of his parish. Eventually, as he grew richer and more powerful, they became *his* people. "We have two Negro schools across the river," Perez informed reporter Velie as he drove the surprised journalist around Plaquemines, "because the light-skinned ones won't mix with the dark ones."[30]

Visitors to Plaquemines were usually struck by the starkness of it all. Mile after mile inexorably pulled vehicles toward more empty miles, swamps, tiny fishing villages, bayous, eddies, and eventually nothing.

It seemed like the perfect place for a fuedal empire, and for decades a clutch of ruthless if elegant plantation barons ran everything in Plaquemines, as well as neighboring St. Bernard Parish. They were refered to with no originality as the "courthouse gang."

"These leaders were not politicians in the ordinary sense of the term," historian T. Harry Williams thought. "They were more like *caudillos* in a Latin country. They might on occasion cajole, but usually they issued genial orders."[31]

They handed out parish jobs by the hundreds to friends and family members, kept control of the local sheriff's office to make certain elections always went their way, and spread lucrative parish contracts and sub-contracts among a few favored businessmen. Those businessmen always offered generous and enthusiastic support on election day.

Foremost among the Plaquemines gang as Perez grew up was a cultivated man with genteel manners and a finger in every parish pie. His name was John Dymond, Jr., the son of a man who greatly advanced the science of sugarcane cultivation in the 1800s. He lived in the Garden District of New Orleans, had graduated from Tulane, and belonged to the exclusive Boston Club downtown. He also had carved out of an isolated island in Bay Adam, west of Buras off the Plaquemines coast, a tropical vacation retreat. Naturally it was called Dymond Island. There he and his wife, Nita, a former Mardi Gras queen, reigned.[32]

Like all men of good breeding, Dymond devoted much of his time to a harmless hobby. His particular obsession was an ongoing study of the Louisiana oyster.

He eventually wrote a small book, *The Oyster in Louisiana*, which went into great detail about Louisiana acreage, the number of canners and vessels, and how fishermen, as Dymond recorded, pulled oysters out of the sea with tongs to cull them on wooden decks. [33]

"As in other animals, the oyster is of two sexes, male and female," Dymond wrote, "but with the peculiarity that the same oyster may be one year male and the next year female."[34]

Dymond, who somewhat resembled the silent film comic Harold Lloyd, hardly looked like anyone's image of a political boss. But in fact, he was a fierce infighter—and nothing about parish political life escaped his attention. If a parish board needed a lawyer, all of a sudden Dymond won the appointment. When the parish voted to contract with a local newspaper to print all of its official business, the paper that just happened to be owned by Dymond's brother submitted the winning bid. Another Dymond sibling was named school board president for the parish.

None of this was lost on a young Leander Perez, whose own father, Roselius, had won election to the parish police jury but was never part of the ruling clique.

By 1910 Dymond had even perpetuated his rule in Plaquemines by making certain that he had plenty of friends in not only the local district attorney's office but also in the 29th District

Court for the parish, making any criminal investigation into his dealings unlikely. By 1916, as captain of the Delta Duck Club, which the New Orleans *Item-Tribune* later called "one of the most famous hunting organizations in the United States," Dymond reigned supreme.[35]

But out of nowhere a handsome man with penetrating blue eyes and a large, flowing mustache said he had had enough of Louisiana's courthouse gangs, of the Dymonds and Old Regulars of New Orleans who ran everything. In 1916 John M. Parker began an assault on the way things were.

A reformer, Parker candidly admitted he preferred to stay in the private sector "because there was so much money to be made." He was a man of painful contradictions: he hated Italians, calling them "just a little worse than the Negro, being if anything, filthier in habits, lawless, and treacherous." In 1891 Parker was one among a handful of white men who incited a riot that led to the lynching of six Italians being held in the Orleans Parish jail for possibly murdering the city's police chief.[36]

Yet Parker also fought for women to have the right to vote and diligently worked to destroy the Ku Klux Klan. A candid man, Parker once remarked: "Do not put me on a pedestal and do not expect too much from me. . . . I have made many mistakes and I will continue to make mistakes."[37]

Perhaps Parker's first mistake was to run in 1916 as a candidate of a third party, which had virtually no base in the state. Naturally, he lost. But not without a nudge by Leander Perez, who had graduated with a degree in law from Tulane in 1914 and was itching to get into public office. Bravely, the young Perez challenged a Dymond candidate in a state representative race and was badly defeated.

But what astonished Dymond was that this young upstart had the nerve to go around the parish bad-mouthing him during the election. When Dymond sought to set the young man straight, Perez "sent word to me that he would not be bossed by me," Dymond later recalled.[38]

When Parker made a return bid for office in 1920—this time as a conservative Democrat—he did not forget that strangely aggressive young man down in Plaquemines who so boldly carried his banner. Just weeks before the 1920 gubernatorial primary, the current judge of the 29th Judicial District was on an early-morning fishing trip with friends when he lost his footing on a slippery deck, fell into the bayou, and drowned.[39]

Just hours later, Parker, almost certain to win the election this time, prevailed upon the outgoing governor to appoint Perez to the empty bench. It would be only a temporary station, as there was only one year left in the term. But Perez quickly accepted and was introduced later that day at a Parker rally in Buras as "your new Judge."[40]

"I shall immediately take the oath of office on coming into the district," Perez solemnly vowed.[41]

But not if Dymond had anything to say about it. He wanted the appointment for himself and petitioned the state's Supreme Court chief justice to block Perez's appointment. "I became convinced he was temperamentally unfit for temporary assignment to the civil district court," Dymond later said of Perez, "and I opposed him."[42]

Dymond's petition would in fact be heard by the full court, but a slim majority, perhaps wary of alienating Parker, voted to affirm his trust in Perez.

Judge Perez. It was a title he would bear for the rest of his life, even after he stepped down from the bench. And he admitted to liking the sound of it himself.[43]

On the bench, Perez, despite his growing reputation for being intolerant, was fair. Weekly at the old gothic courthouse in Pointe a la Hache, Perez presided over dozens of cases, listening patiently to the endless charges against mostly poor people accused of doing everything from operating a still to stealing horses and cockfighting.

Rarely did Perez put a poor man in jail. Almost always he tried to work things out between fueding parties. Perhaps inevitably, the young judge's stature among the working people of the parish grew as they detected in him an incipient populism, a sympathy for the little guy that went unexpressed by Dymond and his men.

"He would give them the decision and they would go back and then the word would pass through the swamp: 'the Judge has said it, that's the way it is,'" remembered A. Sidney Cain, who would clerk for Perez in his New Orleans law office. "That's the kind of leadership he had down there."[44]

But Perez was destined to make news.

"I went to the Judge's bench to show him a record in a case," L.D. St. Alexandre, a one-time deputy clerk of court in St. Bernard Parish, would reveal in 1924. "In looking through his papers, Judge Perez raised one corner of a portfolio on his desk and I saw a pearl-handed revolver under the portfolio."[45]

CLERK TESTIFIES JUDGE PEREZ HAD PISTOL ON BENCH, the *Times-Picayune*, emerging as a Perez critic, duly headlined.[46]

Far more disturbing to Dymond and his friends was the aggressive manner in which Perez appeared to be appointing his *own* men to public office, striving to build a majority of Perez loyalists on both grand juries, petit juries, and general jury commissions, as well as in the office of the clerk of court. Even worse, Perez made a point during one speech in Venice of publicly calling Dymond a "crook and a grafter." Never had anyone dared to say such things about Dymond in Plaquemines before.[47]

"He is a young man, but utterly unbalanced," Dymond said of Perez, before adding, remarkably, "He thinks it right for political purposes to use the power of his office to favor his friends and punish his enemies."[48]

This made Perez a "menace," Dymond added, his anger rising, "a menace to good, honest government," the kind of government Dymond once had complete control of in Plaquemines.[49]

But Dymond failed to take the measure of the man he now

sought to defeat. Running for reelection to the state legislature in early 1924, Dymond suddenly found himself on the
defensive for also serving as president of the state's racing
association. So breezily had Dymond mixed personal financial
gain with political position that it never occured to him that
holding both jobs was a conflict of interest. As Perez began to
raise that very question, Dymond said that he wanted nothing
more than to "promote clean racing as a winter sport in New
Orleans."[50]

But when Dymond took on yet another job for big money,
representing local landowners in a suit against parish trappers, it was one job too many. Perez slammed him across the
parish, noting by the response of the crowds that Dymond was
quickly losing favor with the locals.

"He faces defeat in my parish largely through my personal
effort in exposing him," Perez confidently declared two
months before the January 1924 election.[51]

And Perez, to Dymond's astonishment, was right. On election day, the voters of the parish finally turned Dymond out—
an astonishing upheaval. In a graceless concession speech,
Dymond blamed everyone for his loss: "high jackers, bootleg-
gers and rum runners." The trappers, too, who "believe the
prairies should be open to them, they all voted against me."[52]

He reserved most of the blame for Leander Perez. "The
campaign he made against me," Dymond later said, regarding
Perez's tactics as a disease, "was responsible for my defeat."[53]

But Dymond was not entirely vanquished. Together with
more than fifty former and current parish employees, he drew
up a lengthy brief containing nearly two dozen charges of mis-
conduct against Perez and then called upon the Louisiana
Supreme Court to oust the troublesome judge.

"Judge Perez at various times since he ascended the bench
has been guilty of misdemeanors in office, incompetency,
favoritism, and oppression," the petition began. And yes, "on
one occasion he carried a concealed weapon—a pistol—while
on the bench."[54]

Perez seemed untroubled by Dymond's assault, warning: "The public will get an insight into many othersof Dymond's shady public associations if the case ever comes to trial." He promised a vigorous, if rather creative, defense.[55]

The trial, which began on May 12, 1924, was a big show in New Orleans. A makeshift wooden stand was erected in the Supreme Court's old courthouse in the French Quarter to accommodate hundreds of observers. "The court was crowded to capacity when the case was called for trial," a reporter for the *Times-Picayune* noted as the trial began. "Business in the two parishes below the city was said to be almost at a standstill while the citizens flocked to the trial."[56]

But from the opening hours of the proceedings, Perez turned the tables on Dymond. Through his attorney St. Clair Adams, Perez had read aloud in court all of the many charges of malfeasance he knew of against Dymond. Dymond was astonished, seeing before him the final proof that his adversary was, indeed, no gentleman. Frantically, he looked for a way out.

If only Perez would publicly apologize for calling him a grafter, Dymond suddenly proposed, he would withdraw the suit against him. Perez, relishing the moment, agreed, and shortly issued a letter that was also released to the press, beginning: "At this time, I desire to withdraw the language concerning you which I used at Venice, Louisiana, and which has been published on several occasions."[57]

It was a paltry victory for Dymond. Even Chief Justice Charles O'Neill seemed to have been converted into a Perez enthusiast when he took the extraordinary step of remarking: "I am very glad that this case has ended in this manner."[58]

O'Neill then said of Perez: "He has made some mistakes, but I say that those mistakes were mistakes of judgement. All of the members of this court are of the same opinion."[59]

Press accounts only added to Perez's Very Good Day. In a blaring front-page headline, the New Orleans *States* declared: JUDGE PEREZ WINS; OUSTER SUIT DROPPED. "It is a victory for Judge Perez since the prosecution fails," the paper explained, "and the suit is dismissed at the plaintiffs' costs."[60]

John Dymond never caused problems for Leander Perez again.

III

On the evening that Dymond lost his seat in the state legislature, an ecstatic precinct worker in the cluttered ballroom of the Roosevelt Hotel in New Orleans picked up a ringing telephone and exclaimed: "Oh, Huey! Hello, old man! Huh? Fine! Great! Rolling up a big total in the city and I hear you are sweeping the country."[61]

At the other end of the line, Huey Long grunted. Actually he knew he was not getting much of a vote in the city *or* the country. Of the 1,000 people that day who voted in Plaquemines Parish, only 26 cast their ballots for Long. But, statewide, on a cold wet day that kept many farmers home, Long did finish third and was suddenly seen as the possessor of a promising future.[62]

Only 35 years old in 1924—two years younger than Perez—Long was an upstart and a troublemaker who shared his enemies with Leander Perez. Long promised to throw out the insiders, and Perez was immediately attracted by both his cause and his charisma. When Long announced his second campaign for the governorship in late 1927, Perez rushed to his side. "Huey Long was a very intelligent person," the Judge later said of the man destined for mythic legend. "He was quite a builder, and, of course, he asked [and] sought no quarter and gave none."[63]

Decades later, years after most people assumed Perez simply went over to Long because he saw him as an emerging power—and that was mostly true—the Judge asserted that he also liked Huey Long for his vision: "He was not selfishly ambitious," Perez said of Long. "He wanted power, but he also had a program."[64]

And so did Leander Perez.

Perez's clerk, A. J. Cain, remembered seeing Perez at Huey's Roosevelt Hotel headquarters just days before the 1928 primary—a primary that put him in the statehouse. But how much actual work Perez did for the Long campaign is uncertain. This time Long got 450 votes in Plaquemines Parish, an improvement on his previous 26 but less than half the total won by his opponent.[65]

In the months after Long's inauguration, Perez quietly observed the new young governor and liked what he saw: Long was confrontational, curt, and cynical—but he was also getting things done, enacting a much-needed roads program and laying out the fundamentals for a free textbook program for the state's school children. Long, Perez saw, enjoyed thumbing his nose at his social betters, but even more he was pulling Louisiana into the modern era. In the spring of 1929, however, Long had finally gone too far. In response to his bid to impose a five-cents-per-barrel tax on refined oil, the legislature suddenly passed a resolution calling for his impeachment.

The charges were varied, but Long, for once, seemed entirely derailed. "They've got me," he despaired.[66]

"He went to pieces in the impeachment, gave up, didn't sleep for days," Perez later said of Long. But determined to save his hero, Perez went to the Heidelberg Hotel in Baton Rouge where Long was staying and vowed his support.

"I barely recognized the poor fellow," Perez later told an interviewer. "He was haggard and he hadn't slept a wink for nights."[67]

No one has ever said for certain exactly how Perez came to lead Long's defense team. Harvey Peltier, a Long leader in the House, thought Long himself summoned Perez: "I am sure Huey asked him . . . he invited Perez to be one of his lawyers." A. Sidney Cain, however, thought it was probably Perez who approached Long.[68]

What is certain is that Perez mightily bolstered a wavering team. "Huey was the man being shot at," said Cain. "Perez came in and with just a steady word—'Governor, this will be this way and this will be that way,'" restored Long's "balance of mind."[69]

Perez was defiant. "They can't impeach you," he told Long before setting up a team of lawmakers who would help him run interference in Long's behalf. "The most we ever had was thirty-five," Perez later said of the legislative turnout.[70]

At daily morning sessions, which Perez called "pep meetings," he went over strategy. In the afternoon, Perez sat in Long's law library, pouring over intricate case law and past impeachment cases. "Finally, they began to turn the thing around," remembered Cain of the Perez-Long effort.[71]

On the day of the impeachment hearings, Perez took center stage in a capitol chamber that one reporter said was packed with a crowd that stood behind the railings as "tightly as they could."[72]

Long puffed on a cigar as he sat beneath an overhead fan. Perez addressed the one charge that had finally made its way to the trial: that Long had attempted to blackmail Douglas Manship, the powerful publisher of the *Baton Rouge Morning Advocate*, who had been going after Long's tax bill. He wanted, it was said, nothing more than for Manship to simply lay off. If the publisher failed, it was charged, Long said he would reveal that Manship's brother was in a mental institution.

"There is no cause for impeachment on this act," Perez confidently began to a silent chamber. "What constitutes high crimes or impeachment conduct is not a matter open to question."[73]

The Supreme Court, Perez continued, had held that an impeachment charge must punish a blackmail attempt, "not the ethereal condition of the brain—and intent. Who knows a man's mind unless it is expressed?"[74]

Because Long never specifically spelled out what he expected to get from Manship, Perez argued, "What benefit? What advantage? Nothing!" He then demanded that the charge be dismissed.[75]

It was a sterling performance, everyone agreed. But

unknown to most of the proceeding's observers, Perez had helped craft an even better strategy that would be revealed the next day: a document that soon would be known across the state as the "Round Robin," containing the signatures of fifteen senators who refused to entertain *any* charge against Long.

"We were talking one day and the idea came to one of us," Perez later demurred. But other insiders agreed that Perez was the inspiration behind the brilliant Round Robin strategy.[76]

Long's opposition suddenly collapsed. The trial was over.[77]

"Governor of Louisiana by the grace of the people!" Long yelled to a thicket of cheering supporters outside his office.[78]

An hour later, noted reporter Hermann Deutsch, the chamber was "silent and deserted as it always is between sessions."[79]

The *Plaquemines Gazette*, in which Perez may have by this time had a controlling interest, harbored no doubts about who should get the credit for Long's victory: JUDGE PEREZ DEFEATS MANSHIP CHARGE, the paper declared in a huge front-page story, noting in a later edition: "A surprise party was tendered to the Judge and Mrs. Perez on last Monday at their beautiful home at Promised Land. A crowd of some two hundred or more together with the Pointe a la Hache Band made Whoppee for the Judge and offered congratulations for his wonderful work in defending the Governor against the false impeachment charges."[80]

Several days later Perez hosted a party himself. No record exists of the remarks he made at the joyous gathering attended by more than one hundred Plaquemines and St. Bernard Long supporters, but a reporter for the *St. Bernard Voice* said Perez gave a "brief narrative of the details [of the Senate trial] in a witty vein, loudly praised the governor for his untiring energy and ability, and his unflagging determination to do things for the good of Louisiana."[81]

Perez's energetic defense of Long not only made the two men closer. It transformed the Judge for the first time into a statewide figure.[82]

Meanwhile, on election days Plaquemines Parish was now nearly entirely in Long's corner. In 1930, when Long ran for the U.S. Senate, Perez's parish delivered him 1,913 votes to 131 for his hapless opponent. Two years later, as voters went to the polls to decide on a successor to Long in the statehouse, Plaquemines did even better, giving 3,152 votes to Oscar "O.K." Allen, while four opponents failed to get even a single vote![83]

That same year, another Long candidate for Louisiana's second U.S. Senate seat swept both Plaquemines and St. Bernard parishes with a combined 6,217 votes. This time the opposition was able to manage 204 votes.[84]

Clearly, by the early 1930s, Perez was in contol of Plaquemines and most of St. Bernard too. But his methods for keeping in touch with his constituents, noted A. Sidney Cain, were unique. Remembering a typical Perez hunting trip, Cain recalled: "He'd get off the boat on Venice on a Saturday at 1 p.m. and go up to the bar and order a drink for the house and turn around and over in the corner by the window there's a poker game, and he would take a seat in the game for half an hour."[85]

Then Perez would depart. Next stop: Triumph, and then Buras, and finally Port Sulphur. At each village he would visit the busiest grocery store or restaurant or bar, sometimes playing poker, sometimes eating, always catching up on local gossip, usually offering friendly opinions and advice.

"By the next morning everyone knew he had been there," continued Cain, who was certain word of the Judge's visit had travelled up and down the parish among excited locals. "They had all heard what he had said." And it goes without saying that if the Judge nicely *requested* that the same villagers vote for a favored candidate, they honored his request—absolutely.[86]

What Perez expected in return for his vote-getting magic was more often than not the luxury of simply being left alone. By the early 1930s, Perez had cleverly formed at least one front corporation, the Delta Development Company, which, in turn, was the same company that always won bids from the parish levee board to explore Plaqumines' rich mineral deposits.[87]

Playing both sides against the middle, Perez was soon a multi-millionaire, one of the richest men in Louisiana, if not the South.

And he was determined to protect his autonomy. When Long, in the summer of 1934, returned to Louisiana to solidify his command over the state with a flurry of measures usurping local control in favor of Baton Rouge, a bill was introduced allowing Louisiana to control local levee districts.

Perez instantly figured out what Long was up to.

"I can state without qualification that neither Plaquemines nor St. Bernard will give up its right to local self-government," Perez told lawmakers during committee hearings, revealing his first public disagreement with Long. "We'll not yield that right to any man or power on earth."[88]

Perez then quickly inserted an amendment to Long's bill exempting both Plaquemines and St. Bernard from his legislation. "What have you done to my levee board bill?" Long demanded when he saw how his legislation had suddenly changed.

"Nothing," Perez innocently replied, "I just put on a little amendment to take care of my parish."

"Those are the very levee districts I wanted to take over because there's oil down there!" Long yelled.[89]

Oddly, even as Perez was doing all he could to protect both Plaquemines and St. Bernard from Long's very long reach, he publicly supported Long's "Share Our Wealth" scheme to redistribute the nation's income, a plan that was, by 1935, terrifying the country's millionaires.[90]

Laying the groundwork to run for president in 1936—and probably certain he would have not only the backing of Perez but his financial support as well—Long returned in September of 1935 to Baton Rouge, where he was gunned down in the corridors of the new state capitol.

Days later, Perez arrived at the Roosevelt Hotel in New

Orleans to divide up the remnants of Long's kingdom and craft a winning political ticket to retain Long's seat in the Senate. Perez and Long's top men, including Huey's brother Earl, picked O.K. Allen as the man most likely to follow their orders. It was lost on no one that the man who would escort Allen before the Democratic State Central Committee when he officially declared his candidacy was none other than Leander Perez himself.[91]

Long's heirs in the late 1930s would prove sadly inferior to their mentor. The state was shortly bathed in a series of political scandals that would see the conviction and imprisonment of hundreds of Long cronies—including his eventual successor as governor, Richard Leche—on various charges of corruption and malfeasance in office. Those scandals, in turn, ushered in a wave of reform spearheaded by a conservative lawyer from Lake Charles, Sam Jones, who would be elected governor in 1940, and Hale Boggs, who would defeat a Long man for one of New Orleans' two congressional seats later that same year.[92]

With Long's empire in ruins, Jones turned to Plaquemines Parish with the hope of finally getting rid of Perez, too. The Internal Revenue Service pursued him, as did investigators with Jones's zealous Crime Commission. But Perez simply proved too elusive for his hunters. The IRS, after going over Perez's papers from 1938 to 1941, could find no wrongdoing. A Crime Commision investigator, meanwhile, hit his own brick wall in Plaquemines.

Prodding a parish grand jury to go after Perez, William Joel Blass one day listened with sympathy to the pleadings of one of the jurists. "He told me he just couldn't take on Judge Perez and that when I was older I might understand that sometimes we're forced to do things we don't want to do," Blass later said.[93]

But Jones was not finished with Perez. In the summer of 1943 the governor, incensed that Perez refused to recognize his appointment of a local sheriff, declared martial law in

Plaquemines and ordered into the parish a convoy of 11 trucks and more than 650 state guardsmen, all to take control of the local courthouse.[94]

"We will not accept the military decree of Governor Jones," Perez, wearing hunting fatigues, declared as he armed dozens of quickly-sworn in deputies and ordered the courthouse secured. "As men we know how to handle that situation."[95]

The troops, however, easily pushed through Perez's barricades, while Perez himself fled, disappearing, according to one reporter, "over the levee in front of the courthouse with a number of his courthouse guards just ahead of the approaching militia." Other reports said they saw Perez jumping on a ferry headed for the other side of the river.[96]

Jones won the battle, but the governor's victory was short-lived. The next year Jones was forced to step down because at that time the state allowed governors to serve only one term. When a less resolute successor—cowboy singer Jimmie Davis—took over the statehouse, peace returned to Plaquemines, and Perez's power continued unchecked.

By the late 1940s, Perez's profile began to cast a shadow beyond Louisiana's borders. He led the Southern battle for state control of the Tidelands, a fantastic mineral deposit just off the coast that was greatly enhancing his own personal treasury. In 1948 he helped form a third party in the hope of thwarting Harry Truman's reelection bid. The *New York Times* put Perez on its front page. *Collier's*, one of the country's largest newsweeklies, devoted a two-part series to him. "Perez," *Collier's* journalist Lester Velie wrote, "is emerging as an important national figure."[97]

The New Orleans *Item*, meanwhile, made Perez the subject of a six-part front-page series, one that resulted in a least one death threat from a Perez man against the reporter, David Baldwin, who concluded: "Today Perez is at the peak of his powers. No longer an unknown outside his native state, he has emerged on the nation's political scene as a figure of great and growing prominence."[98]

Yet for all of his power, Perez, by 1951, was worried. A new election for governor would take place in early 1952, and the Judge yearned for nothing more than a man he could control. From New Orleans, a new voice was heard. It belonged to an earnest young reformer named Hale Boggs, who was the heartthrob of do-gooders, the people Perez hated most.[99]

If Perez needed any more proof that Boggs was trouble, he got it when Sam Jones himself thundered out of retirement to declare that Boggs was the "one best hope for Louisiana under prevailing conditions."[100]

Weeks later, Leander Perez made an important decision. The 1952 election could be turned to his advantage, he was sure, but only if he first undertook a preventive action: Hale Boggs would have to be destroyed.

Leander Perez: some people just called him boss. (Courtesy Plaquemines Parish Public Library)

CHAPTER FOUR

Mr. Boggs Goes to Washington

It was not an accident that Lindy Boggs was the first person Hale Boggs turned to as he struggled over the question of running for governor. Almost from their first encounter, when Hale announced to Lindy at a Tulane fraternity dance that he would someday marry her, their relationship had been defined by Hale's emotional excesses and Lindy's unyielding realism; son/mother themes perhaps too complicated for either to understand.

It was Lindy who gave Hale his spine, although, a Southern lady, she was loath to admit it. "He honored me by letting me help him make big decisions," was all Lindy, eloquent of her place and time, would admit.[1]

Yet Lindy's role in her husband's professional life was much more than that. When Boggs, at age 26, seized an opportunity to run for Congress in 1940, he instantly realized that he needed the public support of reform Gov. Sam Jones. Repeatedly Boggs travelled to Baton Rouge with Laurence Eustis, his official campaign manager that year, hoping to meet with the governor and interest him in their campaign.

But Jones, who was notoriously stingy with his political capital, was frustratingly elusive. He either refused to meet with the two young men, or when he did, he dominated the conversation with other topics.

One evening, Boggs and Eustis returned to New Orleans particularly downcast. They just didn't seem to be getting anywhere

with the governor, they told Lindy. "Well, you're just going to
have to go back up there again," Lindy firmly responded.
"That's all there is to it. If you want to run for Congress, you
have to remind him!"[2]

Many months later, Jones finally did give Boggs his official
blessings, only after first making sure that the Old Regulars—
supposedly the reform governor's greatest foes in the city—
had no objection. And even then, Jones' benediction was
hardly enthusiastic. "If there was any opposition to him in our
ranks, it is rapidly disappearing," Jones said of Boggs.[3]

In the end, Jones may have backed Boggs because he had
nothing to lose. The incumbent, Paul Maloney, was that year
conducting an uncharacteristically listless campaign, and
seemed weaker than before. Meanwhile, Jones did owe a big
favor to an energetic group of mostly wealthy women reform
activists from New Orleans who had been an important factor
in his victory. And Lindy Boggs had served as a precinct captain for Jones with that same group.[4]

"Hi, sweetie, how is everyone?" Lindy cooed to old and new
friends alike. "Oh, darlin', do you have to leave now?" she'd
plead with a departing guest. It was impossible not to like
Lindy Boggs. Raised in Pointe Coupee Parish, Louisiana,
Corinne Morrison Claiborne came by the name "Lindy" when
a family nurse mispronounced her father's name—Rolinde—
and began to call Corinne that. The name stuck.[5]

Lindy's lineage was impeccable and included William Claiborne, Louisiana's first territorial governor, a man gravely
concerned that because of the "machinations of a few base
individuals," democracy would most probably never succeed
in Louisiana.[6]

Growing up, Lindy was a serious student who particularly
enjoyed her history and Shakespeare classes at the tiny St.
Joseph's Academy in New Roads before she entered Tulane.
She was also, very early on, a devout Catholic. The nuns at St.
Joseph "instilled in me a lifelong devotion to Mary, the
Mother of Jesus," Lindy later wrote, "that strong and virtuous

woman and unfailing guide to the paths of justice and peace."[7]

"Lindy went to school, rode horses, could bait her own hook, and was always a lady," her outspoken mother, Corinne Claiborne Keller Joseph—always good for a laugh—later said. "She was born with a silver spoon in her mouth—but it never went to her head, just her mouth."[8]

At Tulane, Lindy joined the staff of the *Hulaballoo*, the school's newspaper, as a correspondent covering the soirees and teas of Newcomb College. But it was at that same newspaper that Lindy first became aware of her future husband as she watched him agonize over his wordy editorials on mostly foreign policy issues. Sometimes Hale and Lindy found themselves finishing their copy together before heading off to a downtown printer where they watched the magical process of their written words taking on new life in newsprint as the small paper rolled off the press.

Always, Boggs was thinking or talking about politics: how Franklin D. Roosevelt's New Deal must be given a chance to succeed, how the U.S. should not be drawn into any foreign wars even as Hitler's Nazis were ascendent, why the socialists and even the Communists were at least addressing the nation's economic and social ills.

By her senior year, Lindy was certain: "I was in love with Hale," she said, and equally taken with "the drive he had and his ability to attract people."[9]

While most shared Lindy's enthusiasms for the man who would soon become her husband, not everyone liked Hale Boggs. "He acted as though he had all of the answers," Laurence Eustis later said, "and I think that turned a lot of people off."

Remarked Floyd Newlin, another Tulane graduate from the 1930s: "Hale Boggs could be real arrogant at times. He would tire people out."[10]

But always Lindy would be his saving grace, a grace that endured far beyond their Tulane days: "I did not always agree with Hale Boggs on everything," recalled James Coleman, another Tulane graduate from those same years, "But I could never vote against him because of Lindy. I just loved her too much to do that."[11]

"The one thing you always heard, and I mean *always,* was how insufferable he could be," said Ben Toledano, who would later manager several campaigns against Boggs. "A lot of people did not like Hale Boggs. They thought he was arrogant and full of himself. A big turn-off. But in the same breath they would talk about how much they liked Lindy, how gracious and kind she was. And that's why it was so hard to beat *him*."[12]

"Our parents were the bedrock upon which we built our adult lives," daughter Barbara would later say of Hale and Lindy. "What used to give me a great feeling of warmth and security was hearing Mama kind of giggle at whatever Daddy was telling her in bed at night."

Recalled Lindy: "Hale teased me so . . . you know, I never could tell when he was teasing me for sure, and that's the kind of teasing he liked best, the kind when I wasn't sure."[13]

After his election to Congress in 1940, Boggs lost some of his confidence when he was defeated for reelection two years later. In the middle of World War II he got a job with the Maritime Commission in Washington. Lindy moved back to New Orleans with the children. Lindy's letters to Hale were full of family news: "Barbara and Tommy look magnificent. Barbara actually has a 'tummy' and Tom's round as he is tall," she wrote of their oldest children. "They're wild as little bulls, though."[14]

Cokie, the youngest child, born on December 27, 1943, "tips the scales at an even ten pounds and is simply rolling in fat," Lindy wrote in early 1944. "She smiles and tries very hard to coo and can now follow our movements (not just our voices) with her eyes."[15]

"All our babies are asleep now," she wrote in late 1944, "and the house is so lonely. This is usually the time that we enjoy together so much (when you aren't at a meeting!). Even if you were at a meeting, I could read until you came in."[16]

Yet for all of her devotion to Hale, Lindy was no pushover: "You must be lonely when I don't write because I hate the days when I receive not a word from you," she chided. "You're busy too, I know. But, darling, you have many more moments to call your own than I do."[17]

In a separate letter, Lindy complained: "You know, precious, the responsibility of caring for and protecting our children without your aid is a job I don't relish."[18]

"It is impossible to imagine what would have happened to Hale Boggs without Lindy," pondred Eustis. "I mean, she was so tied up with his success, so much more than anyone knew, even in the earliest days. I just don't know how far Hale would have gone without her."[19]

II

Hale Boggs sprang to life in a family full of dreamers.

His grandfather was Robert Boggs, a frail man with a grand, grey beard who came to the Mississippi Gulf Coast in 1875 to carve out a small piece of property in the nearly-empty village of Long Beach with his wife Eliza Jane Inneriarity.

Robert Boggs was greatly inspired by the natural bounty of the coast. Surrounded by massive live oaks and gray Spanish moss that filtered a soil fertile for grapes, figs, nuts, and apples, Robert Boggs made his own mark on the shore, planting Long Beach's first orange trees along a narrow path of land near the ocean's edge that came to be known as Boggsdale.[20]

An artist, Robert Boggs studied drawing in New York and Italy, where he produced a large oil painting of a dark-skinned girl whose delicate hands enchanted him. Decades later, the painting was still in his possession at Boggsdale, and the girl's hands still entrancing. He was also a poet and a playwright. "Benebach: the Spanish Jew" was the title of one of his works. It is not known if any of his plays were ever performed.[21]

In his later years, Robert Boggs would also become a writer, laboring for hours on a manuscript he said would be his masterpiece. He called it "Man and Money," and would only tell neighbors that it was a treatise on the evils of child labor. At the time of his death, the manuscript remained unfinished and was later lost in a flood.[22]

By the time of Robert Boggs' death in 1919, Eliza Jane had given birth to four children, one of whom, William Robertson, would marry and give birth to six children in turn. From William Robertson's brood Thomas Hale Boggs emerged, discarding his first name as he reached adulthood, but never the insecurity that came from a father who, like Robert Boggs, chased dreams.

His father "jumped around from one thing to another without a sense of direction or inner stability," Hale later said. A sister, Claire Morrison Boggs, sharply disagreed: "Daddy did *not* jump around from one thing to another. He was rather high-strung. But as for his jumping around, that came when the Depression came."[23]

But, added Claire: "Daddy *did* have a low self-esteem about him."[24]

If Hale Boggs as a young boy was insecure, he hid it. In a scrapbook he kept while a student at Long Beach High School in the 1920s, Boggs described his aspirations: "To be true—first to myself—and just and merciful. To be kind and faithful in the little things. To be brave with the bad; openly Grateful for the good; always moderate."[25]

He then added that he felt no fear, and any pain thus far visited only served to "make my joys stand out."[26]

Like millions of kids in the Great Depression, Hale Boggs may simply have been too afraid to even realize he was afraid. Tomorrow would always be a better day.

Slender, tall, and dark-haired, with piercing blue eyes, Hale was also curious, and early on learned to read. "He just always seemed to be thinking about big things, world events, things he'd read about," said Claire. "He was kind of faraway at times."[27]

Another sister, Mary—two years his senior—would remember

that Hale asked "plenty of questions. A person wouldn't realize that he was, when he talked to them, he was getting all sorts of information from that person. And I suppose that was his way of being so interested in people. He wanted to know what they did and how they did it, and just everything he could find out."[28]

His curiosity and reading would soon pay off. In the late 1920s, the young Boggs entered a contest sponsored by the *Times-Picayune* called the Biggest News of the Week. A wildly popular feature that sometimes saw as many as one thousand students from southern Louisiana and Mississippi participating, the Biggest News of the Week challenged high school students to write a small essay on what they thought was the most important news of the preceeding seven days, and why. Winning essays won cash prizes ranging from $3 to $10—very handy money for a kid just as the country was entering the Great Depression.

Throughout 1929, Boggs won so many prizes that the Biggest News of the Week's editor, Beatrice Cosgrove, was eventually prompted to write him: "Pretty soon we are going to find ourselves automatically typing you a letter of congratulations with the close of each Biggest News contest, so chronic are your awards."[29]

Two months later, Cosgrove went public with her praise, writing in her Sunday column: "Hale Boggs has probably put his teeth in to more difficult problems during the course of this year than any other individual essayist." In the fall of 1930, Cosgrove lauded him yet again, telling readers that Hale's most recent essay on global economics was a "typical Hale Boggs theme. It has sound, solid thinking. Events near at home never interested Hale; world problems and results intrigue him."[30]

Coupled with a near-perfect report card, Boggs' participation in the Biggest News contest helped him secure a scholarship in the spring of 1931 to attend Tulane University. The Breaux Scholarship would not only pay for Boggs' schooling, it would also give him an additional $35 for expenses.

"That's all I had," Boggs would later remember. But it was enough to change things forever.[31]

III

Boggs arrived in New Orleans just as the city was falling apart. At least 10,000 people were out of work, many starving, and the papers were filled with tales of individual tragedies. An elderly blind man near death from a lack of food asked only that someone find a good home for his dog and treat him with kindness. "This is the only kind of treatment he knows anything about," said the man, F. R. Walker.[32]

A young father of four, Steve Ridley, was desperate: "It's a tough thing to admit, but I've got just a dime in my pocket this minute, and what I'm trying to figure out is supper for the family tomorrow night."[33]

Alexander Jules Heinemann was doing much better than either Walker or Ridley. The president of the New Orleans Pelicans baseball team, he was also a prominent businessman said to be worth millions. But when the stock market crashed in the fall of 1929, Heinemann lost more than $300,000. One morning in early 1930 he climbed up to the empty grand-stands of the old Pelican Stadium and shot himself in the mouth, dying instantly.[34]

Unlike Heinemann, Boggs never had much money, so he didn't know what he was missing when he arrived in the city nearly broke. But he knew that in order to survive he would have to find work, any kind of work, in his off-school hours. "I just didn't eat if I wasn't working," Boggs later bluntly explained.[35]

He sold Beechnut gum on campus, then moved up to seer-sucker suits, always hustling his fellow students. Finally he got a job digging ditches for the city.

Because Tulane was self-billed as the "Harvard of the South" and was the home to most of the city's elites, it might have seemed like an intimidating place for a poor boy from

Mississippi, but in the middle of the Depression bad times had hit the university too. Hundreds of students could only afford to go to the school on a scholarship. Many of them were the offspring of blueblood families whose royal names hid their depleted savings accounts.

"I had to very often put little specks of linoleum or cardboard in the soles of my shoes to cover holes," Howard K. Smith, also a new student at Tulane, would later admit. "These were not the best of times."[36]

Jimmy Coleman, also at Tulane, remarked: "Most of the kids in school had to work just to keep their heads above water. It wasn't a matter of choice. And Hale worked the hardest. He was always working, and never complained about it."[37]

At Tulane Boggs joined the school debate team and was given the unpleasant task of arguing the case in the 1932 campaign for Republican President Herbert Hoover, whose administration he greatly derided.

"I don't know why they thought a poor boy like me looked like a Republican," Boggs later joked. But he took the assignment, and won the debate, although he made certain to tell the school newspaper that he was, in real life, "a confirmed Democrat from Mississippi."[38]

In fact, Bogg's devotion to Franklin D. Roosevelt was widely shared among his classmates. A campus poll in the fall of 1932 found 243 students backing the bouyant FDR as he sought his first term as president, while only 93 cast votes for Hoover.[39]

More revealing of Tulane student sentiment was the support recorded for the Socialist Norman Thomas, who received 91 votes—only two less than the president.[40]

In fact, Tulane in the 1930s was the home of a small but decidedly busy Socialist movement that reached out to the city's labor movement and even dared to challenge racial segregation. Boggs was quickly attracted to the movement's passion for ideas and debate, although as he entered the school he was not certain whether he wanted to become, upon graduation, a politician or a writer.

That he could have been a very good writer was effectively revealed in the summer of 1932 after he briefly returned to Mississippi and wrote an essay called "The Ones Who Are Left." He interviewed an 87-year-old Confederate veteran along the Gulf Coast.

"He raises his arm and with one of his long, skinny fingers points towards the horizon across the Mississippi Sound," Boggs wrote. "Bluish trees are scarcely visible in the distance."[41]

"Over yonder is Ship Island and Fort Massachusetts, which was then a federal prison," the man told Boggs. "We were brought as captives over there, but they must have been scared of us because they put twelve miles of water behind us and about 100,000 federal troops in front of us."[42]

Boggs encountered his aging soldier at Beauvoir, the imposing home of the legendary Jefferson Davis, president of the failed Confederacy. "It was white and stately, breathing memories of days past," Boggs wrote.[43]

Here he also recorded a surreal scene: the wedding of a 76-year-old woman about to marry her seventh husband. "The bride was not blossoming eighteen nor was she blushing," Boggs wrote.

> She was a little wrinkled old lady whose round, humped shoulders made her old-fashioned, white voile blouse shorter in the back than in the front. She stood unmoved. Not even the waxy white, red-veined petals of the wilting Confederate lillies in her hands trembled . . . on her furrowed, age-yellowed face there was a look of perfect resignation to fate.[44]

One year later Boggs' interest in writing was further whetted when he visited a likeable eccentric named Maj. James E. Crown, the editor of the New Orleans *States*, then the city's second-largest daily.

Approaching Crown in a cluttered newsroom as he was playing poker with a group of reporters, Boggs announced he was looking for work.

"What can you do?" Crown, behind his thick horn-rimmed glasses, asked.

"Anything," Boggs replied.

"Okay, you're hired," Crown said quickly.

"What am I supposed to do?" Boggs wondered.

"You can do anything," Crown answered. "Go ahead and do it."[45]

Crown's paper was a lively sheet celebrating starlet romances, animal stories, and, best of all, political scandals, of which there were many after the death of Huey Long in 1935.[46]

Boggs filed regular reports on Tulane happenings, but increasingly found himself writing about local and state political news, news that seemed nearly uniformly bad as the scandals coming out of Long's declining empire enveloped New Orleans, where the remnants of Long's regime combined with the tough Old Regulars for truly bad government. For Boggs' young, idealistic classmates, the politics of the city quickly had become unbearable.

"People were stealing like crazy," Laurence Eustis, also a Tulane graduate in the 1930s, would later remember of the Old Regular cronies under the redoubtable Mayor Robert Maestri. "The public was ready for reform."[47]

Moises Steeg, a 1937 Tulane graduate, recalled: "There was dual officeholding. Nepotism. Misuse of public office—like the Dock Board people had the use of yachts and they'd go off to these parties on yachts. The conservation books were rigged, all kinds of things that were going on."[48]

Jimmy Coleman, just beginning to set up a practice, felt that "unless you were part and parcel of the political regime, you just didn't stand much chance of practicing in front of the courts, the way they were."[49]

Lindy, who graduated from Tulane's Newcomb College in 1935, was similarly upset: "In order to do any business, whether it was professional, in finance, banking, whatever, the mature people had to necessarily do business with the administration. . . . It was really up to the young people, in a way, to be in front of the opposition."[50]

Those young people, nearly all of them from Tulane, called themselves the People's League, and made it their task to weed out examples of local corruption with the goal of eventually toppling the Maestri/Old Regular regime. Inevitably Boggs, who entered law school upon the advice of Major Crown and graduated in 1937, joined the group and even served as their official spokesman. Politics, in Boggs' mind, had won out over writing. He wanted to enter public life but wasn't certain how to proceed.

One of the few woman attorneys in the city, young Marian Mayer Burkett, remembered telling Boggs that the People's League would be a good place to start. "Whenever there's a public presentation to be made, we'll let you make it so that you get good publicity out of it," she said.[51]

But Boggs' sudden prominent role with the group did not please everyone. When the League filed a series of briefs attacking the lackluster way a grand jury assigned to look into incidences of local corruption was doing its business, they also organized a massive demonstration on the parish courthouse steps attended by more than 5,000 people. Boggs gave the principal speech of the day, getting his name and face splashed across all four of the city's daily papers.

Moises Steeg, however, was hardly amused. "He made this talk to all of the people as though he was the one who handled this whole thing," said Steeg, who did most of the tiring legal footwork in the case, "and I don't remember seeing Hale there at any time before, even during the hearings."[52]

The experience left Steeg with a lasting impression: "Hale Boggs was a person who handled things in the most expeditious manner for the benefit of Hale Boggs. . . . I was always rather circumspect in my relationship with him."[53]

But the enormous publicity that Boggs generated from the People's League movement made him known city-wide, particularly to Uptown reformers with money who desperately wanted to topple the Old Regular/Maestri regime. They got their chance the following year when one of the city's two congressional seats came up for reelection.

By the summer of 1940, Boggs was off and running. It would

be an anti-corruption campaign that was greatly aided by cine-
matic inspiration: Boggs' young effort reminded some of the
popular Jimmy Stewart film of the year before called *Mr. Smith
Goes to Washington*, the story of a young lawmaker who goes to
the nation's capitol to fight corruption. "Mr. Boggs Goes to
Washington" soon became Bogg's 1940 campaign slogan.[54]

Lindy later admitted that there was "no immediate reason
to replace Mr. Maloney," the incumbent Boggs hoped to
unseat. And Laurence Eustis agreed: "Paul Maloney was really
a very honorable fellow."[55]

But that did not stop Boggs who—putting aside his own
previous reservations about the war in Europe—soon attacked
Maloney for not helping to prepare America for war. When
France, in the early summer of that year, fell to the Nazis,
Boggs even managed to somehow put the blame on Maloney.
"For years France has left her destiny in the hands of men
who were re-elected year after year," Boggs said in an obvious
reference to Maloney. "And where is France today but under
the dictator's yoke?"[56]

Boggs then attacked Maloney for failing to bring big
defense dollars to Louisiana, and even suggested that because
of the incumbent's incompetence, Louisiana was actually
prone to Nazi attack. "Louisiana, right in the line of attack
should Hitler move in to the South of us, today stands unde-
fended," Boggs declared.[57]

It was a campaign of relentless assault, the sort of effort that
would have greatly offended Uptown sensibilities had it been
done by an Old Regular or Maloney himself. Boggs regularly
referred to his opponent, decades his senior, as "sleeping" Congressman Maloney, and called Maloney's organized supporters
"common grafters" and "misguided henchmen." When one
pro-Maloney broadside dared to question Boggs' involvement
with a college group now thought to be Communist—Boggs
would soon hear *much* more about this—he called their queries
"fruitless witch-hunting" and "useless lies and slanders."[58]

Bouyed by his Uptown support, Boggs was certain he would

The winning poster of the winning candidate. (From the author's collection)

win in a landslide, one of the biggest victories for a congressional seat in the history of New Orleans, he said. He publicly predicted that easily more than 40,000 people would vote for him and that Maloney would be lucky to get 20,000. But on primary day, Setember 10, Boggs—who had campaigned nonstop everyday for more than three months and given hundreds of speeches—garnered just over 33,000, while Maloney, who barely campaigned at all, came in at just over 25,000.

It was not the mandate Boggs hoped for, but it was enough to make him, at 26, the youngest congressman that year in the nation.[59]

IV

Hale and Lindy arrived in a Washington somber with talk of war. They met their idols, Franklin and Eleanor Roosevelt, in a quick receiving line at the White House and quietly viewed an inaugural parade for the president that was dense with tanks and soldiers.

"Tears were running down my face," Lindy later said of her reaction to suddenly seeing, for the first time in her life, such an abundance of military equipment, "and I didn't even realize it."[60]

Suddenly, Boggs emerged as one of the most bellicose advocates of war, energetically rallying votes for FDR's controversial Lend-Lease Bill, which lent military equipment to a besieged Great Britain. Most important, Boggs urged a national draft, the same draft he once had deplored while a student at Tulane.

"I am a member of this generation of draftees," Boggs said as debate on the draft bill got under way. "I marched up last October 16 and registered with the other sixteen million."[61]

And that was all he did. Millions of his contemporaries registered *and* enlisted. But Boggs just then was beginning his political career. Even after the bombing of Pearl Harbor, when congressmen of draft age resigned and signed up, Boggs resisted.

He had a wife and children, and so could be properly exempted. Plus he was a public official, and the argument could be made that he was needed more in Washington than on the front. But that excuse soon evaporated as a result of the 1942 election. Old Man Maloney suddenly rose from the dead to challenge Boggs.

Maloney, his grandson later said, did not like the cavalier way Boggs had treated him in the last election. He thought Boggs was cocky and needed to be taken down a few notches. Out of nowhere, he waged the kind of tough campaign he had once been famous for and was suddenly seen, by the summer of 1942, as a real threat to Boggs. Things were only made worse when the Old Regulars, who earlier had signaled a truce with Boggs, went over to Maloney.

Talking to First District Cong. F. Edward Hebert, Boggs complained about his sudden change of fortunes. Hebert thought Boggs looked frantic and brought the matter up with Mayor Maestri, who told him the endorsement from the Old Regulars was a done deal. But Maestri, too, was worried about Boggs' emotional state: "If that boy doesn't go back to Congress, he jumps out the window," Maestri predicted.[62]

On September 8, 1942—nearly two years to the day of Boggs' election to Congress—Maloney was returned to office. Once the nation's youngest congressman, Boggs was now the youngest *ex*-congressman in the country.

He was deeply embittered by the results and complained that although the Old Regular opposition had hurt, far more devastating had been the decline in Uptown support, a decline he could not explain. In a letter to his old friend Laurence Eustis, who was by then in basic training at the U.S. Naval Air Station in Quonset Point, Rhode Island, Boggs reported that "old man Maloney" had beaten him by only "several hundred votes." In fact, Maloney's final margin of victory was more than 2,000 votes. Boggs lost, he complained, because he had "absolutely no organization, practically no money, and darn little help."[63]

Clearly his defeat was devastating.

Then, as he neared the end of his letter, Boggs added: "It is the consensus around here that old man Maloney is about to die. I know half a dozen people who are making novenas for that event to come off."[64]

Now out of office, Boggs still managed to avoid military service. He mulled over offers to run for mayor or a seat on the city commission. Not until the fall of 1943 did Boggs finally enlist, shortly thereafter receiving a commission as an ensign attached to the Potomac River Naval Command and the U.S. Maritime Service. Even Lindy thought her husband's lack of active service was a mistake.[65]

Hale Boggs in World War II was nothing more than a "swivel-chair officer who was in command of a complement of stenographers," Henry Vosbein, a World War II veteran who wanted to become the next congressman from the Second District, said in 1946 as Boggs attempted a comeback. Boggs could see that the political terrain of the city had changed in the four years since his defeat.

DeLesseps Morrison was now the young darling of the reform set, having beaten Maestri in the early 1946 mayoral elections. Morrison promised Boggs his support, but between the two young men who shared the same constituency there was always suspicion and envy. Other reformers relished the idea of defeating Maloney for good. But then Maloney surprised everyone by announcing his retirement, thus depriving Boggs of his most convenient target.[66]

Boggs entered the race anyway, calling himself a World War II veteran in his campaign literature, a claim that opponent Vosbein said was "an affront to veterans who were not in a position to pull strings." Boggs avoided active service, continued Vosbein, because he wanted to stay in Washington where "he could go to parties and enjoy his usual life."[67]

Boggs was incensed by Vosbein's remarks. But this time the Uptown reformers, curiously forming under Mayor Morrison a political machine that would rival the worst excesses of the

Hale and Lindy Boggs and their photogenic children: from Louisiana, but of Washington, they

Old Regulars, produced results, giving Boggs a big comeback victory on the heels of what he characterized as a campaign of "abuse and vilification."[68]

Weeks later, Hale and Lindy returned to Washington, the scene of their earlier triumphs. In Congress, Boggs also returned to House Speaker Sam Rayburn's fold, generally voting as a moderate conservative. He was for trade, the United Nations, and an ambitious program to provide housing for all of the returning GIs. Yet he did on occasion break with convention. When President Truman's nominee to head the Atomic Energy Commission was attacked as being insufficiently worried about Communist infiltration, Boggs rose to publicly defend him, winning a personal thanks from Truman in response.[69]

Similarly, when Truman's troubled Secretary of Defense James Forrestal retired and then killed himself by plunging from the sixteenth floor of the Bethesda Naval Hospital, Boggs was among only a handful of congressman who dared to attack Forrestal's critics. Forrestal, too, had been accused being soft on Communism.

In Forrestal's defense, Boggs even dared to point a finger at Walter Winchell and Drew Pearson, undoubtedly two of the most powerful newspaper columnists of their day. In a nation that was becoming, by the late 1940s, increasingly certain that Communists lurked everywhere, Boggs' comments underlined his opposition to what civil libertarians had come to call "Red-baiting," comments that probably came from the heart and won him few if any political points at home.[70]

Civil rights, too, portended nothing but trouble for the young congressman. Democratic Southeners were upset with Truman because of the party's pro-civil rights plank, a plank Truman actually did little to promote but refused to disavow once it was adopted. The vast majority of the Louisiana delegation to the 1948 Democratic Convention took a walk. But Boggs refused, although he thought Truman's nomination meant the "funeral of the Democratic party."[71]

"I will not walk out of the party," Boggs resolutely told a

New Orleans reporter. "We have to do things to keep our group together to stay within the party."[72]

But Leander Perez, seeing for the first time where the sympathies of this young Hale Boggs rested, had other ideas. Less than two months after the 1948 Democratic Convention he stormed into a Democratic State Central Committee meeting and persuaded a majority of the members to remove Truman from the November ballot.

Perez urged his fellow Southern Democrats to follow him into the Dixiecrat Party headed by Gov. Strom Thurmond of South Carolina, a party very much in favor of segregation and equally opposed to civil rights.

"It's a matter of self-preservation," Perez cried, sounding the battle call. "Are we going to lie down supinely and see the resurrection of carpet-bagging in the South?"[73]

Perez additionally invited Louisiana's elected leaders—to some it sounded more like a command—to join him. Dozens fell in line. But not Hale Boggs.

Although Truman's name was eventually returned to the ballot, Boggs after the 1948 convention tried to stay out of the Perez-inspired battles for the rest of the presidential campaign.

"At the moment I have just about decided to retire for good, what with the Dixiecrats, the Semi-crats, and the Donkey-crats," Boggs wrote to a friend that fall. "No kidding, the confusion here today is without parallel."[74]

On election day, both Truman *and* Perez won. Truman pulled off the greatest coup in American electoral history by winning the White House for another term after virtually every pollster dismissed him as a sure loser.

But Perez commanded Louisiana, swinging it—and a good deal of the rest of the South—to his third-party effort. He suddenly gave every appearance of being a king-maker, as Dixiecrats from across the South looked to his leadership for the next presidential election.

Emboldened, Perez flew to Washington to begin his next assault: an attack on the Truman administration's plans for the Tidelands, which proposed that while Louisiana and the other coastal states were entitled to a percentage of any proceeds gained from the offshore mineral treasure, it was still federal property.

"Every man, woman and child in the state of Louisiana is a shareholder in our Tidelands and waters," Perez proclaimed after talking Earl Long into letting him present Louisiana's case in Washington. All of it, even the oysters, fish, and shrimp, belonged to Louisiana, said Perez, who significantly added: especially the "resources of our submerged lands, such as oil, gas or other minerals."[75]

Already disappointed in Boggs for his failure to join the Dixiecrat movement, Perez nonetheless accepted the congressman's invitation to meet with House Speaker Rayburn and several Truman administration figures in the hope of reaching some sort of settlement.[76]

At that meeting, Rayburn made it clear that while Washington owned the Tidelands, Louisiana would get 37.5 percent of all Tidelands revenue outside a three-mile limit beyond the Gulf Coast, in addition to two-thirds of the revenues from all mineral bonuses, royalties, and leases within the Tidelands.

It was a good deal, or so thought Boggs and Lt. Gov. Bill Dodd, who came along for the ride. "The president was offering us far more than we hoped to get," Dodd later recalled. Boggs remembered being "very pleased" with the offer.[77]

Then Perez spoke and thunder struck.

Louisiana did not want 37 percent of anything, said Perez, perhaps thinking just then of all the money he stood to lose if Washington would not get out of the Tidelands, where his investments had nearly quadrupled in the past decade. Louisiaiana deserved 100 percent and was going to get it! He would urge Governor Long, Perez added, to reject any compromise.

"This ain't no compromise," Rayburn, who didn't like to be yelled at, simmered. "It's a gift, and you better take it while the president is in the mood to give it to you."[78]

Perez then made a few disparaging remarks about Tom

Clark, Truman's attorney general. Rayburn then, according to Boggs, "invited him to leave."[79]

And that, added Boggs, "was really the end of the Tidelands settlement."[80]

Perez swiftly departed with Rayburn vowing to never "sit in the same room with him" again.[81]

As he returned to Washington, one thing was clear to Leander Perez: Hale Boggs was not to be trusted. His failure to join the white Dixiecrat movement was suspicious, and his willingness to simply sign over Louisiana's birthright to billions of dollars in mineral wealth confirmed those suspicions.

Months later, as the New Orleans press speculated on Boggs' possible gubernatorial candidacy, Perez gave Boggs a taste of things to come. William Green, the powerful president of the American Federation of Labor, was in New Orleans, and Perez's newspaper—by now nothing more than a mouthpiece for his views—was certain he had arrived to strike some sort of nefarious deal with Boggs.[82]

In a front-page story underneath the headline HALE BOGGS FLIES TO BE HERE WITH BOSS, the *Plaquemines Gazette* reminded its readers that Boggs was a Truman supporter, adding: "Public-spirited citizens are warning that we must be on guard against deceit and double talk."[83]

"Hale Boggs and Mr. Truman are politically welded together," Perez roared, continuing the attack after Boggs finally announced his candidacy for the governorship. Because of his position on civil rights and the Tidelands, Harry Truman by 1951 was greatly disliked among Louisianians, and Perez decided to do all he could to link the president to Hale Boggs.

"I say Mr. Boggs' support in Louisiana today is nil, and he might as well stay in Washington."[84]

As Boggs was shortly to discover, Leander Perez had only just begun to fight.

CHAPTER FIVE

Miss Lucille

Saturdays were mostly quiet days in Plaquemine, Louisiana. It was a small river town of less than 6,000 across the Mississippi River from Baton Rouge that hadn't grown much at all over the past twenty years.

Farmers, foundrymen, and millworkers gathered in a town square dominated by a white stucco City Hall fronted by four paint-peeled columns across the street from the towering St. John the Evangelist Catholic Church with its bright orange tile roof.

For the laborers from nearby sugarcane plantations who came into town on the weekend, Plaquemine, for its size, had lots of grocery, drug, and department stores to chose from. Their names reflected the town's unlikely diversity: on Railroad Avenue alone was Joseph D'Agostino's Groceries, the Weill Department Store, Gomez's Groceries, and Breaux's Drug Store.[1]

Visitors might also wander into Mrs. Cox's Colonial House at the corner of Court and Bayou, "the Ice Cream House of Distinction," which also boasted a stocked magazine rack, or sit on the steps of a store near the town square and cock an ear toward a radio blasting out of a window somewhere, which today probably would be airing the big game between the Louisiana State University Tigers and Ole Miss.[2]

Other radio show offerings of the day included the live call-in *Appliance Auction* on WJBO, the *Hillbilly Jamboree* on WIBR, the science fiction serial *Space Patrol* on WLCS, and the Tulane/Vanderbilt game on WAFB (unlike LSU, Tulane this year was suffering though a losing season).[3]

Not many of the small wood-framed houses in Plaquemine had air conditioning in 1951, and even fewer had a television. For those that did, a test pattern from WDSU in New Orleans was the only daytime fare.

Nighttime shows began promptly at six with *Hop-A-Long Cassidy*, the adventures of a good cowboy always getting into bad trouble, followed by Groucho Marx's *You Bet Your Life*. Then Freddy Martin, successor to Frank Sinatra, whose career in 1951 appeared to be in eclipse, had his own musical variety program. Finally, the local television day ended around midnight with the sign-off *Prayer for Peace*.[4]

Townspeople in Plaquemine, more than a third of whom were black, usually entertained themselves with church socials, square dances, and picnics throughout the year. Evening hours passed pleasantly on front wooden porches— the absence of air-conditioning creating community for what it took away in comfort.

Plaquemine also possessed a handful of nightclubs and music halls, but here racial segregation was at its most pronounced. The Blue Tavern on Iron Farm Road, for example, typically billed itself as "one of the Most Modern Lounges in Plaquemine—for colored only."[5]

A reporter for the New Orleans *States* one day took on ride on the ferry that crossed the Mississippi River to Plaquemine Point and was surprised to discover yet one more of the town's diversions: gambling. Plaquemine, the journalist recorded, was "crowded day and night with persons hunting a chance to play the horses and shoot dice. Sixteen persons were found on one trip yesterday . . . they admitted that they were going to Plaquemine to 'lay some bets.'"[6]

But on this late fall Saturday afternoon something different was going on in Plaquemine. Hundreds of townspeople in their Sunday best gathered near a banner with the happy image of a sun bonnet being tossed into the air alongside a simple message: "Lucille May Grace for Governor."[7]

The mayor, Charles Schnebelen, was there, sharing the stage with W. H. "Little Eva" Talbot, an enormous man at more than 300 pounds, who had been in and out of state politics for more than a decade. Members of the extended Grace clan, as well as the Dardenne family—Lucille May Grace's mother's side—came out as well.

Suddenly the crowd erupted into cheers as the door of a gray sedan opened and suddenly emerged Lucille May Grace herself—or "Miss Lucille" as she was known to thousands of Louisianians—striking in a deep purple suit offset by a large white orchid pinned at her shoulder.

Tall at more than five feet, ten inches, Grace was also attractive, her hair fashioned in a swept-up bob. The handsome clothes, the orchid, and her ladylike poise had the combined effect of radiance. Miss Lucille would be the first to admit she was no Ava Gardner, in 1951 the most popular actress in Hollywood, but she was nevertheless comely and usually in robust health, although she had recently lost an alarming amount of weight—more than twenty-five pounds—and wasn't certain why.

"She has dark eyes under arched eyebrows, an olive skin, and the same square jaw that denoted strength, leadership, and determination in her father," observed Katherine Bourgeois in the *Baton Rouge Morning Advocate*.

Society reporter Patricia Sinclair, visiting with Grace at the French Provincial ranch house in Baton Rouge she shared with her husband, Fred Dent, and their 14-year-old son, Fred, Jr., told readers of the New Orleans *Item* that Miss Lucille's attire rarely strayed from a "well-tailored suit with a soft white blouse" and that she preferred high-heeled shoes which "show off her pretty feet and ankles."[8]

It was a mark of Grace's independence that she refused to relinquish her maiden name.

"But why print that?" Miss Lucille, much more accustomed to hardball political questions, demanded of Sinclair after the two women contemplated her choice in footwear. "It makes me look silly."[9]

And Lucille May Grace was never silly.

Margaret Dixon, the veteran *Baton Rouge Morning Advocate* columnist, once observed Miss Lucille campaigning across the state and wrote: "She is apt to desert her ticket mates for brief stops in filling stations and stores along the route." Grace, thought Dixon, was "indefatigable . . . a good campaigner and a hard-working one." Dixon would know. She had spent years covering the campaigns of Huey and Earl Long and was not easily impressed.[10]

After Grace visited Washington in the spring of 1950, *Times-Picayune* correspondent Edgar Poe became convinced Miss Lucille could someday soon make history and become Louisiana's first woman governor, largely because she had built such a "large personal following and has proved to be one of the greatest vote-getters who ever ran for a state-wide office in Louisiana."[11]

Two other writers for Louisiana's largest paper were similarly impressed. "With organizational support and a good ticket to back her up," E. M. Clinton noted in his Sunday column from Baton Rouge, "she would give anybody a whale of a race—she's that good a campaigner."[12]

Meanwhile Ken Gormin, in confidential correspondence with Hale Boggs in early 1951, warned: "Lucille May Grace is not a candidate to be underrated. Some political figures are doing just that—and I sincerely believe she will upset someone's little applecart."[13]

And it wasn't just the working press that was awed by Grace. "I would rather tangle with anybody except Sister Grace," Earl Long once exclaimed, although he frequently tried. Lt. Gov. Bill Dodd thought Miss Lucille was "an aristocratic woman and a very good politician." Long-time lobbyist George Bown also offered his assessment: "Lucille May Grace was very prim and proper. But behind that facade was a tough woman who wielded raw power."[14]

What undoubtedly surprised most of the men who dealt with Miss Lucille was how forthright she could be in business transactions while somehow always being a lady. "I hate women who act masculine and I hate smirking little 'feminine bits,'" Grace once explained. "So I am just myself."[15]

And when she was herself, she was awfully good. "She had the ability to think like a man, which was important in those days," said Naomi Marshall, a New Orleans businesswoman and long-time Grace friend. "That was her big advantage, and most of the men didn't know that until it was too late."[16]

Miss Lucille could also distinguish, usually by instinct, a talker from a doer. "She could speak with someone and determine right away whether or not that person was a reliable, conscientious person," said Ory Poret, who met Grace in 1947. "And that went statewide—whether it was a sheriff, an assessor, or any other parish official."[17]

Happily accepting a large bouquet of roses, Miss Lucille appeared to bask in the memories and support of the townspeople whom she had known since the days when she was a thin little girl playing hopscotch outside the old Grace family residence on North Street. It was recalled that her father, a determined man named Fred Gumel Grace, had been the long-time register of the state land office and that a grandfather had once been Plaquemine's mayor. Another grandfather from her mother's side served as the parish's first school superintendent.[18]

Suddenly Mayor Schnebelen, perhaps envisioning the wonders to come with a native girl serving as governor, announced that today would be officially proclaimed "Lucille May Grace Day in Plaquemine."[19]

There were more speeches and memories before Miss Lucille spoke, and when she did she created a powerful presence. "She had a very good voice," remembered Poret, who accompanied Miss Lucille on most of her campaign stops in the fall of 1951. "She never spoke above anyone's head. She spoke at their level."[20]

Charming and blunt, Grace directly addressed the question on everyone's mind: Could the state really be run by a woman? "Louisiana needs a housecleaning, and who can clean a house better than a woman?" Grace quipped. "When I say a housecleaning, I don't mean firing conscientious employees, but I do mean getting rid of deadheads."[21]

She then outlined her program. She would fight to maintain the great advances of Long populism as inspired by Huey, while doing away with its excesses, as exemplified by Earl. And unlike Earl, Miss Lucille added, she would not make any promises about pensions. Earl was going around doing just that, she said, and it was unfair.[22]

"Now they are trying to bribe poor unfortunates by promising a raise in old age pensions if they elect the hand-picked candidates," Grace charged. Earl Long and his cronies would do anything to stay in power. In fact, she added—warming now to her task—Earl had even spent $10 million of the state's money getting his nephew Russell elected to the U.S. Senate. Could these same men be trusted forever with the state's money?[23]

"What will happen to the pension program later on if there is a depression?" Grace asked. "That's the woman in me, wanting to save for a rainy day."[24]

Grace's hometown audience was obviously sympathetic. But tomorrow—a Sunday—she would make the same pitch all across southern Louisiana, in Labadieville, Raceland, and Houma. Catholic Louisiana always welcomed a Sunday speech. Protestant northern Louisiana, land of the blue laws, promised religious offense and empty streets for similar Sabbath work.[25]

As she plunged into her campaign for governor in the fall of 1951, Miss Lucille knew she did not have much money behind her, nor the support of any of the state's large political organizations, such as the Old Regulars in New Orleans. But she was convinced that if only enough people could meet her, look her in the eye, and listen to her up close, she would win.

That, after all, was how she had won five statewide elections in a row over the course of the last twenty years.

"The People's Choice," a sign from Miss Lucille's 1951 campaign announced. And like so many other things on Lucille May Grace Day in Plaquemine, the sign brought back memories of another era for the townspeople who knew her family so well. It was the slogan her father, Fred Gumel Grace, a populist, had used for the twenty years he headed up the state land office.

Fred Gumel Grace was once an overseer in a hot, swampy neck of the woods known for its sugarcane and racial oppression. "His attitude to get work out of the negro was wonderful," a town historian would later say of Grace, "based on firmness, fairness, and kindness."[26]

It was also based on some coercion. At the end of one grinding season on Christmas Eve, the black field hands were tired and wanted to go home. It was wet and dark, and everyone, including the mules that hauled the sugarcane over muddy roads to the factory, had had it. But piles of cane were still out in the field, and Grace wanted it sent to the factory while the boilers were still lit.

A business partner had a sudden inspiration: pass around just enough whiskey to keep everyone warm and in rousing good spirits until the work was done. Grace and his workers drank and cut throughout the rest of the miserable night, all the way to the middle of Christmas day, until all of the cane was finally gone and Grace at last told the men to go home.[27]

"Fred Grace was never at any time in his life addicted to strong drink," Desdemona Redlich, the local historian, jocularly concluded, but on the night of the Christmas harvest, he "came painfully near to injuring his good name."[28]

As a young man, Grace sold mill supplies for Woodward and Wright manufacturers in New Orleans, enduring years of hard travel across a state plagued by a lack of passable highways and roads. Suddenly, in 1908, the position of register of the state land office came open, and Grace decided he

wanted the job. He was only 37 years old and had no significant previous political experience. But like his daughter in
later years, Grace thought he could win if he met as many
potential voters as possible.

He even dared to invade New Orleans—then the Old Regulars ran the city—passing out cards boasting his candidacy in
the lobby of the St. Charles Hotel and promising, always, to
make the land office a "people's" office.

How many other hotels, bars, town squares, and festivals
the elder Grace visited is unknown, but his effort paid off. On
primary day he won a plurality of the votes and in the election
that followed received an outright majority.

He would survive twenty years of status quo governors until
a man came along who shared his vision. In 1928 Huey Long
ran a firebrand anti-corporatist campaign and confounded
everyone by winning a big plurality in the primary—including
Fred Gumel Grace's Iberville Parish.[29]

As Long entered office, Lucille May Grace—Fred's oldest
daughter—had already attended St. Joseph's Academy and
graduated from LSU, where she was elected class treasurer in
her freshman year, the first woman in the school's history to
hold a class office.

She was one of twenty-three women graduates at LSU in
1920 out of a total class of eighty-three. And she was also one
of the daring twelve female students who bobbed their hair, a
radical and alarming style that horrified traditionalists.[30]

All of a sudden, young girls like Miss Lucille were wearing
dresses with the hems cut just above the knee. Cumbersome
corsets and petticoats virtually disappeared. Some women
even smoked cigarettes and listened to jazz! F. Scott Fitzgerald
published his first novel the year Miss Lucille graduated from
LSU, the same year that women had finally won the right to
vote, and shocked readers with images of working women din-
ing alone in "impossible cafes, talking of every side of life with
an air of half earnestness, half of mockery, yet with a furtive
excitement."[31]

Lucille May Grace at Louisiana State University: was this the face of a tough politician? (Courtesy Louisiana and Mississippi Valley Collection, LSU Libraries, Baton Rouge)

Miss Lucille played the part of a wealthy New York business-man's wife in *Pink Pierettes*, a play produced by the school drama club, and followed that with her portrayal of Lady Crackenthorpe in *All of a Sudden Peggy*. She also sang in the glee club and was roundly buoyant. The inscription above her photo in the 1920 *Gumbo*, the school's yearbook, reads: "Hap-piness is cheaper than worry, so why pay the higher price?"[32]

By the time of her graduation, Miss Lucille had broken one more tradition—she got a job, clerking in the field note and map department of her father's office. She loved the work, deciphering old state and parish maps and researching obscure tracts. But Miss Lucille also strictly adhered to her father's mission for the office: everyone, poor or rich, must be received courteously, and all mail answered the day of its arrival.

In the fall of 1931, Fred Gumel Grace died unexpectedly, and for a moment the political world that his lively daughter delighted in seemed about to come to an abrupt end. But then Huey Long got an idea: the Grace name was an honored one in Louisiana politics. Why not give Miss Lucille a chance at running her father's office? She was only 30 years old and not very good at giving speeches. Veteran politicos in Baton Rouge were stunned. How could Miss Lucille run a major state office? She was too young. She had never run for office before. And, worst of all, she was a woman!

Huey Long would "never have appointed me had he not considered me the most competent person to fulfill the posi-tion," Lucille May Grace coolly told a reasonably skeptical press on the very afternoon of her appointment.[33]

Just days later, after attending her first professional confer-ence in New Orleans, Miss Lucille displayed the feisty indepen-dence that would soon distinguish her long career. "I let Carl Campbell, who was with my father in the state land office, do most of the talking," Grace said. "However, whenever I differed from them and I thought I was right, I spoke right up."[34]

She would never forget Huey Long. The document to

which Long attached his signature making Miss Lucille the new register became for her a treasured artifact, lovingly shown to visitors years later by a woman still delighted with her good fortune. She also maintained large, bulky scrapbooks that were filled with stories about herself, but more often, about Huey—cartoons, photos, and lengthy features.

"His mind was so far ahead of the others," Grace would later say of her mentor. Huey Long "had already seen things they hadn't thought about."[35]

And one of the things Huey Long could see was trouble. Suddenly Long began to hear rumors that someone in the Grace family tree was black. In a racially hegemonic South, this could be dynamite. He would not, of course, drop Miss Lucille based on idle gossip alone, but now it was up to her to prove to his satisfaction her lineage.

That she was compelled to do so infuriated some of Miss Lucille's most ardent supporters, but she raced back to Plaquemine and gathered old yellow birth and baptismal records to give evidence of her heritage.[36]

Huey studied Miss Lucille's evidence, declared himself satisfied, and promised her that her place on the 1932 ticket was secure. Miss Lucille, in return, bore Long no grudges. "I knew he'd see me through," she later said. "I never worried." Her goal for the 1932 campaign was to somehow just to get through it. Her standard speech, she said, was only "five lines long, written on the back of an old envelope—I think it actually took me just a minute and a half to deliver it." At one stop, O.K. Allen—tapped by Long to succeed him as governor—instructed Grace to "make it short."[37]

"If I make it any shorter," Miss Lucille replied, clutching the worn envelope in her hands, "I would simply get up and take a bow."[38]

Before primary day, she would also have to contend with the perhaps inevitable speculation that Long appointed her to her office because they were romantically involved. Similar rumors also pegged Alice Lee Grosjean, Long's pretty secretary, as the recipient of his attentions. Miss Lucille also worried, with Long, about the women's vote. "Huey told me that he thought the men would vote for me, but he didn't think the women would," she later said. "But the women must have, because I won."[39]

And she won big.

In a sweeping victory that saw every member of the Long ticket elected, no one won as big as Miss Lucille, who drew more than 233,000 votes to the 130,000 of her four opponents combined. That she even got more votes than O.K. Allen was undoubtedly lost on no one.[40]

In subsequent elections, Lucille May Grace, soon to be married to Fred Dent, a well-liked Baton Rouge businessman, proved that her 1932 victory was no fluke. She was easily reelected in 1936, receiving more than 367,000 votes to her opponent's 163,000 during the emotional peak of Longism in Louisiana, just months after Huey's assassination.[41]

But four years later, when anti-Longism was suddenly the rage, Grace astounded the experts again, winning more than 65 percent of the vote. And in 1944, when all of Louisiana was falling in love with Jimmie Davis, the conservative singing cowboy, Miss Lucille won by roughly that same percentage.[42]

Tired of reform governors, Louisiana in 1948 returned to Longism, and brother Earl led the charge. After her seventeen years in office, some wondered if the bloom was off Miss Lucille's rose. This time she was facing a woman opponent, Ellen Bryan Moore, who was also a veteran of World War II. "I thought I had a real chance to beat Miss Lucille because I thought people might be tired of her," Moore later said.[43]

But Moore, like so many of Grace's opponents in the past, was wrong. On election day, Miss Lucille won her fifth straight victory. [44]

Louisiana had never seen anything like it. Not only had Grace, by 1951, been in office longer than any other elected official of the state, winning stunning reelection triumphs, but she had done so as a woman.

"I'm telling you, she was tough as nails," Naomi Marshall

remembered. "That was what made her so successful both as an administrator and a candidate. No one could put one over on Lucille May Grace."[45]

Tough as nails. When Grace heard rumors that Moore—whose slogan was "More with Moore"—might challenge her, she sought to head off her would-be foe. "No one can run against me," Miss Lucille bluntly told Moore, promising retribution on election day. "She threatened me," Moore later claimed. "She could be tough that way."[46]

When another opponent, reviving old rumors that Miss Lucille and Huey Long were once intimate, persisted in calling her "Lucille May Grosjean," Miss Lucille was livid. "If you ever use my name in connection with that other woman again, I'm going to have my husband beat the hell out of you," Grace promised her tormentor, who wisely moved on to other topics.[47]

Even when the somber Robert Kennon telephoned Miss Lucille one afternoon as she was sitting on her front porch, announcing that he was running for governor and that he was considering her as his running mate, Grace had a quick response that must have startled the normally serene Kennon: "*I'm* running for governor, Bob. Why don't you be *my* lieutenant governor?"[48]

The young woman who in 1931 had claimed to be "scared to death" in front of large crowds had bloomed, by 1951, into a full-fledged campaigner who, noted reporter Bourgeois, "likes people, likes to talk to them, and firmly believes that quality to be a first prerequisite of holding a public office."[49]

Fred C. Dent, Jr., Grace's son, thought his mother was a particularly effective politician because of her astonishing memory. "If she met you on the streets of Marksville and then five years later ran into you in New Orleans, she'd remember your face and name," he said. "It was amazing."[50]

Miss Lucille was also popular because she knew how to work the state's political network. On the night Huey Long was shot, Grace and her husband were in the state capitol and heard the shots ring out. Frantically, Miss Lucille tried to find a doctor who could save Long's life. The next day and a half were torture. She and her husband stayed by Huey's side until it was too late, and were among the mourners at the massive hot September funeral that followed.[51]

But after Long's death, Miss Lucille became much more connected. She and her husband threw countless lavish parties at their Baton Rouge home, late-night celebrations thick with lobbyists, reporters, and anyone visiting the state capitol. "Am completely worn out today," she confided in a letter to First District Cong. F. Edward Hebert in the spring of 1941. "Saturday night eighty-eight sorority girls had a picnic out at home—last night we had a barbeque supper for two hundred florists gathered here for their state convention. It was really a party, believe me."[52]

When the local symphony society asked Grace to host an event for a traveling diva, she was only too obliging. Expect about seventy-five guests, they said. "I thought I better be ready for about one hundred," Grace thought. Then more than two hundred people appeared, sending Grace into the kitchen where she contemplated the night's finger cakes. "I knew I didn't have enough," Grace decided. So she personally cut each cake in two, "and everything went fine."[53]

She grew close to Congressman Hebert, called him "Eddie," and visited with Hale and Lindy Boggs in Washington, where she shared her gardening hints with Hale. "I'll tell you how to be successful with the talisman climber," she would remark. "You have to train it horizontally, along the trellis—you let it go up, or it won't do well."[54]

"One time when she had been in Washington, we had her in for dinner, and she sat near this hydrangea she had given Hale," remembered Lindy, who regarded Miss Lucille as her friend. "It was a beautiful flower with pinks and purples, and when we moved we took it to our new house where it just expanded and blossomed, a lovely reminder of a very sweet person."[55]

Above all, Grace loved being on the inside of politics.

"I am wondering if you have heard the sordid details of

what took place," she wrote to an overseas Bill Dodd in 1944, more than eager to entertain him with the latest Louisiana political machinations. "It's too much of a story to write . . . but I will try and give you some of the *highlights* and only wish I could tell you all about it."[56]

Eventually, Lucille May Grace also came to know Leander Perez—and she liked him. He frequently visited her office in the state capitol and her home on Highland Road. To Grace, the Judge was a figure of wonder. He had the same stubborn independence that she so admired in Huey Long, and an equal brilliance to back it up.

Observing Perez working the legislature during the 1950 regular session of the legislature, Grace reported to Hebert: "The Judge seemed very, very busy—noticeably with the Senators from north La. I know something is 'cooking' and it will be good."[57]

Grace was unimpressed with most of the men who had succeeded Huey Long in the statehouse. But Perez was something else altogether: "If he doesn't take over and assume the leadership," Grace said of Perez, "the Lord only knows what's going to happen to the state's affairs."[58]

Perez, in return, was more than happy to keep such an admiring friend in office. In 1948, as Ellen Moore thought she was about to win the endorsement of the Old Regulars, Grace prevailed upon Perez for help. All of a sudden the Old Regulars announced their support of Miss Lucille.

"They weren't going to support her as a unit that time," Moore later asserted. "But Perez got them to do so." Considering the closeness of the final results—Grace beat Moore by only 43,000 votes out of more than 560,000 cast—Perez's efforts were probably pivotal.[59]

II

But even with her many political skills, Miss Lucille could never have remained in office for so long without giving the voters something to reward their confidence in her. And that was her management of the state land office.

"It was a service-based office," said Poret, who went to work for Grace in the fall of 1947. "We could only do good. It didn't matter if a man was wearing khaki clothes or a tuxedo, he was given the same attention. We were strictly a service office."[60]

"It was a wonderful place to be if you were a cartographer or interested in anything that had to do with the history of certain parcels of land," remembered Fred Dent, Jr., who would often visit his mother in her statehouse office. "There were old maps and documents everywhere; some things dated back to the era of Spanish rule. It was a magnificent place."[61]

Created by an act of the legislature, the state land office from the time of its inception into the early 1930s was a relatively unnoticed berth in the state's bureaucracy, charged with maintaining the records on all of the land owned by Louisiana. This was hardly an easy task. Some of the documents dated back centuries into the era of French and Spanish rule.[62]

In addition, some of the land, thousands and thousands of acres, had since been deeded to private owners. Other land was leased to utility companies, oil and gas corporations, and individual speculators.

Other property that also came under the register's purview was known as "military boundary land," land that years ago had been given to Civil War veterans in the hope that they might carve out a future on the vast empty spaces.

Other land was leased to railroad companies. It helped them lay tracks through thick woods and across deep swamps with wooden bridges as they tried to haul people and cargo from one end of the state to the other.[63]

Each year the register's small staff filed a report with the state auditor that listed every public land transaction from the previous year. And each year the report showed the same thing: there just wasn't much interest in the more than 10 million acres of swamp land to the south and exploration offshore.

"People just had no desire to buy those lands," Poret said of the swath from Plaquemines Parish to Iberville Parish. "They didn't see the swamp as having any potential for them at all."[64]

More alluring throughout most of the 1920s was central and northern Louisiana, where the far smaller number of swamps could be drained and exploited for exploration. Oil wells sprang up everywhere, on wide-open, unfarmed patches of land as well as in the fixed platforms set in any number of small and medium-sized lakes.

Wildcatters, ignoring the swampy south, did their prospecting in places like Caddo and Bossier parishes, where they frequently hit paydirt. In the spring of 1928, for example, a dozen new wells were drilled in just those two parishes alone, with nine eventually producing either gas or oil.[65]

And this small boom was not only good for Louisiana's prospectors, but also benefitted geologists, chemical engineers, patent attorneys, and the manufacturers who produced drilling rigs, pumps, compressors, casings, and tools.

In 1925 there were less than twenty-five new wells dug in the state. But by the late 1930s that annual number was up to 150.

Of course, with the new drills came a dramatic increase in the amount of money the state land office generated from properties the oil and gas companies leased.[66]

As early as 1932, Huey Long knew the value of Grace's office. When O.K. Allen, trying to save state money, refused to approve an appropriation to buy Grace a new car for $1,500, Long hit the roof.

"Are you out of your mind?" he demanded of Allen. "Don't you realize how many millions of dollars that office brings into the public treasury every year through royalties and payments?"[67]

Needless to say, Miss Lucille got her new car.

That revenue, reaching a new high of $1.4 million in 1937, made some of the state's politicians nervous. The boom times, they warned, could not last forever. They pushed the state to move away from its dependence on oil.[68]

But Grace remained calm. She knew of the large numbers

of fields across the state that had not been tapped yet. "It is fair to say, I think, that the surface has only been scratched," she said. And, just as certainly, revenues more than quadrupled over the next seven years to reach $8.4 million for 1944.[69]

The drilling eventually unearthed a wholly unexpected source of revenue: the vast reaches of the Tidelands off the Gulf Coast, which suggested a pool of oil so deep and wide as to be almost unimaginable. In a short three years—from 1945 to 1948—some 548 new leases were given their approval by Miss Lucille, all allowing for further offshore acreage exploration.[70]

Suddenly oil revenue shot up to $29 million, and then, in 1949, it surpassed $55 million. And there seemed to be no end in sight.[71]

"I realized from the very beginning just how much the revenues from this area would mean to the state," Grace remarked in 1951, "since it is my duty to collect the funds."[72]

Washington and the Truman Administration, however, saw it differently, insisting that the Tidelands belonged to the nation and that a percentage of those funds would only naturally have to go to them.

Grace was incensed. Very soon the issue became something of a crusade for her, she later admitted, "something personal and sacred to me," because she so much wanted to see Louisiana succeed, and the money from the Tidelands belonged to Louisiana.[73]

As long as Washington and Louisiana quarreled over ownership of the Tidelands, tax revenue from it could not be used. "Think of what is going to happen if we keep delaying," Grace worried. All of that money, money that could be used to fund Huey Long's free schoolbooks program for poor kids or to pay for state pensions or to retire the debt, would remain simply unused! And what Miss Lucille could not get over was that the money belonged to Louisiana in the first place.[74]

Visiting Washington nearly half a dozen times between 1945 and 1951 to argue Louisiana's case, Grace soon grew embittered toward the federal government and particularly the Truman Administration. Increasingly in her public speeches she spoke of the dangers of big government. "Creeping socialism," she began to call it, and very soon she had even another word for it: "Trumanism."[75]

"This fight is bigger than any one of us," Miss Lucille declared during a visit to New Orleans. "We must join hands—the press, the people, and all officials, city, parish and state—or we will suffer an irreparable loss."[76]

If Washington took the Tidelands from Louisiana, she added, what would stop them from someday seizing the port of New Orleans, or the city's lakefront airport, or even the entire inland waterway system?

But not everyone in Louisiana shared Miss Lucille's alarm. Earl Long and Lt. Gov. Bill Dodd hoped for a compromise. Hale Boggs, meanwhile, didn't seem to be much involved in the matter at all. "I can tell you from personal knowledge, because I have attended all Tidelands committee hearings in Washington since 1946," Grace acidly observed, "that Congressman Boggs never as much as put in a single appearance at any of those committee meetings."[77]

Even worse, Boggs, too, was in favor of a compromise.

Grace was dumbfounded.

Other things about Boggs began to bother Miss Lucille as well. He seemed too close to the Truman Administration and wasn't concerned enough about the effects of socialism on American life, let alone Communism. Then Boggs himself seemed to confirm Miss Lucille's worst suspicions when a television interviewer in June of 1951 asked his opinion of socialism. And Boggs replied that he was a "middle of the roadist."[78]

Grace leaped. "One cannot be half American and half socialistic," she declared in a statewide radio address several weeks later. "We must take our stand one way or the other. But one cannot, as T. Hale Boggs publicly announces, be a middle of the roadist on socialism."[79]

There was one man, of course, in Louisiana who *did* bravely go to battle for the Tidelands. And for that, Miss Lucille's admiration for Leander Perez suddenly knew no limits. When the Judge argued Louisiana's case before the Supreme Court, some observers thought he bombed badly. Perez, said Bill Dodd, was "humiliated and embarrassed by Chief Justice Vinson and several of the other justices, who literally and physically turned their backs on Leander while he made a political speech instead of a legal argument for our case."[80]

Grace saw it differently. Perez, she said, did a "remarkable job" in front of the court, despite the antics of the justices. "I have never seen such rudeness and indifference as was shown by the judges of the court," Miss Lucille said. For all of his work, Grace thought, Perez "might as well have been whistling in the bathroom."[81]

Repeatedly, throughout the summer of 1951, Grace scorned the likes of Hale Boggs and Earl Long, both of whom she said were traitors to the state for their stand on the Tidelands. Just as often she lauded Leander Perez.

On September 13, the Judge returned the favor: "I think the best man in the race is a woman," he dryly remarked as he announced his endorsement of Miss Lucille, the one candidate "we know will not sell Louisiana down the river."[82]

This was a very promising turn of events for Grace. Already Perez's *Plaquemines Gazette* was giving Grace frequent and fawning front-page coverage. Now she naturally wondered if the fantastically wealthy Judge would not only bankroll her campaign but put his men to work for her, setting up phone banks, distributing fliers, just getting the word out that the Judge was serious when he said he wanted to see Miss Lucille as the next governor.

Soon a booklet written by Maurice Gatlin—a New Orleans attorney with ties to Perez—appeared, lauding Grace as an "experienced and competent public servant who has demonstrated her capacity to get votes."[83]

Just as certainly Gatlin, who probably released his work with Perez's approval, called Boggs an "amiable but colorless young man."[84]

Perez's swift backing of Grace meant the immediate support of both the St. Bernard and Plaquemines Parish Democratic committees. Meeting in Pointe a la Hache, precinct captains from those two parishes quickly ratified Perez's decision without even taking a vote. But St. Bernard Sheriff C. F. "Dutch" Rowley surprised the locals when he said he was going his own way. "I am a single swimmer," he declared.[85]

Three weeks later, someone had talked to Rowley, and now he was once again floating with the pack when he announced: "Judge Perez didn't indicate to me how far he intended to go backing Miss Grace. But I am ready to go along with him."[86]

As she entered the fall campaign, Grace was ecstatic. She was drawing big crowds, receiving positive press coverage, and had the support of one of the richest and most powerful men in the South.

Then on the evening of October 15, a Monday, everything changed. Miss Lucille entered the gold-paneled elevator doors to the American Bank Building in downtown New Orleans on her way to Perez's private office. She exchanged greetings with the Judge's secretary. Perez then handed her a thick stack of documents that he promised would turn the campaign upside down.

Here, Perez said, was stunning proof that Hale Boggs was far more than just a supporter of the Truman Administration, a liberal, or even a socialist.

Hale Boggs, Perez continued, was in fact, a Communist.

And it was now up to Lucille May Grace to do something about it.

Louisiana's first woman governor? (Courtesy Fred Dent, Jr.)

CHAPTER SIX

Red Corpuscles

"Liberty against Socialism!" declared the colorful Republican banners and red-lettered pamphlets that seemed to turn up everywhere in the dark 1950 elections.[1]

The Grand Old Party had a grand new cause: Communist subversion at the highest levels of Washington, a theme loudly expounded upon by Sen. Joseph R. McCarthy of Wisconsin who, in February of that year, claimed to know of at least two hundred Communists currently on the federal payroll, "working and shaping the policy of the State Department."[2]

Across the country Democratic incumbents were under siege, accused of being Communist dupes, or much worse, their sympathizers. In Maryland Democratic Senator Millard Tydings, a tough old man, was stunned one day to see of one several thousand doctored photos making the rounds across his state showing him amiably chatting with the head of the American Communist party. Tydings was naturally enraged and judged that the murky composite image actually illustrated only one thing: the "moral squalor" of his opponents. But Maryland's voters failed to share Tydings' outrage, retiring him from office in a decisive landslide.[3]

In California the fiercely partisan Richard M. Nixon was on fire, scorching the state with charges that his opponent, one-time Hollywood film actress Helen Gahagan Douglas—erudite and hardly a match for Nixon—was "pink right down to her underwear." Nixon, never a lady's man, was not really interested in Douglas' underclothes. But he was taken with the notion that any foe could be casually painted as a Communist sympathizer and that those colors could not be washed away in time for the election. Gleefully Nixon distributed half a million copies of what he called the "pink sheet," a document that compared the votes in Congress Douglas shared with the only Communist serving in the House, New York's Vito Marcantonio. Nixon cleverly neglected to mention that many other Democrats and even some Republicans had similar records, mostly voting on routine matters.[4]

Douglas was quickly reeling. "Thou Shall Not Bear False Witness," she naturally protested in full-page ads in response. But on election day she, too, disappeared under a landslide.[5]

Across the continent, in Florida, crusty Claude Pepper, folk hero of unpopular causes who thought many of the Cold War's worst problems could be lessened if the U.S. and Soviet leadership would at least negotiate, was undone in his own party primary by a 49-page booklet called *The Red Record of Senator Claude Pepper.*

"I was like a hummingbird fallen into a nest of screech owls," Pepper would later say of his electoral drubbing, adding that he had quite simply failed to anticipate the "slander, innuendos, and vituperation" that marked the effort against him.[6]

"In every contest where it was a major force," columnist Marquis Childs observed after the 1950 election returns were counted, "McCarthyism won."[7]

The GOP picked up a big twenty-eight new seats in the House and five in the Senate. At the White House, President Truman was feeling overwhelmed. His wife, Bess, said she had rarely seen her normally chipper husband so downcast. "They did just about everything they could think of, all that witch-hunting that year," Truman later said, calling the Republican anti-Communist crusade "the worst in the history of the country."[8]

Truman added that McCarthyism and the new inclination among the Republicans to call any opponent a Communist made him fear for the future of the republic. "The Constitution has never been in such danger," he would later reflect.[9]

But neither Truman nor his fellow Democrats could deny the most salient lesson of McCarthyism: it won elections.

II

The papers that Lucille May Grace filed with the secretary of the Democratic State Central Committee on the evening of October 15, 1951, were bathed in legalisms and nuance, yet clear on one point: Hale Boggs should be disqualified from running because he belonged to a known Communist organization, and Louisiana party rules quite clearly prohibited Communists from running for office.

Grace's petition, Boggs had angrily declared to reporters, was a smear, a deceit, nothing less than "the big lie," he called it. Boggs would gladly fight her charges, he vowed, as well as Leander Perez, before the DSCC, and failing that, in court.[10]

But as Boggs huddled with his attorneys over what must have been an anxious defense, he was plagued by memories of an intellectually energetic past; reality and illusion collided; epic battles with storybook heroes, years of brave words and sometimes foolish deeds rushed back in a flood of forgotten sensations to haunt him.

Boggs was only 21 years old in 1935 when he first began to write about war. He found work that summer as an emcee— every night in a white coat with his dark hair handsomely parted—fronting a dance orchestra at the trendy Markham Roof. Far from the sun-baked shores of Gulfport, Mississippi, were the footsteps of soldiers in Hitler's Germany or Mussolini's Italy, but Boggs read the papers and listened to the stacatto dispatches of radio broadcasters. War's flames licked the European canvas—how long until America became involved? How long until the country would send its own young to battle?

"There is no telling what we, as ordinary cannon fodder, must face," Boggs descriptively pondered as he returned to the Tulane campus that fall.[11]

In his preoccupation with events in Europe, Boggs was not alone. Author John P. Dyer, in his history of Tulane, thought students on campus during Boggs' years there were nothing less than cattle on their way to a "giant slaughterhouse.[12]

"And they rebelled against this," Dyer recorded, "against man's inability to create a world in which depression and war would not rob youth of its hopes for a life of usefulness and happiness."[13]

"We did not want to be in any more wars, and we were complaining about it to everyone," James Coleman said as he recalled being afraid. In small groups or in large auditorium settings, Tulane students gradually committed themselves to a peace offensive, urging pacifism through a series of busy rallies, parades, and seminars.[14]

And the mood stretched far beyond Tulane. It traveled, almost magically, from campus to campus across the country, creating a network of good cheer and fierce intentions.

A Gallup poll in 1935, for example, revealed that nearly 40 percent of the country's college students would refuse to serve in the military unless the U.S. was attacked first. A smaller faction—comprising 31 percent of the students—were more radical. Identifying themselves as "absolute pacifists," they vowed non-violence even if the country *were* attacked first.[15]

By November Boggs was prepared to make his first appearance at an anti-war event, a seminar at the gray-stoned Gibson Hall, where he introduced Rabbi Louis Binstock of the nearby Temple Sinai, already a prominent voice in local anti-war circles. "We are on the verge of another world war," Binstock told his concerned young audience, "unless the machinery of peace is strengthened to prevent it."[16]

This meant one thing to students: agitate for peace.

"War is caused by greed, by foolish nonsensical financial conflict, by insidious propaganda, by economic jealousy," Moises Steeg, on the Tulane campus with Boggs, declared during the first large anti-war rally at the school in the spring of 1936. Meeting on the cool, wet grass in front of the university library on the morning of April 22, students at the rally consulted their watches. At precisely 10:30 hundreds of other rallies on hundreds of other campuses across the country were set to begin.[17]

The Tulane students excitedly gathered around two wooden tables serving as a makeshift platform as Steeg, wiry and intense, explained the meeting's purpose. Suddenly a freshman named Shelby Moore ran up yelling, "This is a Communist meeting!" A group of boys quickly pushed him away.[18]

It was not the first time Tulane's peace demonstrators had encountered resistance. Howard K. Smith recalled a group of angry World War I veterans, whom he called "very right wing," marching onto the Tulane campus in search of pacifists.[19]

Calmly, Boggs met the men and sought to placate them. "He talked them out of their march," said Smith. "He talked them into believing we were not the radicals they assumed."[20]

But now Boggs outdid himself. Introduced as "General Boggs," he gamely jumped feet first on the tables and performed a Mussolini strut. He wore a green band jacket, blue trousers, and a cap. His chest jangled with medals. The audience, startled, laughed and cheered.[21]

"As Washington marched, as Caesar the Unconquerable marched, as Alexander the Great marched," Boggs began, so now would the "Veterans of Future Wars!"[22]

These "veterans" were a peculiar bunch. They had not actually served in any wars yet, but they wanted their GI benefits *now* so they could be enjoyed while they were still alive.[23]

"Arise to the occasion and show your patriotism," Boggs continued. "Heed the call of your country. What's the use of having an army, good-looking uniforms, and lots of medals if we can't fight?"[24]

His audience yelled in response: "WE WANT WAR!"[25]

It was all supposed to be great fun. But not everyone was amused. "They were Communists, pure and simple," judged Maurice Clark, Jr., "and my father was one of them."[26]

Maurice Clark, Sr., was only 21 years old, but typical of the young activist spirit then spreading throughout Tulane and the city. A resident of the tough working class neighborhoods off the Industrial Canal, Clark proudly belonged to the American League Against War and Racism, and, as he proudly revealed, was "one of them," a small group of disaffected leftists, socialists, and even Communists who gathered throughout the city to make their views known.

With his now-prominent role in pacifist circles, Boggs was suddenly exposed to an improbable group of idealists like Clark who were convinced that America was ready for revolution. They held rallies and handed out pamphlets written with the language of alarm until the police approached and moved them along.

One of their busiest meeting spots was the second and third floors of a three-floor brick building in the French Quarter, a block dominated by galleries and shops. This was the official home of the New Orleans Socialist Party, and at least once a week local activists hiked up a long wooden staircase to enter a salon where they recited poetry from the laborer's perspective, presented oral reviews of recent leftist books, and mulled over the coming revolution.[27]

"Public meetings every Thursday at 8 p.m.," a flyer for the group announced. "Headquarters open daily from 1 to 5 p.m. . . . Enroll now! Insist upon your place in this world! Establish a Worker's World!"[28]

The discussions were always spirited and far ranging. Many of the activists yearned for a dramatic restructuring of the nation's wealth and were certain FDR's New Deal was not going far enough. They talked about the large number of unemployed and frequently starving people in New Orleans; sharecroppers across the state who were prevented—sometimes brutally—from organizing; the war in Spain, where the forces of democracy were being crushed by pro-Franco fascist forces.

It was a curious assortment: Stanley Postek, an activist for the Marine Workers' Industrial Union, who was trying to form a local chapter down on the docks; Alice Simmons, a black

The movie that enraged. (Courtesy United Artists)

seamstress who marched for integration; Louise Jessen, a gray-haired, middle-aged Newcomb student who was both ardently religious as well as a Socialist Party organizer; and Mack Swearingen, a controversial Tulane history professor whose classes were so popular, recalled Abe Kupperman, an undergraduate in 1936, that students "monitored his course not even for credit. They just wanted to sit in on his lectures. He was very, very interesting, and of course, if a professor was controversial, that was even more interesting."[29]

Town and gown mixed amiably. When in the fall of 1935 a downtown movie house featured the United Artists picture *Red Salute*, which starred Barbara Stanwyck as a young leftist duped by Communists, the French Quarter activists complained, handing out pamphlets in front of the Tudor Theatre protesting the film's heavy-handed message. They even sent a telegram to Mayor T. Semmes Walmsley—then in his final months in City Hall—asking that he do something to stop the film.[30]

Walmsley, who enjoyed movies, did nothing. But Hale Boggs did. In his column printed in the *Hulaballoo*, the Tulane student newspaper, Boggs complained about *Red Salute* and mistakenly accused William Randolph Hearst—at the time a huge supporter of the military—of having something to do with the film. "The finger of Hearst, the most rabid opponent of free speech and constructive economic improvement in America, is undoubtedly in the production," Boggs charged.[31]

So casual had leftist activism on the Tulane campus become that one student, John M. Blair, proudly mentioned in his 1935 *Jambalaya*—the school's yearbook—listing, that, yes, he was a member of the debate and golf teams, but he was also an officer in the Student League for Industrial Democracy, a group that by then was widely suspected of harboring Communists.[32]

"The Tulane campus then was magnificent," remembered student Floyd Newlin. "It was active, my God. It was wonderful." It was a place populated with students, Newlin added, who were excited about "being involved in something."[33]

Perhaps only naturally some of the college activism was

shrouded in schoolboy pranks, such as Boggs' appearance as "General Boggs," a performance that annoyed some of the more serious organizers. Coleman remembered somehow getting hold of a large swastika symbol and waving it around as a joke at a rally.[34]

"We did crazy things," he tried to explain years later. "It didn't mean a thing."[35]

Laurence Eustis, who always claimed to enjoy drinking more than protesting, remembered a favorite slogan of the agitators: "Butter, not battleships," he laughed. "We said that all of the time. It meant the country should spend its money on people starving here at home and not worry about some far-off war."[36]

Years later Eustis would add that he was never very serious about the issues that so drove the Tulane and French Quarter activists. "It wasn't something I thought about everyday," he said. "I wasn't that kind of student."[37]

But Boggs was. In his *Hullabaloo* column after the big April peace rally, Boggs wrote: "America—young America—the part that is clean and untouched by profits, investments, and what have you—does not want to fight. Young America declares that it will not participate in war unless it will be in defense of the nation itself."[38]

The equally young writer Gore Vidal, swept away by the same youthful passions that consumed Boggs, joined a Veterans of Futures War unit at Princeton. Another student, Eric Sevareid, who would one day be a commentator for CBS, declared: "We began to detest the very word 'patriotism,' which we considered debased, to be a synonym for chauvinism, a cheap medallion with which to decorate and justify a corpse."[39]

Across the country more than 350,000 students participated in dozens of rallies similar to the one at Tulane. And reporters noted the movement was growing: in 1934, for the same one-day protest, only 25,000 students had turned out.[40]

And soon emerging as the largest of the peace groups was

DR. BUCHANAN
Interesting facts about —Tulane
Main Teacher—See Page 1

POLL
Results of student opinion re-
viewed by reporters—See Page

The Tulane Hullabaloo

Volume XXXII   NEW ORLEANS, LA., FRIDAY, APRIL 23, 1937   No.

STUDENTS STAGE ANTI-WAR RALLIES

Announce Summer Schedule

GET PICTURES

Picture parade of fraternities and campus organizations used in the Jambalaya may be secured from the annual's office this afternoon from one until five o'clock. The Jamb headquarters is located in the basement of Gibson Hall.

Funds will be delivered only to presidents or authorized representatives of the fraternities and organizations, announced Leo Meyers, in charge of distribution.

Recitation Set For June 12 And 14; Classes Begin June 14

June 12 and 14 have been set as registration dates for the 27th annual session of the Tulane University Summer School, with classes to begin on June 14 and end July 24, it was announced this week by Dr. Edward A. Bechtel.

The amount of credit which may be obtained by a student in the Summer School is three hours for the six weeks' course. University undergraduates, graduate students and teachers are eligible to summer School are accepted toward a degree and a certificate of credit will be issued for the satisfactory completion of any course.

Guest instructors for the 1937 session include Robert L. Bechtell, Mississippi State College for Women, Emma P. Cooley, and Zillah M. Mayer, New Orleans Public Schools, Paul C. Lacroix, College of Medicine, Julio del Toro, University of Michigan, and George W. Frasier, Principal Marshall High School, Long Island, N. Y. of the ...

Mayan Exhibition To Dominate Texas Fair

By Tula von Kurnatowski

To the Greater Texas and Pan-American Exposition in Dallas will go the Tulane Department of Middle American Research this summer to put on display exhibits from its library and museum in the giant Texas State Building of the exposition.

So announced Frans Blom, director of the department, on his return this week from conferring with officials of the exposition in Dallas. The D.M.A.R. will also show some of its special art pieces of Fine Arts, now the Texas State building, cooperating with some of the leading museums of the United States.

Selected as the nation's obvious center for getting a cross-section of the Latin-American peoples that is both ancient and modern—the Tulane department has been assigned the dominating position in the huge fair where millions of people are expected to see its exhibits during the four months of the exposition.

The Texas State building stands at the end of the principal avenue of the fair and faces the main entrance of the exposition. Because of this commanding position, practically every visitor to the fair will pass through the building after ...

8 To Vie For Burke Medallion

Debaters To Compete Before Oratorical Society Tuesday Night

Eight students have registered to compete for the coveted Gleudy Burke medal, Leon Pradel, speaker of the society, announced Wednesday.

Order Of Coif Initiates Five Law Seniors

Charles L. Rosen Is Named As Honorary Member By Fraternity

Order of the Coif, honorary legal fraternity, initiated five seniors in the Law School library, at a meeting Tuesday at 8 p.m.

They were Moise W. Dennery, Ashton Phelps, Charles D. Marshall, Hugh McCloskey, and Jules S. Sterg, Jr. Charles L. Rosen, New Orleans attorney, was elected an honorary member, Charles E. Dunbar, Jr., president of the general chapter, and a local attorney, presided.

Dr. Rufus C. Harris, dean of the college, talked on "The Lawyer and His Public" and as customary at the initiation the newly elected honorary member spoke. The subject of Mr. Rosen's talk was "The Young Lawyer of the Future."

Hulla Wins Top Honor In Rating

Tulane Paper Gains Coveted All-American Standing On Survey

Scoring 850 out of a possible 1000 points, the 1937 Hullabaloo received All-American rating, the highest honor available, in the annual critical survey conducted by the Associated Collegiate Press. Twenty-five college weeklies merited similar distinction.

Besides an excellent paper, both in its news coverage and feature material. There are few papers that achieve the same standard of excellence," the judge noted in the score book. The editorial page was also commended.

Three hundred and fifty-five college newspapers of all classes: dailies, twice and thrice weeklies, weeklies, bi-weeklies and monthlies entered the critical service. The names of 291 from this group were included in the honor ratings made public on April 15 in the A.C.P. monthly bulletin. Forty-seven were listed as All-American or "Superior." Of these, seven were also designated as "Pacemakers." Other honor ratings are as follows: First Class, "Excel- ...

Briefs Ready In Moot Court Competition

Shattles Will Lead Juniors Next Semester

Tulane, Newcomb Join In Protests Against Fascist

Sug·Jest

Miracle of miracles! Someone placed a suggestion in the Suggestion Box outside the Student Activities office in Gibson Hall!

Miss Pendergrast, Randy Feitus' able secretary, after long and fruitless opening of the box, Wednesday afternoon found it contained a'teasily enveloped message. All was agitation until the contents could be read.

The suggestion:

"I suggest you suggest Mr. Feitus suggest more students suggest in the Suggestion Box."

"Undoubtedly, you will suggest Mr. Feitus suggest that I don't suggest in the Suggestion Box."

SUG·GEST."

Merely suggested.

"Now Closer to W Than 1913," S; Kupperman; Fo Others Talk

Students of Tulane and comb joined in a national celebration of the anti-war move and Fascism yesterday mor at 11 o'clock on their indiv campuses. Arranged by the lane Student Union under the rection of President J. David Neil, junior law student, the was demonstration had the proval of university authorities. A huge rally was taps as th sembly was called to order the meeting dedicated to thousands of students who lost lives in the Great War."

T. Hale Boggs, senior law dent, as chairman of the meeting said: "We are here in a r and patriotic movement. ridicule on any one societies but to democrat feeling of students and the versity and some 1,000,00 ...

Student life in 1937. (Courtesy Tulane Hullabaloo)

the American Student Union, which by 1936 was also housing members from the Young Communist League as it sought a permanent place on the Tulane campus.

Boggs was only to happy to welcome them. "This week a significant step was taken on this campus with the formation of a local branch of the American Student Union," he wrote in his front-page column on December 11, 1936, calling the ASU a "national organization seeking to promote the economic and social welfare of students in America."[41]

But Boggs did more than offer the ASU moral support. He helped organize the Tulane chapter and was put in charge of a committee to support a student activities building, one that could be used to promote increased student activism.

Finally it was all too much for a middle-aged man who viewed Tulane's growing peace movement—and Boggs' participation in it—with dismay. Arthur de la Houssaye was a prominent Uptowner, a member of the prestigious Boston and Stratford clubs, and, according to journalist and editor Walter Cowan, "a flag-waving nut."[42]

"He could with one smile charm the birds out of the trees," de la Houssaye's daughter Helene would later say of her strong-willed father. "Or with one look he could bomb them out."[43]

The daughter never forgot how her father operated. One day, discovering a pack of cigarettes in Helene's purse, he "took one look at me, drew himself up to his fullest height, and looked down that imperious nose and said, 'You don't know how you've hurt me.'"[44]

Helene never smoked again.

Now de la Houssaye, on his way to becoming president of the Sons of the American Revolution, went to work on Hale Boggs.

Although fourteen years older than Boggs, de la Houssaye was interested in his young charge because both men belonged to the Beta Theta fraternity at Tulane, which sponsored little brother/big brother relationships among its members. Boggs fraternally called de la Houssaye "Icky," while de la Houssaye referred to Boggs as "in-kai."[45]

The solemn de la Houssaye genuinely liked Boggs, who could always impress an older, powerful man. Plus that fact that Boggs was now escorting Lindy Claiborne, the daughter of a family whose roots reached back through Louisiana centuries, was not lost on de la Houssaye, who revered a noble lineage.

But in the fall of 1936 de la Houssaye had other matters on his mind. Subversives, he decided, were running amok in New Orleans, threatening the republic itself. With a small group heavy with Uptowners, de la Houssaye helped form the Louisiana Coalition of Patriotic Societies, a group that would uncover and battle Communist subversion wherever it lurked.

"We want to call to your attention that within the past three years there has been a vigorous campaign conducted to inculcate Communistic doctrines in our schools, colleges, and churches," the group announced in a fund-raising letter released in early 1937. "Their work here in New Orleans is only a part of a national program to weaken our military and naval forces so as to make this country defenseless in case of a national emergency."[46]

And the American Student Union very shortly became de la Houssaye's number one target.

Reading in the *Times-Picayune* of Boggs' involvement with the ASU, de la Houssaye asked his ever-enthusiastic counterpart to visit him in his downtown law office. "I told Hale there was some indication of Communist infiltration" in the ASU, de la Houssaye later said he told Boggs.[47]

"Hale then left my office and had nothing further to do with any of the groups that were raising sand on the Tulane campus," de la Houssaye then descriptively added.[48]

Indeed, by the summer of 1937, Boggs had suddenly severed all of his ties with the city's leftist groups. But not everyone was so easily converted. Moises Steeg took one look at de la Houssaye's group and thought it was a joke. In response he announced the formation of a mock group called the Coalition of Red Hunters, whose mission, he mournfully declared, was to ban *everything* red on the Tulane campus, including red lipstick, neckties, dresses, "even red corpuscles."[49]

But by the beginning of 1937, most leftist activists in New Orleans had little to laugh about. The New Orleans Police Department, with the implicit encouragement of new Mayor Robert Maestri, unleashed a violent campaign against activists, to the point, said one later historian, of beating up organizers for one local labor group "in the back room of the Tenth Precinct."[50]

Henry Hermes, the secretary of the New Orleans Socialist Party, was arrested and beaten for inciting a riot when police caught him distributing literature in the summer of that year. That same summer Irene Scott, the wife of a black sharecropper trying to organize a union, was mauled outside her small farm house by a group of men. "They were all white men, sixteen altogether I counted," Mrs. Scott later said in an affadavit, "and all of them were well-to-do farmers against the union."[51]

When the New Orleans police busted into the local offices of the International Longshoreman Association, they arrested all of the women there, said organizer Lucille Pettyjon. She recorded: "Apparently they were searching for weapons, because one of them perceived an old door learning against the wall behind me and he looked behind it and found a small stick lying there and remarked 'Okay, Captain, here are your weapons.'"[52]

When Bernard Mintz, a young attorney and friend of Boggs, protested the confinement of Pettyjon and six other women, he encountered John Grosch, the city's tough chief of detectives. Mintz asked him why he was holding the union women in jail, and Grosch had a simple response: "Because I want to," he calmly said.[53]

When he subsequently learned that he could not even talk to the women, Mintz again asked Grosch why. And Grosch again calmly answered: "Because I want to."[54]

Several days later, Grosch and three detectives forced a separate group of Socialist and union organizers to quickly flee New Orleans, escorting their car late at night to the Huey P. Long Bridge, where Grosch delivered a memorable farewell address: "If we ever see you within 50 miles of New Orleans," he promised the activists, "we'll kill you."[55]

Maurice Clark, his son recalled, one evening answered a knock on the door of his Industrial Canal home and was abruptly hauled off to jail, but not before the New Orleans police rifled though pages of printed socialist material he had in his living room. Tulane professor Swearingen, publicly labeled a subversive by de la Houssaye, was fired by the university. Louise Jessen's husband, Otto, was mysteriously fired from his job, forcing the Jessens to flee to Hawaii, where she eventually took her life.[56]

"Everyone ended up having to pay a price for their activism," said Trude Wenzel Lash, the wife of Joseph P. Lash, national secretary for the American Student Union, in New York.[57]

But Joseph Lash, at least, had a powerful protector. Eleanor Roosevelt, who admired the young boy's idealistic fervor, shielded him from the worst excesses of the coming anti-red crusade.

Boggs, of course, had de la Houssaye. But the lessons of the depleted fortunes of activists such as Clark, Swearingen, and the Jessens, as well as many others, could not have been lost on him.

Suddenly, Boggs no longer talked about pacifism or the efficacy of anti-war movements. Just as swiftly, he no longer had anything to say about the American Student Union and fiercely denied that it ever existed at Tulane. Even when confronted with stories printed in the local press *at the time* of the ASU's formation at Tulane, Boggs had nothing more to say.

It was all an illusion, he maintained. There was never an American Student Union at Tulane.

But others told a different story. F. Edward Hebert, a reporter for the New Orleans *States*, with many connections on the Tulane campus, said there was never any doubt in his mind that the ASU had a Tulane chapter and that Boggs was an active member. "He *did* belong to a left-wing, a Commie outfit," Hebert later charged, adding that he even told Boggs to stop playing games and tell the truth.[58]

"Say, sure you belonged to them," Hebert advised Boggs. "You were in school, you had chicken pox, you had measles, you had fever, sure; but you're a grown man now, you've out-grown that foolish stuff."[59]

Boggs, Hebert added, swiftly rejected his counsel.

Another person, who was a student on the Tulane campus at the time, offers even more contradictory evidence. "There is no question that the American Student Union had Commu-nist influence and that we knew about it *at that time,*" Floyd Newlin later adamantly declared with a hint of anger in his voice. "Swearingen made that clear. He explained to us the issues and what the principles were." And Boggs, Newlin added, *"belonged* to the American Student Union. He defi-nitely belonged to it. He was a campus leader in it."[60]

But if Boggs would deny the existence of the ASU in 1937, just as the anti-red movement gathered steam in New Orleans, he had little incentive to do otherwise in 1951, as anti-Com-munism reached a fever pitch across the country and Leander Perez was hot on his trail. Already Perez was handing out copies of an irregularly published newspaper called the *Federa-tionist,* which reproduced photos of Boggs in his band uni-form giving what the paper called a "Communist clenched-fist" salute.[61]

And that was about all Perez had. He was still short of prov-ing anything. In fact, Perez never would find a formal charter application for the ASU at Tulane. But there was one for the League for Industrial Democracy, which the *Nation* in 1934 would say was "extremely active" at Tulane.[62]

In 1936 the League had merged with the larger ASU and assumed its name. Together they formed the largest Commu-nist-front group in the country.[63]

Because the ASU inherited the League's chapter on campus, it eluded the normal charter and designation procedures at Tulane.

There was only one thing Boggs still did not know: how much of any of this had Leander Perez—a man with an obses-sive need to know—put together fifteen years later?

CHAPTER SEVEN

Full of Politics

In clover, Leander Perez was a sage lion. Nothing pleased him more than catching prey by surprise.

"The Judge," a stubby-fingered guard with a broken nose would say, "is a brilliant man."[1]

"He always liked to have the upper hand," thought Rosemary James, a New Orleans journalist who interviewed Perez and suspected his bellicosity tempered by a bit of the blarney. "It was *fun* for him to yell at people or act outraged about something, challenging them, trying to get them mad at him," James said, "but it was all part of the act."[2]

Reese Cleghorn, assigned by *Esquire* magazine to find a genuine Southern demagogue, only naturally turned to Perez. The man would have made Tennessee Williams blush, greeting Cleghorn on his Idlewood plantation in an immaculate white suit and holding forth on the differences between "darkies" and "niggers."[3]

"He would slam his fist on the table so hard that my tape recorder kept jumping around," Cleghorn later recalled. "He was *all* showman."[4]

And nowhere was the Judge's worth as an entertainer more on display than in the vaudeville of his dreams—the Democratic State Central Committee, which met regularly in the House chamber of the capitol. There Perez was at his oratorical best, cajoling, thundering, transforming himself into a thespian of Shakespearean dimensions, surely the equal of a Laughton or a Barrymore.

To readers of another time, the DSCC must seem like a throwback to a hazy postbellum, horse-and-buggy day when white men made all of the decisions, leaving women and blacks efficiently disenfranchised.

But to those who understood how power in Louisiana worked, the DSCC was a bit like the Mafia, College of Cardinals, and Politburo all rolled into one. Its power primarily derived from the state's devotion to the all-white Democratic Party and the millions of voters who loyally supported the system.

For more than a century, from the days of Andrew Jackson to Franklin Roosevelt, the Democrats in Louisiana reigned supreme, winning every state office in sight, while the party's presidential nominees easily won 90 percent of the vote and more.

In fact, only once in a century had Louisiana voted for someone else on the presidential level, and that was in 1948 when Leander Perez had an idea.

"We of the Southern states believe that custom, laws, and people go to make up a sovereign state," the corpulent W. H. "Little Eva" Talbot—a Perez supporter—declared that summer, "and these cannot be legislated out of existence by a Congress, a party, or a political platform."[5]

Talbot saw himself as the last of a beseiged Southern calvary, "retreating in good order with our flanks protected," as he dramatically left the national Democratic Party.[6]

F. Edward Hebert took to the pulpit to "drive the infidels from the party church," while New Orleans attorney Hugh Wilkinson, an Uptown lawyer with fantastic connections, issued a news release: "A line has been drawn between the North and the South and there is only one side upon which a Southerner can stand."[7]

What men like Talbot, Hebert, and Wilkinson were so worked up about was the loss of a "way of life," the racial segregation that they had known and accepted since their youths, an order that now was being challenged by the moderate civil rights program endorsed by the national party in its summer convention. To change things now, they cried, would be a tragedy of catastrophic consequence.

President Truman saw it otherwise. The South, he believed, was "living eighty years behind the times." He called for a ban on lynchings, poll taxes, and segregation in the nation's armed forces. Even more, Truman sought to promote racial equality in federal jobs that, in Louisiana, once went entirely to white men.[8]

Talbot, Hebert, and Wilkinson were nostalgic, anticipating the end of an era.

But Perez, at least, was going to do something about it.

Walking into the DSCC on September 10, 1948, the Judge unveiled a stunning plan: Truman's name—the name of the president of the United States—should be removed from the Louisiana ballot, he said. Calling the president a "political renegade" who was making a "demagogic bid for minority votes," Perez informed the committee members that only one name should appear on the fall ballot: that of Strom Thurmond, the governor of South Carolina and presidential nominee of the segregationist Dixiecrat Party.[9]

"It is time for the Democrats to reassert themselves," Perez declared, labeling the current national party a coven of "demagogues, pinkos, and Communists." In what reporter Ed Clinton thought was a "swift, well-engineered movement," the DSCC followed Perez's lead and kicked Truman out of the Louisiana Democratic Party.[10]

Perez once again emerged from the DSCC as its master. Only this time he took a president down with him.

Of all the many Democrats holding state office in the late 1940s, only Earl Long—the governor—could rival Perez's influence with the DSCC. By 1950, political reporters thought Long, with a smart use of patronage, had a working majority on the committee. "I got my people here," Long taunted Perez during one angry meeting. "I can get them here anytime—they're all on the state payroll."[11]

Long's control soon seemed so certain that at least twenty-five members of the DSCC did not even show up for one meeting, simply handing their proxies over to the governor to do with them as he pleased.

And one thing that pleased Long very much was axing Talbot from the Democratic National Committee—the Louisiana seat on that committee was determined by the DSCC—primarily because Talbot was a Perez loyalist.

Perez was outraged by Long's tactics. But Talbot seemed serene. "I've helped elect two governors," he would later said of his efforts for Jimmie Davis and Earl Long. "The honeymoon lasted a couple of weeks with one and a couple of months with the other."[12]

Now, appearing before the DSCC on October 2, 1951, Talbot promised to never be led astray by a man again. He would run on Lucille May Grace's ticket for lieutenant governor, supplying needed comic relief in the process. "I've been married to the same woman for twenty years and we get along fine," Talbot explained, "so this time I'm with a woman for governor."[13]

Just as DSCC members contemplated a Miss Lucille/Little Eva administration, Judge Perez walked in with a surprise of his own. "Every time the Judge had something to say, we listened," remembered Camille Gravel, a pro-Long member of the committee. "He was always trying to pull something."

This time Perez wanted the DSCC to change the way delegates to the national Democratic convention were selected, claiming that his only worry was that Truman—"a disgrace to the presidency"— would somehow trap Louisiana's delegates in his snare if he ran for reelection in 1952.[14]

Observers immediately realized Perez was up to something. Truman had no chance at all of winning Louisiana's delegates, no matter what system was used. In reality, Perez proposed a different system as a way of weakening Long's influence over selecting Louisiana's delegates.

But the biggest surprise of the day came when Hale Boggs, appearing before the DSCC to make his candidacy official, *supported* Perez, arguing that the Judge's proposal "allows the people to determine the issue. I believe in representative democracy."[15]

Boggs, not yet aware that Perez was soon to be his mortal enemy, here revealed his Uptown inclinations when he added: "It is difficult to understand why our outgoing governor would oppose a democratic way of selecting our representatives to the next Democratic convention."

Uptowners frequently extolled the "democratic way" if it meant weakening a Long. But as the committee members tried to decipher exactly what it was that Perez was up to, Uncle Earl himself observed: "Mr. Perez sometimes puts up things that no one understands but himself."[16]

This was too much for one Perez fan, old Frank Looney of Shreveport, who snapped: "Anyone who says he can't understand this is unfit to serve on this committee."[17]

Long could afford such insults—he knew he had a working majority. When the committee voted on Perez's idea, Long won: 52 of his men slapped Perez down, 21 voted in the Judge's favor, while a big 27 did not even bother to show up.

For reporters covering this October 2 meeting, the Long-Perez confrontation got most of the attention. Whenever these two titans met, it was worth plenty of good copy. But, according to Ory Poret, Miss Lucille's administrative assistant, the Long-Perez sparks weren't always what they seemed. Recalling a similar public feud between the two men, Poret remembered being shocked minutes later to see the same Long and Perez walking out of the rear door of the capitol, loudly laughing, "like they were the best friends in the world."[18]

Those same reporters took marginal note of two other important DSCC actions on that day. For the first time since Reconstruction, Negroes would be allowed to vote in what was previously called the "all-white primary." It was noted that in Louisiana prohibitions against black voting—unlike most of the rest of the South—were casually enforced. In fact, more than 65,000 Negroes in southern Louisiana alone had voted in one recent election. Making things legal, it was thought, would not change things much, although it might add as many as 30,000 more black people to the rolls in time for the January 1952 primary.[19]

But a second resolution passed overwhelmingly by the DSCC greatly diminished the effects of the first: Communists or anyone "associated with a Communist or Communist front organization" would be prohibited from running. The black *Louisiana Weekly*, speaking for the black leaders it surveyed, suspected an eerie connection between these two committee actions. "All that glitters is not gold," the paper warned its black readership. If Communists were prohibited from running, most black leaders would be, too, mainly because so many civil rights groups had connections with various Communist organizations.

Ironically, even the American Student Union, the Communist-front group Boggs could not these days get far enough away from, had a sterling civil rights record.

In a suspicious time, Negroes had a right to be suspicious. But at least one man went his own way. He was Kermit Parker, a New Orleans pharmacist with horn-rimmed glasses and a pencil-thin mustache who promptly declared his candidacy for governor. The idea of a black governor in 1951 was even more shocking than a woman candidate. But Parker promised a vigorous campaign. Naturally, like almost everyone else, he was for reform.[20]

Less than two weeks after this quirky DSCC meeting, Perez welcomed into his office Lucille May Grace, handing her a stack of documents as he instructed his secretary to place what she later called a "person-to-person call to Tallulah."[21]

Perez was trying to locate Henry G. "Happy" Sevier, his long-time fishing buddy and the chairman of the DSCC. "My father and Judge Perez always got along well," Sevier's son, Henry, Jr., remembered. The father, who also served in the legislature, would regale his sons with tales of the latest doings of the Longs and other legendary Louisiana politicians. But his stories about Perez were particularly fascinating, the son remembered, because his father always cast a wary eye at the Judge.

"I like Leander," Sevier laughed to his son, "but, you know, Leander *will* get you in trouble."[22]

Unable to locate Sevier, Perez's secretary tried to reach Jesse Webb, the secretary of the DSCC. Again, no dice. Finally, Miss Lucille left Perez's offices with the important papers in her hand and drove with her husband to Baton Rouge, where they found Webb and handed to him a document entitled "Objections to the Candidacy of T. Hale Boggs."[23]

Webb informed Miss Lucille that only Sevier could properly receive such documents. It was now past 11 p.m., and Sevier at that moment was sleeping in his suite at the Heidelberg Hotel. Worried, Webb woke Sevier with his telephone call and told him about the papers Grace had given him.

"Send telegrams out early tomorrow and then follow them up with letters and proxies," Sevier instructed Webb, as he wondered how he could get the full 100-member DSCC to Baton Rouge in the next two days to hear Grace's complaint.[24]

In the French Quarter that same night, Boggs looked at his own copy of Miss Lucille's suit and promised to officially respond within the next two days. "It's not a hard answer to file," he said. "It's just a question of denying a group of Perez lies."[25]

But it was more than that, and Boggs knew it. If Perez and Grace somehow convinced the DSCC that Boggs had, indeed, belonged to a Communist-front group, he wouldn't have a chance of defending himself on the campaign trail. Suddenly he remembered the DSCC vote taken just two weeks earlier that prohibited anyone in Louisiana from running for office if they belonged to a Communist group. That proposal was strongly supported by Perez's allies on the committee and now suddenly seemed like a noose waiting to hang the young congressman from New Orleans.

A separate charge was equally curious. Grace claimed that the state constitution specifically prohibited any federal official—and Boggs was certainly that—from running for a state office, although she never said where or how she came to that conclusion.

In an interview with a reporter the following morning, Miss Lucille expanded on her petition, charging that Boggs "publicly and in writing stated that Communism should be adopted as a solution for our national problems." Then she added an ominous note. As far as she knew, Miss Lucille continued, Boggs might *still* be a member of the ASU, as there was no evidence of his resigning the group.[26]

Talbot and Perez were in equally fine form that morning. "He's got nobody to blame but Hale Boggs," Talbot said of Boggs. "We will show on the trial of this case considerable evidence of Mr. Boggs' Communist tendencies."[27]

Perez quickly weighed in: "No name-calling or personalities can erase his own record," Perez said, sounding like a displeased teacher. "No petty or vicious personalities directed at Judge Perez can efface the record made by Boggs himself." And that record, Perez continued, clearly showed Boggs as a Communist.[28]

Boggs scrambled to defend himself. New Orleans Mayor deLesseps Morrison, who did not publicly endorse Boggs until an angry Lindy told him to, issued a press release of his own, exclaiming surprise that Perez would "hide behind a woman's skirt to make these charges."

House Speaker Sam Rayburn wired a quick statement of support, as did a group of House Democrats who declared: "To say that Hale Boggs is pro-Communist is like saying the American flag is the Hammer and Sickle." But at least one of the congressmen—Frank Chelf of Kentucky—privately admitted he came to Boggs' defense because Rayburn told him to.[29]

Even Lyndon Johnson, the Senate Minority Leader, sent Boggs a wire intended for public release: "Am amazed that any question would be raised concerning your loyalty to the Democratic Party or your Americanism," LBJ said. "During my many years of service in the House I know of no man more admired, respected, or beloved by his fellow members than you."[30]

But some of Boggs' defenders, in their zeal, strained credulity. "I still recall with pride his leaving Congress to go on active duty with the Navy during World War II," New York Cong. Daniel Reed remarked of Boggs, forgetting for the moment that Boggs "left" Congress because he was defeated for reelection and that his "active service" was a desk job stateside.[31]

Boggs also received the public blessings of a unique holy trinity: Monsignor Charles Plauche, chancellor of the Archdiocese of New Orleans, Rabbi Julian Feibelman, and the Baptist Rev. J. D. Gray, all of whom lauded Boggs' citizenship. Certainly Boggs was doing a good job rallying his troops, a fact made even clearer when the New Orleans *Item* condemned Perez as a dictator in an unprecedented front-page editorial underneath a huge banner headline reading: THE ISSUE: PEREZ VS. THE PEOPLE.[32]

For the next two days Boggs would huddle with attorneys from the prestigious law firm of Monroe and Lemann in the old Whitney Building in downtown New Orleans. His counsel would be further assisted by two city attorneys Mayor Morrison dispatched at taxpayers' expense.

Together the men decided that Boggs could best save himself by demanding a full and open hearing on the matter. In this his greatest ally was Leander Perez, who wished for the same himself.

Perez departed from New Orleans for Baton Rouge by way of Airline Highway. Here was a stretch of road to be appreciated, with signs of the progress Perez so worshipped everywhere. New hotels boasting of air-conditioning and television, ranch steak houses, and mysterious neon-wrapped nightclubs. None of this had been here in 1940, but with the advent of the post-World War II suburban sprawl, Airline Highway thrived. Now Perez could survey from his air-conditioned sedan with its white walls and shiny crome the future everywhere.[33]

But even progress could not obscure the potential danger ahead. There were stretches of Airline between the two cities that were barren and surrounded by swamp. Just to make certain, Perez kept in the glove compartment of his car a small revolver.

Arriving in Baton Rouge, the Judge found the capitol oddly quiet. For the past two days, Boggs had frantically wired every member of the DSCC and begged them to appear for the hearing. But it was the more important telephone calls from Governor Long that were making the difference. "I guess it's my duty to attend," Long said of the coming Boggs-Grace-Perez showdown, as he proclaimed only a passing interest in the matter.[34]

In fact, Long was vitally interested in the proceedings, and quickly passed the word among his people that the protest against Boggs must be defeated.

Was this a sudden stand against McCarthyism? Reporter Alex Vuillemont of the New Orleans *States* had his own explanation: "The governor, in a last-minute emergency meeting with many of his leaders, reminded them of the New Orleans fight in which one candidate stepped out of the race in favor of another, thus setting up the reform administration headed by Morrison."[35]

Translation: in order to dilute the reform anti-Long vote, it was necessary to *keep* Boggs in the race. Thus Earl Long, of all people, would emerge tomorrow as Boggs' greatest advocate, grandly declaring "let the people decide" in defense of a ballot listing for Boggs.[36]

Friday, October 19 was a cloudy, cool day in Baton Rouge. Radio listeners in the city, expecting to hear the "Platter Party" on station WTDS, or the courtroom drama "Perry Mason" on WWL, or the dance show "Dixieland Matinee" on WNOB, instead tuned in to hear the soft Southern accent of "Happy" Sevier as he attempted to gavel the DSCC meeting to order.[37]

"You've never seen so many people in one room," recalled Abe Kupperman, a former Boggs classmate called to serve as a factual witness. "It was complete chaos."[38]

"Everyone I knew was there," remembered Helene de la

Houssaye, also there with her father, Arthur, to testify for Boggs. "I looked around and saw every political leader in the state. It was very exciting."[39]

"It was out of control," thought Camille Gravel. "There was a lot of tension and anger in the air and a huge crowd in the gallery, the biggest group of people I've ever seen at a meeting of the committee."[40]

"I am going to ask all those who are not members to move back so the members of the committee will have ample seats," Sevier began. Loudly, dozens of people moved about, some carrying Boggs posters. Mayor Morrison, taking a prominent seat near the front of the chamber, brought with him dozens of city workers instructed to cheer at every mention of Boggs' name.[41]

"This is a serious matter and I want to be here to hear all of it," remarked Miss Lucille to a reporter, who described her as "extremely tense." Sitting next to her, Little Eva Talbot was bursting with confidence: "We are ready to fight this thing all the way, from here to the highest court," he declared.[42]

But before even this first battle could begin, Sevier, who was also running for lieutenant governor, had an important announcement to make. "I realize that this is one of the most important meetings that has ever been held by this committee and one of the most important matters ever brought before it," he began, before openly wondering if he should recuse himself because he was an active candidate in the race.[43]

Counsel for neither side objected, nor, by a unanimous voice vote, did the members of the DSCC.

It was just past 11 a.m. Hale, Lindy, and their three children entered the chamber to a flood of applause. Hale took a seat with his counsel while Lindy and the children sat prominently behind him. There was far less cheering—and even some booing—for Perez. Clearly, Boggs owned the gallery.

Scowling, Perez took his place at a small wooden desk behind Boggs, a lit cigar jutting from his frowning face.

As soon as Sevier gaveled the session to order, a member from Natchitoches, Arthur Watson, rose to propose a measure that would specifically allow anyone serving in Congress to also run for a state office at the same time.

Already the Long forces were exhibiting their control.

Suddenly Earl Long himself strode into the chamber. Laughing and waving in a navy blue suit offset by a colorful Confederate tie that had recently been given to him by the equally colorful governor of Alabama, "Kissin' Jim" Folsom, Uncle Earl took center stage. He shook hands with various members of the committee before finding a seat at the press table, where he would jump up and down for the rest of the session when he wasn't observing the proceedings with a look of benign mischief.

Perez quickly objected to Watson's measure. This clearly was an attempt to gut one of his arguments against Boggs' candidacy—although it was obviously the weaker of the two— and he would not let it go without a violent resistance. Citing state laws, the constitution, and even the bylaws of the DSCC, the Judge began a lengthy explanation of his suit. But the Long majority on the committee cut him off by voting to move the question.

Suddenly Earl jumped up. "Since I have urged and advised and have gone so far as to promise additional funds, if necessary, to pay the expenses of other members of the committee, I find it necessary as a member from Winn Parish to be here myself or be accused of double talk," Long began to laughter from the galleries.[44]

Perez quickly turned: "Will the Governor yield?"

"No!" Long shot back, resuming his speech.

Perez tried again: "Will the Governor yield?"

This time Long was even louder: "No! I might say that Judge Perez has been making two-hour speeches to this committee for twenty years, and this is my first time, and I take full advantage of the privilege."[45]

A roar of applause greeted Long's remarks as he began a wandering commentary on the gubernatorial race. Again Perez objected: "You are making a political speech," he growled.

"And it is a good one, too," Long answered to laughter.[46]

From Miss Lucille's table, Little Eva prodded Long: "What have you been doing, brother?"[47]

But Long ignored this plump challenge, turning his attentions instead to Miss Lucille, whom he said was "far out of her line of duty and has practically vacated her office to run for governor."[48]

Again, Perez: "The governor is making a political speech."[49]

"The Judge might be right," Long responded, momentarily reflecting. "If you want to know my opinion, it is full of politics!"[50]

With that, the gallery exploded in a hail of cheering. Sevier tried to gavel the session back to order. "Let's conduct this in an orderly manner," he pleaded.[51]

But Long was on a roll now. He next turned his sights on both Boggs and Perez and brilliantly suggested that the whole hearing could be the result of some sort of sinister collusion between the two men.

"I witnessed Mr. Boggs joining hands with his vote and later with his statement with my good old friend Leander Perez," Long said in reference to the October 2 DSCC meeting when Boggs and Perez had, in fact, become brief allies. There was something fishy about it all, Long concluded, before astutely observing: "With this charge, Judge Perez is aiding Boggs three times as much as he is injuring him in the eyes of the people."[52]

Bill Dodd, also a candidate for governor that year, later reflected that Long was a master of creating doubts about his opponents. If even 5 percent of the radio listeners now somehow believed that the Perez charges against Boggs were part of some put-up deal between the two men, that could be enough to make the difference in a close race.[53]

Finally, Long said he supported the right of any congressman to seek any state office he pleased. "It is the democratic thing to do," he remarked, "the fine thing, to allow Hale

Boggs or Leander Perez or anyone else who wants to run for governor of this state."[54]

Again, a torrent of applause erupted. This was what the Boggs people wanted to hear. But Boggs himself was feeling glum. Being allowed to run was one thing, but being allowed to run without mounting the defense he had planned against Perez's charge was another. Smoothly, Long was putting Boggs exactly where he wanted him.

"We are going to have order here or else I am going to ask the sargeant-at-arms to maintain order," Sevier warned the Boggs crowd. Then he asked for a vote. The result was a blowout, with 92 members supporting Long's proposal that a congressman be allowed to run for state office, while only 8 were opposed.[55]

This was too much for Perez, certain now that Long would probably simply adjourn the meeting without ever addressing his charges against Boggs. Angrily he demanded the floor: "The members of the committee should know the truth," he cried.[56]

Incredibly, Boggs now came to Perez's aid. He, too, begged the committee to conduct a full hearing.

"Will the gentleman yield?" Boggs addressed Perez.

"Yes," Perez calmly responded, "I will yield."[57]

Then Boggs, his blue eyes sparkling in a field of crimson, stood up and declared: "I say to the chairman and the members of this committee and the people of Louisiana that I welcome an open hearing here."[58]

His hands were shaking, but Boggs continued in a confident voice: "I want Mr. Perez to put his witnesses on the stand. I want to look at them in the eye and cross-examine them," he said as he moved towards Perez.[59]

Then suddenly thrusting his finger in Perez's face, Boggs, his voice rising, challenged: "And I will tell you something, Brother Perez, when you questioned my patriotism, you took a big bite that you are going to regret!"[60]

Photographers rushed to record the confrontation as pandemonium swept the proceedings. "Order!" Sevier yelled, smashing his gavel on the wooden desk in front of him. But the galleries were out of control, cheering, whistling, and stomping their feet.[61]

Perez turned to survey the noisy, menacing crowd and observed: "Mr. Chairman, I recognize the fact that Chep Morrison, the mayor of New Orleans, has send hundreds of his city employees to this hearing to create disorder . . ."

Boos poured from the gallery. "Order!" Sevier once again demanded.

Angrily, Perez added, "I mean to prove that."[62]

But before Perez could prove anything at all, Long wanted to quickly conclude the hearings. "It was so clear that that was all he wanted to do," remembered Kupperman, "just get the thing done with as quickly as possible."[63]

As Boggs and Perez feared, a Long man on the committee suddenly moved to dismiss Grace's suit on the grounds that it had been improperly filed. It seemed like a perfect out. By a 68 to 24 vote, the DSCC agreed. Just three hours after it began, the hearing was officially over. "The committee stands adjourned," Sevier dryly announced.[64]

But Boggs would not, could not, let it end there. He grabbed the House microphone in front of him and rhetorically asked: "Was this protest filed against me?" The statewide radio broadcast was connected. "No," he continued, "it was directed against you—the people. It was a confession of lack of faith in the people, of fear on the part of this man who time and time again has done the same thing in Plaquemines Parish, as everybody knows."[65]

Boggs turned toward Long and continued: "Here stands Governor Long—and I'm fighting him now with everything I've got—but I'll say he was mighty fair here today."[66]

Was it possible that Boggs still did not know Long was playing him as a pawn?

He then denied, again, that he had been a member of the American Student Union. "They say I'm a Communist because I went to some meetings when I was a college boy," he

The climax of the DSCC meeting: Hale Boggs confronts his greatest foe.
(Courtesy Photofest)

remarked. The committee members, officially done with their business, had no choice but to listen.[67]

"I went to a meeting to try and preserve the peace," Boggs added. Observers glanced at Lindy and noticed her eyes were wet. "I'm glad I did. If we had succeeded, we wouldn't have so many graves and crosses all over the world today."[68]

From Miss Lucille's table, Little Eva started to heckle Boggs, while Long, always wanting more, asked, "He hasn't rented this building has he? How about giving me fifteen minutes for my side?"[69]

But Boggs would not be silenced. First, he gazed at Little Eva and remarked: "I want to tell you about Eva. In 1944, when I went to him and said 'How about running Jimmie Davis' campaign?' I never saw him grab so fast, and I never heard him say, 'Hale, I can't do that because you're a Red.'"[70]

"About a week after Jimmie was elected governor, he said 'For God's sake, get that fat man away from me.' He almost drove old Jimmie Davis crazy," Boggs declared. With laughter engulfing him, Little Eva said nothing more.[71]

At that moment, Boggs' microphone went dead. Did a Long man pull the plug? Boggs didn't stop to wonder. He approached the speaker's platform and concluded: "I've talked too long. But I had a right to."[72]

At least Boggs had his say. Perez, trying to get the last word, declared, "You have just heard Hale Boggs take some free radio time on the air."[73]

But by now the audience was loudly leaving the galleries. Outside, a huge crowd cheered Boggs. It seemed as though he had won the day. All he wanted, he said, was to resume his campaign.

Inside, Miss Lucille gathered her belongings as Perez busily prepared his next step: a suit against Boggs in court. Naturally it would be filed in Lucille May Grace's name.

Throughout it all, noted one reporter, Miss Lucille had maintained "a tight-lipped smile."[74]

Now she just wanted to go home.

CHAPTER EIGHT

Not a Single Witness

On the following morning, Leander Perez and Lucille May Grace went to court some ten blocks south of the state capitol.

As they did, they entered a chamber loaded with political irony.

Perez and Grace filed suit protesting Hale Boggs' candidacy in the Nineteenth Judicial District Court of East Baton Rouge Parish. Judge Coleman Lindsey, one of four justices on that bench, immediately put his signature over an order directing Boggs—"as required by law," the form read—to formally respond within five days.[1]

Because Louisiana judges were elected to their positions, courthouse reporters oftentimes entertained themselves guessing how a particular judge might rule in a case based upon the political faction from which he emerged. Lindsey, for example, was a Long man—a one-time floor leader for Huey Long in the state Senate. Presumably he would receive kindly the petition of two other Huey Long devotees: Perez and Grace.

But in the next 24 hours, the Nineteenth Judicial would be joined by a new jurist, and his past professional affiliations indicated that he might be more sympathetic to a reformer like Boggs.

"I am an independent candidate and have never been identified with any political group or organization," the balding, genial Jess Johnson declared during his campaign for the

Nineteenth Judicial seat. "This is the first time I have ever offered myself as a candidate for office."[2]

Johnson was elected to fill the unexpected vacancy left by Carlos Spaht, who stepped down from the bench after Earl Long anointed him as the Long faction's candidate for governor.

Long, under pressure from local attorneys worried that a vacancy would create a logjam in the Nineteenth, then announced a special election for Spaht's seat. Upon the urging of a group of local businessmen and attorneys, Johnson announced his candidacy. He was a widely liked man, so popular, in fact, that when the members of the Baton Rouge Bar Association voted in secret to endorse a candidate for the race, Johnson—out of a field of eight—won going away, getting more than twice as many votes as his nearest opponent.[3]

Initially, Johnson was a reluctant campaigner. He had heard stories about the kind of compromises candidates for the bench in Louisiana were forced to make if they expected to get elected, and he wanted none of it. But his supporters would not let it go at that, petitioning him in early September to run. "Clients, businesspeople, laborers, and people of all walks of life have urged me to cast aside my personal reasons and become a candidate for this high office," Johnson revealed when he finally agreed to run on September 20.[4]

One week later, Johnson placed first in the primary, and easily won the October 16 runoff election. "I don't think any judge accepting his office is as free of political or group influences or alliances as I am today," Johnson declared on the morning of October 23 when he was sworn in.[5]

Wearing glasses and a light charcoal gray business suit, Johnson, standing beside his wife of more than thirty years—Ada, a professor of English at Louisiana State University—appeared uncommonly robust for a man of 64 years. And for good reason: he was. Every weekend, to push out of his mind the briefs and petitions and lawyers and witnesses that were a daily part of his life, Johnson would get on a horse just outside the city and ride.

"He loved nothing more; that was when he was really

With his wife, Ada, Jess Johnson awaits the Boggs-Perez-Grace fireworks.
(Courtesy the *Baton Rouge Morning Advocate*)

happy," recalled his son, Jess, Jr., who shared with his father the same passion for horses, but later laughed as he wondered whether he could ever equal the old man's stamina.[6]

Not only did Johnson, in colorful western garb, ride with the local sheriff's posse in city rodeos, he also liked to saddle-ride across the state.

The entire state.

"It was amazing for me to see him do that," Jess, Jr., said.

> Sometimes he would go with a riding partner and a trailer with two horses. One guy would lead off, the other would follow, and the two of them would leap-frog one another, one riding on the horse, the other driving the truck up ahead to meet him, for miles. They never tired the horses, either; but they always kept going.[7]

Every year, to commemorate the first 300-mile Pony Express run from Baton Rouge to Texarkana, Johnson and his horse would gallop past murky swampland, dense pine forests, and, by night, the faraway lights of a distant city, until he arrived above Shreveport, in Texarkana, feeling in his body the pain that never deterred an earlier generation.[8]

Although as a candidate Johnson decried the politicization of judges running for office—"My one desire is to perform my duties without fear or favor," he said—any reporter piecing together Johnson's long career could see that for decades Johnson had been, at least, closely associated with the anti-Longs.[9]

In his early twenties, Johnson clerked for Sen. Joseph Ransdell, a man who detested Huey Long not only for unseating him in the 1930 U.S. Senate race, but also for the moniker Huey gave the aging goateed lawmaker: "Old Feather Duster." After Ransdell, Johnson formed a partnership with an even more determined foe of Huey's, former Gov. J.Y. Sanders, who once chased Long through the lobby of the Roosevelt Hotel in New Orleans, eventually striking him for an earlier insult.[10]

Now, by random assignment on the morning of his swearing-in, Johnson was chosen to hear the Boggs-Grace-Perez suit. Fellow jurist Caldwell Herget, with a smile, shook Johnson's hand and jokingly offered his condolences.[11]

Roughly five hours later the civil sheriff of Orleans Parish, accompanied by a group of reporters, marched up the front walk to Hale Boggs' two-story, stained-glass home in the Garden District and officially notified him of Miss Lucille's suit. Boggs, playing it confidently for the press, said he would file a formal response immediately.[12]

He added that Perez—"the protector of the last citadel of interstate racketeering in America"—was in pursuit because he worried about the negative effects a Gov. Hale Boggs would have on his Plaquemines kingdom. Then Boggs added: "I have complete confidence in our courts. They are made up of outstanding jurists—men of honor, integrity, and good Americans."[13]

There would be more of this to come. Suddenly Boggs was the most patriotic man in Louisiana. He extolled the flag, the Constitution, the Bill of Rights, anything that would reassure voters that he, too, loved his country and was a 100 percent American.

It was Perez, Boggs argued, who was the un-American one. His mud-slinging and guilt-by-association tactics were the antithesis of American fair play. On the evening of October 22, Dayton Boucher, a state senator and Boggs supporter, ran with this theme in a speech that was written for him by Boggs' staff. Recalling the DSCC hearing, Boucher, in a statewide radio hook-up, said, "I pinched myself to make sure I was not in Russia listening to arguments for a controlled ballot rather than in Louisiana where free elections prevail."

During that same broadcast, aired after the *Railroad Hour,* a popular musical variety show, Boggs played back for his listeners favorite moments from the DSCC hearing. The following day, the Boggs caravan traveled nearly 300 miles north to the small city of Ruston, where he warned: "You can predict a lot of things in politics, but no slander, no meanness, no vilification will stop me from our program of trying to get our people together. Let the slanderers slander, let the winds blow," he said, "give us a chance to end this hate, bitterness, and malice."[15]

Nearly another 200 miles to the south and the candidate was in Sunset, just above Lafayette, a small town of open vistas near the heart of Acadiana. He charged that Perez was "afraid of the people for he knows that if you give the people a chance they will always do the right thing." And Hale Boggs, he told his audience, "is of the people."[16]

"He is afraid of Hale Boggs," the candidate yelled into the wind. "And he has reason to be."[17]

Meanwhile, in New Orleans Perez was going through the material he never had a chance to present before the DSCC meeting. "When the truth about Boggs' Communist-front connection is bared for the people of the state," Perez told the press, "I say Boggs will be ready to quit the governor's race."[18]

By now Miss Lucille had recovered from what had been for her a bruising DSCC meeting. On October 25, angrier now with Earl Long than with Hale Boggs, she remarked in a radio address from New Orleans that "Boggs threw his arms around Governor Long's neck and thanked him publicly for a good dictatorial, undemocratic job of suppression."[19]

In Albany, a small farming town just outside of Baton Rouge, Earl Long was now joyfully in the middle of things, climbing on the back of a small pickup truck as he theatrically remarked, "A lot of people are saying mean things about ol' Earl, but they can't prove them."[20]

Then Uncle Earl opened up on Grace, charging that her husband, Fred Dent, had once tried to close an unsavory deal with the state Highway Department to sell and distribute cement. He put an end to it, Long said, saving the state thousands of dollars. Then there was the matter of Miss Lucille's pension. She "had a bill passed that would enable her to retire on $4,500 a year," Long claimed—good money in 1951.[21]

"It's a question of whose ox is gored now!" Long proudly crowed, convinced he had given Lucille and Fred something to worry about.[22]

That question would presumably be answered in Judge Johnson's Division C courtroom, which was packed to the walls on the morning of October 29. Perez, accompanied by his sons, Chalin and Lea, arrived holding up a huge photostatic copy of the *Hullabaloo* newspaper, which he was certain held the key to Boggs' future with the evidence of his past.[23]

Boggs, wearing a double-breasted dark blue suit and maroon tie, removed his fedora to pose for photographers before entering the courtroom. But absent was one member of his defense team: New Orleans lawyer Henry B. Curtis, who was suddenly rushed to a nearby hospital after he almost passed out in the courthouse. Curtis' wife later told a reporter that there was no doubt what led to her husband's collapse. He was overstrained "from working on the Boggs case."[24]

"Everyone was tired. You just can't believe how tense and angry we were," remarked Barbara Rathe, Boggs' longtime secretary in Washington. Returned to Louisiana to help in her boss' campaign, Rathe added, "A lot of us were at the breaking point."[25]

Even Lindy, normally buoyant with an ample reserve of good cheer, was depleted. When she saw her children punching the air with their fists after listening to one radio broadcast about their father's now-epic battle with Perez, she worried about the corrosive effects hate might have on them.

Yet she could not deny that Perez was trying to destroy the father they loved. Finally, she came up with a solution that honored her Jesuit education. The children were instructed to pray for "Mr. Perez," she said, because a man as vengeful as he needed all the help he could get. "It was the only thing I could think to do," Lindy later said.[26]

Lindy was also worried about her husband. Although the old and wise attorneys who made up his defense team advised him not to take the Perez challenge personally, he could not help it. He was increasingly emotional, given to moments of great euphoria and deep depression.

Usually protective of her husband, Lindy on the first morning of the hearing in Judge Johnson's courtroom had other things on her mind. Son Tommy had suddenly been rushed to the hospital for an emergency appendectomy. Lindy entered the courtroom with her husband, steadying his nerves, but just as quickly she left.

"I dashed out," Lindy later wrote, "feeling torn between abandoning Hale in the courtroom and being with my little son."[27]

Just before Lindy left, Lucille May Grace looked across the crowded courtroom at the Boggses and whispered to her husband an incredible observation: "I am so sorry that this is being done to Hale because I am very fond of [him] and his wife."[28]

Wearing a dark green dress and black hat, Miss Lucille never uttered a word in court. She sat mute, a mere observer to a highly destructive suit that was filed in her name and was now going to be handled nearly completely by the man who talked her into it in the first place—Leander Perez.

More than two hundred people crowded into the courtroom, pressed against the white plastered walls and windows shaded by metal blinds. "You could just sit back in your chair and get ready for the show," recalled Ory Poret, who did just that as he found a chair where he could be near Miss Lucille. "You just knew you were going to be watching something with a lot of explosives."[29]

Judge Johnson, reigning in a large wicker-backed chair, gaveled the proceedings to order after placing a small notebook in front of him. Unknown to almost everyone in the courtroom, Johnson was a trained stenographer capable of recording every phrase and word in court. When a small smile crept along the side of Johnson's face, it was usually in response to the bewildered looks of Boggs and Perez as they heard Johnson repeat verbatim something long and complicated that had just been said in court. How did he do it, they wondered?[30]

"That was a very valuable skill to have, considering his profession," laughed Johnson's son, who skipped his law classes at LSU to watch the proceedings. "But it sure seemed to annoy the lawyers who were arguing a case."[31]

As the proceedings began, reporters were shocked to learn that while Boggs had brought with him dozens of witnesses, Perez had none at all.

It wasn't for a lack of trying. "He called several of us, offering

all kinds of enticements if we would say certain things," Floyd
Newlin, who knew Boggs was concealing much about his
Tulane days, later recalled. "Perez called me and he called Moi-
ses Steeg. But neither of us would cooperate."[32]

Perez, however, had other ways of getting information.

One night Lindy drove up to the front of her home only to
see a man with a flashlight lurking near the house's windows.
Slamming the door to her car, Lindy approached him, "Don't
you know there are children in that house?" she demanded.[33]

Startled, the man retreated, before admitting that he was a
"private investigator for your opposition."[34]

The opposition? The sober Robert Kennon? The jocular
Bill Dodd? The soft-spoken Carlos Spaht?

Recounting the story decades later, Lindy felt no need to be
specific. But when asked directly if she thought Perez was
behind the incident, she responded directly: "Who else?"[35]

"All I can do is decide whether to annul the action of the
Democratic State Central Committee and send it back to the
committee," Judge Johnson remarked as the proceedings
began. "I don't see how the court can order the committee to
print or leave off a name on the ballot."[36]

This was a bombshell, one that Perez hoped to quickly dis-
mantle. An annulment of the DSCC vote would be fine, he
said, but a court order removing Boggs from the January 15
ballot would be even better.

Calmly, Johnson said he would hear arguments and witnesses before considering the case on its merits. After the
plaintiff and defense presented their closing arguments, he
would—within 24 hours—render a verdict.

"It was going to be an exciting case," said Jess Johnson, Jr.
"Here you had two very dynamic people—Hale Boggs and
Leander Perez—and everyone else involved with the case was
strong-willed, too. Plus, it was a highly inflammatory case.
There was no telling what might happen."[37]

The opening hours of the case, however, were tedious as
counsel for plaintiff and defense traced the trail of the suit

itself in order to get the case history on record. Mundane to observers, this was crucial information for the Boggs team, who hoped to prove that Miss Lucille's complaint had been filed improperly to begin with.

Not until mid-day did Johnson give an indication of his thinking, and that was when Charles Rivet, serving as Perez's co-counsel, began reading aloud one of Boggs' far-left editorials from the *Hullabaloo*.

"Just a minute," Johnson interrupted. "I want to state right here that this court is not going into the charges of his mental beliefs and processes, what he belongs to and all that . . ."[38]

A faint sound of wheezing may have been heard as the air escaped from Perez's balloon. Johnson, less than three hours into the proceedings, was about to gut the very heart of Perez's suit!

"I don't know of any law that suggests or prescribes the qualifications of mental beliefs and processes for nomination to office," Johnson continued. "Before you get into that, I want to make that perfectly clear."[39]

Bad news for Perez, Johnson's declaration was even worse news for Boggs, who wanted nothing more than to give a speech explaining his "mental beliefs."

"If your honor please," Boggs interrupted.

Attorney Rivet was sharp: "I object to the witness interfering with the trial of this case. He can only answer questions. He cannot talk."

But Boggs would not be quiet: "I will have plenty of time to talk, brother," he remarked, as several people in the court-room laughed.[40]

Rivet quickly regained control of his presentation, reminding Johnson of the recent DSCC vote prohibiting a Communist from running for public office in Louisiana, Rivet concluded that a discussion of a candidate's "mental beliefs" was, in fact, entirely germane.[41]

"Then my ruling is wrong," said Johnson, allowing Rivet to proceed.[42]

But Johnson still remained reluctant to completely center a trial around beliefs. He wanted facts, tangible things based upon precedence and law. "If you are going to prove membership in some organization, you should prove membership," Johnson suggested.[43]

This was not a cryptic remark. In essence, Johnson contended that written thoughts—editorials—could not show if a person was a Communist or belonged to a Communist organization. Documents, such things as a card proving membership or a receipt of dues paid, would.

"I merely asked him if at Tulane University, if he was connected with the Tulane *Hullabaloo*, is all I asked," said Rivet.[44]

"Is it contended that the *Hullabaloo* was some kind of un-American activity?" Johnson wondered, as the courtroom spectators laughed.[45]

Rivet may have smiled in return, but he would not give up. His only goal, he said, was to determine if Boggs' writings in that newspaper might indicate Communist leanings.

"I don't know," Johnson paused, "but go ahead.

"Let him go ahead," Boggs again interrupted, his voice challenging.

"I object to the witness interpolating remarks," Rivet complained.

Said Johnson: "Mr. Boggs, confine yourself to the answering of questions."[46]

Rivet then attempted to draw Boggs out, asking him to describe his role with the *Hullabaloo*, how it was put together, who wrote the columns, and who was responsible for the paper's editorial contents.

But Boggs resisted the bait. He granted that for a year he was the paper's editor-in-chief, but he was never responsible for *everything* that appeared in the paper. The *Hullabaloo* was a chaotic affair, put together by students and sometimes not even laid out until moments before it went to press.

"It was not the *New York Times*, Mr. Rivet," Boggs said.[47]

Besides, he continued, he had always had plenty of other

things to do during his Tulane years than worry about the *Hullabaloo.* "I had to work for a living. I worked on the *States* and *Picayune.* I sold suits. I sold Beech-nut chewing gum."[48]

This was far afield and Johnson would have none of it.

"We are not interested in that, Mr. Boggs," Johnson cautioned.[49]

Rivet then introduced into evidence one editorial after another, all carrying Boggs' byline, and all espousing far-left sympathies. Impassively, Boggs listened as Rivet droned on.

But suddenly Perez stood up. Approaching the witness stand he bluntly asked: "Mr. Boggs, I understand that you were a member of the Tulane Student Union, one of the purposes of which was to build a student activities building. Is that correct?"

"That is positively not correct," Boggs corrected him, a reporter noting that he "alternately smiled and scowled."

"I was never a member of the Tulane Student Union, nor was I a member of the American Student Union."[50]

Perez then pushed a newspaper clipping into Boggs' hands. It was an article from the *Times-Picayune,* dated January 18, 1937. As Boggs looked at the piece of paper, he read: "Officers and committeemen of the recently-organized Tulane University chapter of the American Student Union were named Thursday at a general meeting of the charter members."[51]

This was bad enough, but there was more: an attached list, printed with the article, clearly named Boggs as a member of something called the "activities building committee" under the auspices of the American Student Union.

"I have seen this thing a million times," Boggs remarked disdainfully. "It has circulated in every campaign I have been in."[52]

"Does that refresh your memory?" Perez asked, ready for his kill.

Proving that he, too, was a lawyer, Boggs responded: "It refreshes my memory that there was an article in the newspaper," he said. "But I deny positively that there was a chapter formed at Tulane, and I deny most emphatically and deny positively that I was a member at any time."[53]

Suddenly Perez shifted gears. Did the defendant recall the now-infamous photo of him wearing a band uniform and giving some sort of clenched-fist salute at the Student Strike for Peace rally in April of 1936? "Do you recognize the pictures of General T. Hale Boggs on the left side of the page?"[54]

Boggs replied: "Your honor, please. I don't know what the gentleman is trying to prove. I have never participated in any seditionary movement anywhere in this country."[55]

"Did you participate in these movements at that time?" Perez demanded, ignoring Boggs' last answer.

"Judge Perez, I made not one speech but a dozen speeches in behalf of world peace," Boggs answered, "and I'm sorry we did not have it."[56]

It was almost as though Perez did not hear his answer. Instead, he began to read aloud press accounts of Boggs' activities on that day, his mocking speech, the description of him as "General T. Hale Boggs," again, the clenched-fist salute.

"It was a facetious meeting," Boggs, misrepresenting the purpose of the rally, insisted. But Perez was now ignoring him, reading yet more editorials signed by Boggs—there were dozens of them—as he repeatedly instructed the clerk: "Introduce and file in evidence . . ."[57]

Finally, Perez brandished a small pamphlet entitled *Guide to Subversive Organizations and Publications,* a publication issued by Congress listing political and labor groups thought to be Communist.

He handed the pamphlet to Boggs, but Boggs had had enough.

"Let me interrupt you, Judge," Boggs began. "I am familiar with this, Judge Perez. I have sent out about a million copies to all of my constituents. I am very familiar with that."[58]

"Is that statement of a million exaggerated or not?" Perez snapped.

"It may be a little bit," Boggs reluctantly replied.[59]

Perez asked Boggs to read the part of the pamphlet listing the American Student Union as a Communist group. But

Boggs refused. Perez asked him again and got the same response.

"My answer was that I knew it was three or four or five years ago," Boggs replied, although in reality he had known about the ASU's true character for nearly fifteen years.[60]

"And the witness also said he distributed a million copies?" Perez, never one to cede a point, pounced.

Defeated, Boggs agreed: "That's correct, Judge Perez."[61]

Boggs was shortly excused by the court, although he would return to testify on his own behalf later. But first a parade: an impressive list of important men who found their way to Judge Johnson's court to say all they knew about Hale Boggs—and all they knew was good.

Rep. John S. Wood, the chairman of the House UnAmerican Activities Committee, was first, followed by Mississippi Rep. William Colmer. Then came Cuthbert Baldwin, president of the Louisiana Bar Association; Louisiana congressmen James Morrison, Ed Willis, and Henry Lacade, Jr.; and finally the president of Tulane University, Rufus Harris.

Adjectives were exhausted in Boggs' praise. But each witness, before leaving the stand, was forced to endure the scrutiny of Perez, who asked all of them a simple question: how well did they know Boggs? Did they know he had once written articles espousing Communism or led an anti-military demonstration? Were they aware that in Congress—this was a new theme—Boggs had even advocated a one-world government that would have subjected the U.S. to foreign domination?

This was not the Hale Boggs they knew, the men said. In response, Perez condemned the men for their ignorance. Then he craftily wondered: if these men did not know such crucial things about the defendant, how could they be trusted to know anything at all?

The sun set just after 5 p.m. that day. In New Roads three boys were sentenced to lifetimes at hard labor for raping a young mother on a lonely rural lane. In Natchitoches a battalion of soldiers fanned out over a ten-mile grid of woods to find a sandy-haired five-year old boy missing for two weeks.[62]

Those weary of the troubles on earth could seek escape that night in the stars: Jupiter, late on October 29, could be seen high in the Southern sky, making its first appearance some twenty minutes after Johnson finally adjourned the day's proceedings.[63]

"I'm engaged in a campaign for governor," Boggs pleaded with Johnson when he earlier sought to call it a day. But now, after twelve hours of testimony, everyone was tired—except, perhaps, Boggs and Perez—a feeling confirmed when Perez was about to recite the contents of yet another Boggs editorial. Johnson snapped, "Don't read those things anymore."[64]

The following morning courtroom observers thought Miss Lucille looked like she was the one on trial. "The whole thing was really begin to drain her," remarked Poret. Carlos Spaht, Johnson's predecessor on the bench, felt sad for Miss Lucille. "You could see it was really dragging her down."[66]

Leadoff witness was Ivor Trapolin, past president of the Young Men's Business Club of New Orleans and a guiding force behind the group's anti-Communist efforts. On the stand, Trapolin revealed that for years he had monitored local subversive groups and never ran across Hale Boggs' name. If anyone needed proof they could study his files, Trapolin offered.[67]

"Then I object that that would be hearsay and I am not asking for hearsay," Perez exploded.

Suddenly he drew a bead on the unsuspecting Trapolin: "Are you a lawyer? Have you ever practiced criminal procedure?"[68]

This was too much for Wood H. Thompson, Boggs' cocounsel. "The witness has a right to be questioned in an orderly manner. Mr. Perez is insulting in the very manner in which he is asking questions," Thompson insisted.[69]

"Opposing counsel is interrupting my questioning," Perez, perhaps not in a good mood this morning, complained.[70]

Judge Johnson, prepared for another long day, was patient: "Now, we are not going to indulge in any debate on courtesy," he remarked before directly addressing Perez. "The witness is doing the best he can, Mr. Perez. Try to put a little smile on your face when you ask the witness a question."[71]

"Very well, your honor," responded Perez, who liked to smile only when he had something to smile about.[72]

In a more rational moment, Trapolin would have been Perez's kind of guy. He was a booster who enthusiastically spearheaded campaigns to rid New Orleans of litter, labor unions, and indecent literature. In 1950, honoring his efforts against Communism, the Junior Chamber of Commerce bestowed upon Trapolin their Outstanding Citizen Award.

But now, as Perez faced Trapolin, he saw only a witness sympathetic to Hale Boggs. Trapolin may as well have been Karl Marx.

In his investigation of subversive activities in New Orleans, had he surveyed Tulane, Perez asked?

Trapolin responded affirmatively.

Did Trapolin then read the *Hullabaloo*?

"No," Trapolin replied.

Perez, whose thick eyebrows danced wildly when he was surprised, was astonished. "You mean to tell the court under oath that you were investigating activities at Tulane and did not even read the *Hullabaloo* to find out activities on the Tulane campus?"[73]

"Judge Perez," Trapolin began, "I put the *Hullabaloo* in the right order of importance. There is no importance as to the publication as far as information is concerned."

Trapolin added that he did not read the *Cincinnati Times* either.

What was this? Sarcasm? "Why do you refer to the *Cincinnati Times*? What has that to do with the Tulane campus?" Perez, never very good with irony, asked.

"Judge, a man is only human," Trapolin responded. "A man can only read so much. I have a hard time reading the *Loyola Maroon.*"

Again, Trapolin's remarks were lost on Perez. "What would the *Loyola Maroon* have to do with the investigation of the Tulane campus subversive activities?" he asked.[74]

By now Trapolin probably wished he had never made the

trip to Baton Rouge. But Perez was not done with him. Responding to a series of rapid-fire questions, Trapolin unintentionally aided Perez's cause when he admitted that it was *possible* a subversive group at Tulane could have existed without his knowledge, and that the name of that group could have been the American Student Union.

Quickly trying to repair the damage, Trapolin added: "If such a thing did exist, it was of so little importance nobody paid attention to it."[75]

Now Perez was getting some place, but Johnson intentionally cut things short when he remarked: "I think you have grilled the witness sufficiently." Trapolin, who had endured, said the *Baton Rouge State-Times,* a "grueling cross examination," was told to step down.[76]

Suddenly there was a rustle in the courtroom as Boggs stood up and walked purposely to the witness stand, where Johnson reminded him he was already under oath.

Boggs viewed his testimony on this day as a panoramic spectacle that would dramatically survey the valleys and mountains of his life, his origins as a poor country boy, how he worked his way though school and rose to the highest levels of government through his diligence and perseverance.

" I worked," Boggs began, as he talked about his early days at Tulane, "as a representative of the Beech-nut Packing Company. Ten dollars a week."

"Well, that's all right," his own counsel, Jacob Morrison, interjected, hoping to move things along.

But Boggs was not to be denied. "I had a great many jobs," Boggs continued. "The first job I had was selling suits. Four dollars a piece, incidentally."[77]

"Congressman, let's not go into too many things about that," Morrison gently suggested, this time not giving Boggs a chance to continue but plunging in instead with the pivotal question:

"Did you belong to the American Student Union?"

"No, sir, most emphatically no," Boggs replied as reporters scribbled down his remarks.[78]

He also cut finely his anti-war demonstration speech: "I have never participated in any meeting that the object was to discourage young men from defending the United States in war, when I was at Tulane University or at any other time."[79]

Morrison, who privately loathed Perez, then wondered if Boggs had ever done anything to *help* the military.

"Not once, but many times," Boggs answered, before reading a long list of the many military appropriations bills in Congress he had supported.[80]

Perez, naturally, objected, labeling both the question and Boggs' response to it "self-serving."

"We admit that it is," Morrison happily responded.

"Under the rules of evidence, a self-serving declaration is inadmissible in court," Perez countered.[81]

Johnson overruled, allowing Boggs to continue. When Perez objected again, Johnson explained: "There are specific charges made in opposition to the candidacy of T. Hale Boggs, one of which is he publicly and in writing stated that Communism should be adopted. I cannot consider that the defendant would be so confined, as I stated yesterday, to a mere denial of that."[82]

Not until several hours later did Perez get his last and best shot at the congressman. He began where he left off, naturally, with the *Hullabaloo*. Was Boggs, as editor-in-chief, responsible for statements that appeared in the paper?

"I was responsible for them—depending upon what you mean by responsible," he answered. "It was a very loosely organized publication."

Perez: "But as editor-in-chief you would make editorials generally, didn't you?"

Boggs: "I wrote some of them, a lot of people wrote them."

Perez: "You do not mean to say that a lot of people just indiscriminately wrote editorials for the *Hullabaloo?*"

Boggs: "Yes, I would say that."

Perez: "And they were published without your knowledge or consent?"

Boggs: "Yes, I would say that."[83]

Suddenly Perez changed course and challenged an assertion appearing in Boggs' campaign literature that his vote in Congress—and his vote alone—kept the U.S. Army funded in the crucial months just before the beginning of World War II.

"Were you the last member of the House of Representatives to vote for that bill?" Perez wondered.

"The bill passed by one vote," Boggs was dismissive. "I think that speaks for itself."

But Perez would not let it go. "When the next to the last vote was cast, the vote on the bill was a tie?" he asked.

"It may have been."

Perez continued: "Who cast the last vote—the decisive vote. Was it Hale Boggs or some other representative who you do not recall at this time?"

Boggs seemed annoyed but unwilling to cede the point. "The answer is obvious. Without my vote, it would not have carried."[84]

Unexpectedly, Johnson came to Perez's assistance: "Every other person who voted for it would say the same thing."[85]

At least Perez was building the case that Boggs sometimes had a volatile relationship with the truth. He next turned to the list of anti-Communist legislation Boggs had claimed to sponsor. Was it not so that Boggs had merely attached his name to legislation sponsored by others? This time Johnson took the point away. "It is immaterial whether somebody else introduced the legislation," Johnson declared.[86]

Finally, Perez introduced his last piece of evidence. Years ago one of Boggs' opponents in New Orleans had called him a Communist, and Boggs promised to sue, but never did. Before he could get a reply, however, Johnson stopped Perez cold, deciding the matter was hearsay.

Thus ended Perez's cross-examination of Boggs. Boggs returned to the defense table relieved. Not only was his courtroom ordeal now nearly over, but Perez had failed to bring up the matter of how the American Student Union and the League for Industrial Democracy ended up being the same group, thus missing his best opportunity to put the lie to the Boggs defense.

Perez's closing argument was anti-climatic. He had run out of ammunition and knew it. He spoke for two hours, but he failed to say anything new.

Morrison, perhaps sensing Perez's weak closing, offered that there was still no proof that his client had done anything wrong, "in spite of the forensics."[87]

Morrison asked that the case be dismissed.[88]

With that, Judge Johnson adjourned the court. It was after 10 p.m. He requested opposing counsel to report first thing in the morning.

November 1 dawned gray and gloomy, making unpleasant the annual pilgrimage of the state's Catholics, who spent every All Saint's Day cleaning and repairing family tombs, leaving behind crosses made of multi-colored carnations.

Johnson gaveled his court into session at 9 a.m. and took note of the unoccupied table for the plaintiff. Neither Perez nor Grace had bothered to appear.

Johnson reiterated Perez's case against Boggs, but added that he was surprised that the plaintiff "did not call a single witness in support of the charges contained in that document."[89]

Instead, Johnson went on, Miss Lucille and Perez rest their case "upon cross-examination of defendant Boggs and his witnesses, all of whom denied the charge."[90]

This was a deep flaw etched in their case, Johnson thought. He rejected in particular the notion that he could order the DSCC to strike Boggs' name from the ballot. Only the secretary of state had the power to do that, Johnson believed, "and he is not a party to this suit."[91]

With that, Johnson dismissed the entire suit against Boggs on the grounds that it had been improperly filed. Grace and Perez, then, lost on a technicality. Boggs did not win by proving he was *not* a Communist, but it was victory enough for him. He leapt to his feet and ran to the bench to shake hands with Johnson.

"This is a complete repudiation of the most un-American smear in the history of Louisiana," Boggs declared as he left the courthouse.[92]

Out of character, Perez offered no public comment on the matter at all, even as stories appeared criticizing Perez's courtroom performance.

Writing in the *New Republic,* Irving Ferman, a New Orleans attorney, said in three words what many others whispered: "Perez," he concluded, "was trounced."[93]

CHAPTER NINE

"He's Not a Communist, He's a Catholic"

In ways that neither could imagine, Lucille May Grace's Communist charges against Hale Boggs would haunt both of them up to election day and to an eternity beyond. Boggs bounced out of Judge Johnson's courtroom on October 31 convinced he had beaten back his accusers. Now, he said, he would embark upon an extensive tour of the state. "All of the activities of the campaign had been geared to the court case," admitted Lindy, "and it really put a crimp into the organizational side of the campaign."[1]

Voice lowered, Lindy added, "And, of course, it drove some people away."[2]

Meanwhile, hoping to keep the connection between Boggs and Communism in the news for a few more weeks, Leander Perez petitioned for a writ of review after Johnson's decision, a petition that was unanimously refused by the Louisiana Supreme Court without comment on November 19.[3]

Unwittingly, Boggs gave aid to Perez's cause with a dramatic announcement in the small lumber hamlet of Ida on November 16. "I am filing charges of slander against this tinpot Stalin from Plaquemines, and I am going to insist on a speedy trial," Boggs declared as he began a grueling week-long, fifty-town tour.[4]

Perez was now his greatest foe. But the more Boggs talked about Perez, the more it reminded voters of the Communist charges levied against him. Imitating Huey Long, who loved to pin an unflattering nickname on an opponent in an effort to diminish him—New Orleans Mayor T. Semmes Walmsley was forever "Turkey Head," simply because Huey said so—Boggs came up with a less effective moniker for Perez: "Tinpot."[5]

"Now that the Democratic State Central Committee and the courts have thrown out this un-American smear of this slimy tinpot Stalin from Plaquemines, I have a suggestion to make to him," Boggs remarked. "Tinpot should set up his own court where he could be chief justice; he could immediately disqualify every candidate for governor and declare himself elected."[6]

This, Boggs, claimed, was the only way "Tinpot" could maintain his kingdom, as he continued to pocket his "crooked, ill-gotten oil revenues at the expense of the people."[7]

The gubernatorial election, Boggs added, was set for January, with a May inaugural to follow. Only then would Perez's hold over Louisiana become unravelled, Boggs suggested. "Take a look at the calender, Perez. May isn't far away. Don't you hear the bells tolling on you? The people of Plaquemines and St. Bernard will soon be free."[8]

Boggs was only warming up. On November 20, in an address before Mayor deLesseps Morrison's political workers in New Orleans, Boggs noted of Perez: "What he's for, I'm against. For twenty years I have waited for someone to end his arrogant dictatorship, and I'm happy its going to fall to my lot to do it."[9]

Six days later, Boggs was once again in New Orleans. This time he told an audience, "Just take a look at that little would-be dictator. He hates people."[10]

Even Lindy was finally drawn into Perez's web. Appearing with Mayor Morrison at a ward function, she described the Communist charges against her husband as a "tremendous ordeal," but added: "The people of Louisiana resent this attack against a man who they know is their friend."[11]

With so much attention, Perez was only too delighted to keep his broadside against Boggs current. He claimed that he only took on Boggs because of those "seditionary editorials" that had appeared in the *Hullabaloo*. Stopping such a man from becoming governor, Perez added, was nothing less than his patriotic duty.

"A man who has held such ideas in his heart does not shed them as a snake does his skin when he's a candidate for public office," Perez argued in Baton Rouge on November 15. He added that because Boggs was a Communist, he would not be able to serve as governor, even if elected, because his Communism prevented him for taking an oath "to support the Constitution."[12]

Oddly, there were many other issues to talk about as the 1951 campaign neared its climax. But no one could tell that from listening to either Boggs or Perez.

The past winter Tennessee Sen. Estes Kefauver had arrived in New Orleans to conduct nationally televised hearings investigating local crime in the city.

For years there had been rumors of payoffs at the highest levels of city government. Now Kefauver hoped to unveil everything seamy about political life in New Orleans. Kefauver was particularly interested in the role played by Mafia kingpin Carlos Marcello, whose empire was based in southern Louisiana and would, before Kefauver, plead the Fifth Amendment more than one hundred times, even in response to such questions as "Where were you born?" and "How old are you?"[13]

Nervous city officials came up for air after Kefauver left the city with little tangible evidence that City Hall was run by the underworld. But then, in the late fall of 1951, Sheriff C. F. "Dutch" Rowley, out of St. Bernard, charged that Mayor Morrison knowingly allowed some five hundred gambling operations to go about their business in New Orleans unfettered.[14]

Suddenly gambling was a major issue in Louisiana, but Boggs did not have much to say about it.

The same held true for Angola, the state's huge, aging penitentiary. Conditions at the notorious facility, said a citizen's committee report issued in the spring, were nothing less than barbaric. At least there dozen prisoners, in fact, had taken razor blades to their tendons in symbolic protest.

Angola, Mary M. Daughtery remarked, was nothing less than a "sewer of degradation." Daughtery, a member of the citizen's committee, urged reform, but she did not catch Boggs' ear.[15]

In November New Orleans attorney A.P. Tureaud, one of only seven black lawyers in the entire state, presented a petition to the all-white Orleans Parish School Board asking them to begin the slow process of desegregation.

The board was caught short, telling the eloquent Tureaud that his proposal would be the end of a kind of public education that was as old as the city. Tureaud readily agreed.[16]

In the summer, photographer Clarence John Laughlin published his landmark *Ghosts Along the Mississippi,* a mesmerizing study of decaying plantations that Laughlin was certain would prove "the past cannot ever be wholly dead." Laughlin's book reminded thousands of Louisianians of their architectural heritage and was the opening salvo in what would later become an important movement for preservation.[17]

But Boggs continued to focus on Leander Perez.

II

"Governor Long came along with me on most of my campaign stops," recalled Carlos Spaht, Long's horse in the gubernatorial race. And when Uncle Earl came along, he came along loudly, jeering Spaht's opponents from the audience, yelling out embarrassing questions and comments.[18]

At the South Louisiana State Fair in Donaldsonville, Long took off after Miss Lucille, calling her a "woman candidate who won't get enough votes to wad a shotgun." Miss Lucille responded by kicking Uncle Earl where it hurt the most, noting that it was she and not the governor who stood and fought for the legendary Huey Long. "Where was Earl Long when his brother Huey was with me?" she asked. "He was fighting his own blood brother."[19]

Snapping his bright red suspenders, clicking his false teeth, his voice an unsettling combination of Yosemite Sam and Walter Brennan, Uncle Earl liked to hide behind a clump of trees or the side of a building as he listened to a candidate making a speech, then he would spring into view with a loud question or point of order, challenging the surprised speaker to respond.

The happiest man in Louisiana: Earl Long. (Courtesy John Dominis/TimesPix)

"You're talking on my time!" Long bellowed from the audience in Mansura, in central Louisiana, as Boggs was speaking. In Plaucheville, Uncle Earl critiqued Boggs: "His voice is too harsh—these are gentle people," he told a reporter for *Life* magazine. In Alexandria, he wildly waved his arms in the air and went on the attack against both Boggs and Russell Long, who had endorsed Boggs.[20]

"Earl called us the Gold Dust Twins from Washington and said we were plucked too green and that we went around the state telling folks how pretty we thought each other was," Boggs later remembered.[21]

"You had to admire what he could do in a speech," observed Lindy, who listened to several of Long's diatribes against her husband. "He was very clever."[22]

But not until the final weeks of the campaign would Lindy and Hale Boggs realize how clever.

"Hale Boggs ain't no Communist," Long proclaimed. "He's too good a Catholic to be a Communist."[23]

To outsiders, this may have seemed like a pleasant remark. But in northern Louisiana, where Long made sure he repeated his observation several dozen times a day, it was poison. "I really believe that some of those people up there would have *prefered* to vote for a Communist over a Catholic," said reporter James Gillis, who covered Boggs' campaign. "That's how deep-seated religious prejudice was in those days."[24]

"Do you think a good Catholic like Boggs, a devout Catholic whose brother is a Jesuit priest, would be a Communist?" Long asked another northern audience. "I just don't believe it."[25]

Lindy, in her memoirs, recalled yet another version of the same song: "You know they say if Hale Boggs wins, the pope of Rome will come over here to run Louisiana," Uncle Earl began, just warming up. "Now, you know the Pope is a busy man and those Catholics have a smart archbishop down in the big city of New Orleans where Hale Boggs comes from, and that archbishop and Hale Boggs are just like that," he added, pressing two weathered fingers together for the benefit of his audience.[26]

"Earl Long loved to toy with Hale Boggs," remembered Baton Rouge lobbyist George Brown. "He'd call him 'Hale Boggs, Full of Grace"—yet another reminder of Bogg's religion, but this one somehow managing to sweep in Miss Lucille too. "Earl could do things like that very well because he had this ability to manipulate the other person with his words, the way he portrayed things. I don't think for a moment that Hale Boggs had any idea what was hitting him."[27]

"He could destroy you in two seconds," F. Edward Hebert later said. "He would say anything that came to his mind."[28]

As the campaign reached its final week, Long was not quite done with Boggs. "If you can't vote for Judge Spaht [Long's chosen entry], vote for Hale Boggs," he dramatically announced, making it seem as if he had entered into some mysterious compact with Boggs.[29]

Knowing that Boggs' pure reform supporters would desert their man in droves if they thought he had anything to do with a man they regarded, at the least, as an unsavory hillbilly, Long's remarks finally nailed tight Boggs' coffin. "This tactic made it appear that Hale was secretly a Long candidate and would do Earl's bidding," Lindy later exclaimed. "Nothing could have been farther from the truth, but we had little time to counterattack."[30]

By the last day of the primary campaign, Boggs knew his effort was desperate. But he still had enough money to pay for lavish full-page ads that ran in all of the state's major newspapers, as well as a handful of both television and radio broadcasts. His signs covered the neutral grounds and front lawns of Uptown New Orleans like so many flowers.

That same day, Lucille May Grace's campaign was almost invisible. She had run out of money, the landscape was barren of her signs, and on the eve of the election she made only one small radio and television broadcast.

Grace's troubles were noticeable as early as December 9 when the New Orleans *Item* interviewed a handful of political experts and concluded: "Miss Grace appears weak now.

Although she has many friends in the state, here, again, is the candidacy of one without organized support."[31]

But the *Item*'s team also said there was another reason why Grace's campaign was dying: the Communist charges she had levied against Boggs, they thought, "did much harm to Miss Grace throughout the state."[32]

It was true. While most political observers seemed to instinctively understand that it was Leander Perez who pushed the case against Boggs, Grace was getting the blame—perhaps because so much more had been expected of her.

Then came a final blow. Incredibly, Perez—watching Miss Lucille's support dry up—took back his endorsement and even claimed that he did so at the urging of Grace. "Miss Grace has released us, that's all there is to it," Perez said, adding that "six or seven weeks ago," she had confided to him a reluctance to continue her campaign, citing her weak standing in the polls.[33]

Miss Lucille was livid. "I want to make it clear that I never made any statement to Judge Perez or any other peson that I could not be elected governor of Louisiana, nor have I ever 'released' him or any other person," she countered. "I have never sought the support of persons or groups who want to buy the governorship of Louisiana."[34]

But she knew she was finished. "Anyone could see what was happening," recalled Naomi Marshall, Miss Lucille's longtime friend. "Leander Perez had used her and now that he had no other purpose for her, he dumped her. And all of that talk about him giving her big money was just that—talk. In the long run, she never got a cent from him."[35]

"It was a humiliating thing, what Perez did to her," said James Gillis. "It wasn't just that he made a fool of her, but that the whole state knew about it. It was the big talk of the campaign, how Perez had exploited Lucille May Grace for his own purposes. You had to feel sorry for her."[36]

Witnessing the collapse of Grace's campaign, Boggs could not resist yet one more swipe at Perez: "There is no one now in Louisiana who detests and despises Leander Perez . . . more than she does," Boggs said at a New Orleans rally in mid-December. "Perez cut her to the heart by using her and throwing her aside."[37]

Once a major contender, Miss Lucille was now reduced to the sidelines. "I have no large newspapers behind me and I have no large slush funds," she admitted towards the end. As her funding dried up, so, too, did the size of her audiences and with that went any significant newspaper coverage as well.[38]

But she would not be vanquished, certainly not without a fight: "Oh, some manipulators have tried to sell her out," Miss Lucille said, refering to herself in the third person. "Others have formed a conspiracy [of] silence. Some newspapers have faked stories."[39]

"But none of this," bravely vowed Lucille May Grace, "will budge Lucille May Grace."[40]

"She was absolutely heroic," recalled Ory G. Poret, who noticed Miss Lucille looking drawn and wane in the final days of the campaign. "It was all going down the drain for her and she knew it, but still she would not give up. She would never give up. That's how she was."[41]

Throughout December, she invaded the central and northern parishes. In early January, she spoke in more than two dozen small towns in one week. On one day alone she spoke in Slidell at ll a.m., followed by a noontime visit to Mandeville and an afternoon tour that included Folsom, Franklinton, Varnado, and Angie—small towns north of Lake Ponchartrain where she had always gotten a good vote in elections before. A final night rally in Bogalusa ended the day's activities.[42]

She visited with patients at the old leprosy colony in Carville on January 4. On that same day she was driven to Clinton, where she promised to raise the salaries of Louisiana's teachers by at least 15 percent. In Oakdale she said she had always been an honest administrator and "always will be."

In New Orleans two days later, she reminded listeners of the Lucille May Grace that was, before she entered a campaign that so shattered her good reputation. "No one has been able to question in any phase or part, my record, my integrity, my honesty, and my ability to handle public affairs," she said, perhaps, too, remembering the days when that was so.[43]

On January 12 she returned to Baton Rouge a gravely sick woman. She would be told by doctors that she suffered from malignant hypertension. She was also afflicted with a form of Hansen's Disease, which causes leprosy. The New Orleans *Item* discovered Miss Lucille was confined to bed.

"Reports were that her illness was not serious but largely a result of exhaustion from her gubernatorial campaign efforts," a reporter for the paper said. But this was window dressing. "We didn't know just then how ill she really was," said her son, Fred Dent, Jr. "But by the end of the campaign anyone could see that she was very sick."[44]

"I don't know how she managed to keep going," said Poret. "But she just wouldn't stop campaigning until the doctor told her she had to. I think she felt she owed it to the few remaining people who were still with her to go out there and really put up a fight."[45]

On the day of the primary, the fight was gone from Miss Lucille. She knew she faced a humiliating defeat. She could see it in the things that weren't happening: the telephones that weren't ringing, the highways and town squares that made it to election day without her signs, the newspapers that failed to endorse her, and the reporters who, this time, did not come out to her house on election eve.[46]

It was an empty feeling, a forlorn quiet, preceeding the virtually certain end of a long career.

Boggs' coming defeat, was, at the least, much noisier and more fun. Hundreds of people pushed into the St. Charles Hotel in New Orleans on primary night. Mayor deLesseps Morrison marched in with the cheer of his workers. Sen. Russell Long, quiet and serious, was there too. As was Claire

Boggs, his mother, who beamed when she told reporters that her only wish for her sixtieth birthday was to see her son elected governor. Two women in shawls, listening to the frantic returns, meandered from room to room in Boggs' headquarters, clutching rosaries as they sought a power greater than the local precinct captain.[47]

"Look, Hale," Russell Long advised, as he shoved the results of precinct voting from Lake Charles into Boggs' hands. "This is strong, it's good. Don't worry."[48]

But Boggs was enormously worried. A huge rally at the Municipal Auditorium fired up more than 3,000 people who yelled out their support for him. The women members of the famous "Broom Brigade," the political activists who in 1946 had helped sweep Morrison into office, were there, too, as was a marching jazz band.

But Boggs, bouyed by his New Orlean support, was worried about his appeal beyond the city. That was where the election would be lost or won. His first-place finish dissolved into second place by midnight. By sunrise the next day, Boggs had sunk to third, falling just 18,000 votes short of a runoff that saw more than half a million people vote.

"We made a great fight," Boggs told his crying supporters. "I'm sorry we lost."[48]

Yet no one could deny that Hale Boggs was now an important man whose words and movements would be the stuff of intense front-page coverage. The campaign, for all of its unpleasantness, had made him a bigger man. He was returning to Washington, where everyone knew a thriving career awaited him.

Miss Lucille woke up on the morning of January 16 to a chilling discovery. She had placed second to last out of a field of nine candidates. She even placed behind Kermit A. Parker, the New Orleans pharmacist and first black candidate for governor in a century, a man who was never given the slightest chance of winning.

But at least Parker's friends stood by him, casting their ballots against the chilled winds of fortune.

AS YOUR GOVERNOR

I WILL

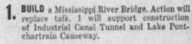

1. **BUILD** a Mississippi River Bridge. Action will replace talk. I will support construction of Industrial Canal Tunnel and Lake Pontchartrain Causeway.

2. **WORK** with your local officials and legislators for a better community.

3. **SPONSOR** reallocation of present state tobacco tax to provide more funds for cities and towns.

4. **INAUGURATE** State recreation program.

5. **WORK** to lower taxes through efficient businesslike government.

6. **REBUILD** main highways. Black-top farm roads.

7. **IMPROVE** and modernize state hospitals.

8. **MAINTAIN** and improve old age pensions—with fair treatment to all. I will end unfair politics in the pension system.

9. **APPOINT** trained penologist to run Angola. Separate youthful prisoners from hardened criminals.

10. **INSTALL** school health program. Provide free hot lunches for every needy child.

I WILL FIGHT

● *For Home Rule and States' Rights to Restore Independence of Legislature.*

● *To Abolish Deducts And Deadheads. To End Forced Political Contributions And Labor.*

● *To Restore And Strengthen Civil Service By Constitutional Amendment. Provide Real Job Protection.*

● *To Work For New Industries. After Helping Bring Kaiser Aluminum Here, Believe I Am Qualified To Work For More Plants And Payrolls.*

● *Continue My Fight For Louisiana's Oil Tidelands.*

● *To Eliminate Present Waste, Duplication And Inefficiency In State Government.*

● *To Extend Voting Machines For Fair Elections.*

● *For Permanent Registration. Above All, I Will Bring Integrity Into Your State Government And Will Re-establish Confidence.*

The ambitious campaign of a besieged campaigner. (From the author's collection)

Lucille May Grace woke up friendless. The woman who won more than 400,000 votes in one of her campaigns for the state land office this time could not find 5,000 people in all of Louisiana who would support her for a higher office.[49]

Robert Kennon, who would go on to become the new governor, got more than 158,000 votes.

His closest opponent won 154,000.[50]

Lucille May Grace ended her primary campaign with the votes of 4,677 people.

In Orleans Parish, where more than 200,000 people voted on January 15, Miss Lucille got only 933 votes. In Plaquemines Parish, Perez's machine threw a token 53 votes her way. But even in her native Iberville Parish, a place where her last name meant something, she won only 179 votes of the more than 4,200 ballots cast that day.[51]

"It was an overwhelming defeat," remembered Fred Dent, Jr., "really, just a gigantic loss."[52]

"It almost destroyed her," said Naomi Marshall. "I mean, she was humiliated. She didn't even come close. Never did she imagine she would do that poorly."[53]

"She, heretofore the acknowledged greatest vote-getter in Louisiana, finished next to last, and was crushed by this blow," columnist Hermann Deutsch later wrote. "Aforetimes, it would have been said that it broke her heart. . . . It did break her health."[54]

In the bleak weeks following her defeat, Miss Lucille lost another ten pounds. Although she would not officially leave office until May, she mostly stayed home and was ordered by her doctor to put everything behind her; the election, the job, politics in general.[55]

But this she could not do.

"My heart is crushed and I cannot let my emotions run away with me again," she confided to F. Edward Hebert, who invited her to leave her Louisiana troubles behind for a visit in Washington.[56]

Miss Lucille declined. Her life now was a mess, she said, a

mess created by "my lack of judgment, over-ambition, and all that goes to make me a fool."[57]

Two weeks after the primary, Fred C. Dent—Miss Lucille's husband—wrote a letter to Hale Boggs. "In her thirty-five years experience with the State, I believe this episode is the first time that she has followed such foolish advice," Dent wrote, trying to explain how his wife had come to attack Boggs as a Communist in the first place. "She is a very sick person at this time and it seems that all the talk is about apologizing to you and bemoaning the fact that she was ever so foolish to be a part of such an action."[58]

One month later, in New Orleans—Naomi Marshall said Miss Lucille was then in a wheelchair—she rallied enough to be driven to a political event at the Municipal Auditorium and there encountered Hale Boggs.[59]

The apology that had eluded her during the heat of the campaign came easily to her lips now. In response Boggs was gracious, but, still determined to prove a point, asked her to put it in writing. Nine days later Grace wrote an extraordinary letter of contrition, perhaps the sort that only one person raised in Catholicism could impart to another.[60]

She had been too weak to return to her office, she explained, to dictate the letter. But that did not stop her from letting him know of her "deep and sincere regreat in having been a part of the vicious court action against you in the recent gubernatorial campaign."[61]

"It is something I will regret for the rest of my life," Miss Lucille continued. "I realize that there is nothing I can do about it now, other than let you know the feelings that are in my heart. One pays for mistakes, and I assure you that I have already paid a terrible price for this one that I made."[62]

Then came the sentence that Boggs was waiting for: "There is no doubt in my mind that you are a good American."[63]

Boggs could "make use of this letter," if the matter of her charges against him was raised again, she added. Just three days later Boggs did just that, circulating Grace's correspondence to his colleagues in Congress.[64]

"My family and I have at no time blamed you for what happened," Boggs responded to Miss Lucille on March 4. "We felt then and we feel now that you were victimized by an evil man."[65]

"It was all very sad," Lindy later observed," seeing how things turned out like they did for Miss Grace. And it really was too bad because she was one of the most wonderful women."[66]

Boggs also sent copies of Grace's letter to his supporters across Louisiana.

"Sure it was some satisfaction to you to have the *only* person in the state of Louisiana who *might* have felt the accusations were true, admit that the whole thing was a hoax," Ellen Bryan Moore, no fan of Miss Lucille and her successor in the state land office, tartly observed to Boggs.[67]

Years later, Moore added: "I mean, none of the rest of us believed the things that were being said about him, so why did she?"[68]

Forgiving Lucille May Grace was easy for Hale Boggs.

And he also soon put behind him his troubles with Earl Long. In later years Boggs laughed when recalling Long's "Communist-Catholic" speech, the memory of which, wrote journalist Rosemary James in 1971, "to this day brings a smile to Boggs' face."[69]

"You had to be admiring of the way it was done," even Lindy said, recalling Uncle Earl's delicious slicing of her husband.[70]

How could anyone not like Uncle Earl?

"He was not one who stood on formalities," Boggs would say of Long, recalling how in later years he received a young John F. Kennedy in his hotel room attired minimally in his BVDs.[71]

"You know, those one-piece underwear things," Boggs explained. "I wore them when I was growing up, as a youngster . . . and Earl Long wore them all of his life, after he got through wearing his long winter undies that came down to his ankles."[72]

Boggs also remembered how Long would retrieve the dentures from his mouth and "rub them and polish them up and examine them, regardless of the visitor who happened to be there."[73]

Returned to office in a landslide in 1956, Long enjoyed telephoning Boggs early in the morning. "Get that feller up!" he commanded Lindy during one sunrise summons. "He's a lazy feller."[74]

What was Uncle Earl calling about? "I don't know," Lindy laughed. "Nothing in particular."[75]

They could have been talking about civil rights. As racial issues pressed in upon the South in the 1950s, Hale Boggs and Earl Long, once unquestioned foes, emerged as unlikely allies, resisting fire-breathing white racists who drew angry lines in the sand that said, in effect, you are either with us or against us.

In the face of enormous pressure, Boggs and Long would go their own way—and both would pay for it dearly.

III

There was one person Hale Boggs would never forgive. And his name was Leander Perez.

As early as November 8, 1951, one week after Judge Johnson dismissed the suit against him, Boggs was on the phone with New Orleans attorney Thomas Furlow. It is not clear who initiated the conversation, but considering that Furlow yearned to work in the state attorney general's office if Boggs got elected governor, it was probably Furlow.

Furlow urged Boggs to launch a broadside against Perez by investigating every aspect of his Plaquemines kingdom. He also hoped Boggs would hire him for the effort. "I know more about the kingpin down there and his methods, as well as local conditions, than anyone else they could find," Furlow claimed.[76]

Furlow thought Boggs could most easily settle the score with Perez by looking into voting fraud in Plaquemines. A powerful case against Perez could be made, Furlow added, but only if "you take enough time to get the matter of indictment and prosecution settled. Do that, and I promise you that the results will come emphatically and quickly."[77]

Despite Furlow's optimism, Boggs was wary, only sporadi- cally corresponding with the New Orleans attorney between November of 1951 and the spring of 1953. Repeatedly Furlow pressed Boggs on pursuing Perez, and just as often Boggs kept Furlow at bay, responding to one lengthy Furlow correspon- dence: "I will continue to proceed as best as I can in this mat- ter and will keep you advised."[78]

It was not, of course, that Boggs did not want to pursue Perez. He just wanted to do it right.

It was only natural, then, for Boggs to turn to the New Orleans law firm of Monroe and Lemann, not an old firm, but one of the city's most powerful.

The principal partners in Monroe and Lemann were cau- tious men who served their clients' interests well by offering them precise, if sometimes conflicting, appraisals concerning the likely result of any legal action.

This they did for Hale Boggs, who was socially comfortable with the firm's founders—Jules Blanc Monroe, Monte Lemann, and J. Rayburn Monroe.

Just days after Boggs publicly vowed to pursue Perez with a libel case, in fact, Monroe and Lemann counsel Jacob Morri- son—who helped present Boggs' defense in Judge Johnson's court—said he liked the idea of going after Perez, but only cautiously. "This suit will have to be very carefully prepared and the research done thoroughly," Morrison said to Boggs on November 23. "We don't want to pull any 'turkey a la Perez.' Above all, we don't want to sue in his bailiwick."[79]

Several months later, Morrison, who, with his wife, Mary, was a liberal activist in New Orleans, pushed for an all-out assault against Perez. "All the spleen, spite, and venom that my carcass is capable of are directed against that man," Morri- son admitted. "I would glory in seeing him humiliated (again and again and again) and I would enjoy giving him untold trouble until the day he dies, when one of the most evil, brazen, arrogant and selfish individuals passes from the Louisiana political scene."[80]

J. Rayburn Monroe was more hesitant, telling Boggs on March 18 that even though Perez "represents a large issue in that he is the embodiment of evil in Louisiana politics," he is "not going to be destroyed by a suit for libel. Nor, in my opinion, would such a tactic even be effective as guerilla warfare."[81]

Boggs had already compiled a defense against Perez's attacks that was now part of the record as a result of the trial in Judge Johnson's courtroom and could be used for action later. But to rush into another courtroom battle with Perez so soon after the election might be foolhardy, Monroe thought. "We have our powder dry. Let's use it when it will have good effect."[82]

But Boggs could not get his mind off Perez. Frantically he reached out in a dozen different directions, obsessed with the idea of retaliation.

In February Boggs asked Mabel Simmons, an editor at the *Times-Picayune*, to send him an index of stories that that paper had compiled on Perez. Eventually, those very articles would be sent to Boggs' office at taxpayer's expense through the Library of Congress' Legislative Reference Desk. Boggs then stuffed the articles into a folder that would be labelled the "Perez file."[83]

Boggs also began to correspond with J. Ben Meyer, a colorful figure in Plaquemines Parish who had an on again/off again relationship with Perez. In early 1952, Meyer was off again and offered to tell Boggs everything he knew about Perez's empire, particularly how he had made so much money. "It is most preposterous that this Chicken Thief should be running around," Meyer said of Perez.[84]

Although Meyer was able to confirm for Boggs that Perez owned the *Plaquemines Gazette*" lock, stock, and barrel," he could offer no information on the *Federationist*, the paper that called Boggs a Communist, which Perez himself distributed during the campaign.[85]

"This paper regularly sells ads to the people of New Orleans," Boggs informed the Better Business Bureau of New

Orleans, as he tried to find out whether or not Perez had any financial interest in the publication. "During the most recent campaign it was used for the vilest kinds of political purposes and carried the worst type of libelous matter."[86]

Boggs then turned to the House UnAmerican Activities Committee. Soft-speaking John Wood of Georgia was HUAC's chairman in 1952, and his credentials as a Communist hunter were without question. Would HUAC review the charges made by Perez against Boggs and issue an opinion?

Surely, Boggs thought, a public vote of confidence from HUAC would go a long way toward restoring his lost luster.

But this was just shadow boxing. Boggs knew Wood would never attack him. Indeed, Wood had already praised Boggs during the campaign for his "devotion to Americanism, freedom, and democracy."[87]

It was no surprise then when on March 21 HUAC voted unanimously to condemn what they termed the "type of campaign conducted against you in your recent race for governor by one Leander Perez," adding that there was no evidence that Boggs was a Communist.[88]

Like the letter from Miss Lucille, Boggs made sure all of his friends in Louisiana—this time including the press—got a copy of HUAC's resolution.

It soon dawned on Boggs, however, that no matter how many times he revisited the campaign, he could never make things right. The postmaster general informed him that there was no precedent for investigating the *Federationist,* because there was no law requiring the disclosure of a paper's principal owner. Attorney Furlow, once so bullish about pursuing Perez, was now forlorn: "It is obvious that the case against Perez and his associates cannot be developed by interviews with any of them," he reported on March 19. "They are well aware of the investigation and have 'clammed up.'"[89]

Finally, on April 1, Boggs reluctantly decided to abandon the idea of suing Perez for libel. "I assure you that as far as I am concerned the question of courage is not involved,"

Boggs, rather defensively, told his attorneys. "I believe I demonstrated that I was willing to take on Perez, and I certainly haven't backed away from taking him on."[90]

But, Boggs admitted, he worried that such a suit would in the long run only project Perez "back into the picture," in a manner that might "help rather than hurt him."[91]

So, Boggs would finally just drop the matter, but not before revealing the extent of his contempt: "Sometimes I think that the greatest single mistake I made was not taking a horsewhip and using it on Perez. I am inclined to believe that this is the kind of direct action best understood by the people. I am not sure they understand or particularly care about libel suits."[92]

Said Boggs, years later: "I came as close to hating Leander Perez as any man I can imagine, and I found this to be a very consuming thing. I really prayed that the Good Lord, then and now, would get the hate out of my system, and He did."[93]

In a letter to Louisiana State University law school dean Robert Lee Tullis, who thought Perez was reminiscent of Mephistopheles, "the emissary of the devil," Boggs even managed to sound serene, remarking: "The older I grow, the more faith I have in God, and I believe that He usually rights things."[94]

Because of Sam Rayburn, Boggs was emerging as a real power in Washington. Cleverly, he used that power to open other doors: beginning in 1952 he became close to Adlai Stevenson, the Democratic party's nominee for president. Stevenson adviser Jim Rowe was particularly pleased to see Boggs at one planning event for Adlai: "As you know," Rowe rightly surmised, "Boggs is Rayburn."[95]

As before, Lindy was there to support her husband's newest pursuits, which included a determined desire to court Washington society. To that end, every spring the Boggs family would host a lavish garden party in their Bethesda home that brought Louisiana crawfish, gumbo, and jazz to Washington. Supreme Court justices, high-ranking members of the Senate and House, and, eventually, even the president of the United

States, joined a guest line that started at the front of the Boggs home and snaked its way to a backyard garden flush with buffet tables lit by lanterns staked between the azalea bushes.[96]

Her husband, Lindy would joke, was responsible for the weather—she was in charge of everything else. But leaving nothing to chance, Hale and Lindy summoned up the spirit of that good protector, St. Fiarca, a legendary Franciscan monk whose stone likeness surveyed the yard's lush surroundings.[97]

IV

Life was somewhat less glamorous for Lucille May Grace after her defeat.

When she finally managed to appear at the State Land Office weeks after the election, she was gaunt.

"The time has come for me to relinquish the duties of register of the State Land Office," she remarked sadly on May 22, 1952—her last day in office.[98]

She was 51 years old. But Miss Lucille's future seemed behind her. Reporters rarely called. She had little contact with the new governor, Robert Kennon. "The uncertainty of the immediate future has caused me a great deal of concern," she confided to F. Edward Hebert on April 8, 1952, "but I guess everything will work out and will not be as bleak as it looks to me now."[99]

The days of the big parties she and her husband hosted on Highland Road were over, too. They sold their spacious ranch house and moved into an apartment building in New Orleans just a block off St. Charles Avenue. "Have found a real nice apartment—so just as soon as we sell the place in Baton Rouge, I'll bring my furniture down and fix the place up," Grace told Hebert. "It has great possibilities."[100]

She slowly regained some of her strength and wanted to work for her husband's freight-forwarding operation, Dent Incorporated, convincing him that the connections she had made in more than two decades of public life must be worth something. "I like this business very much, but must admit that shipping is off," she told Hebert in the summer of 1953, "so in the meantime I am learning the hard way and making as many contacts personally as possible."[101]

"I think she wanted to get on with her life," said Naomi Marshall. "She had been through a terrible ordeal and now just wanted to put it all behind her."[102]

Eventually even her wry sense of humor returned. When the janitors at the Trade Mart office where Dent Incorporated was located accidentally disposed of the cards carrying the names and telephone numbers of recent contacts she had made at a trade show in Tulsa, Grace remarked: "I had to laugh, for I wondered just what could happen next."[103]

She did not have to wonder long. By 1955 Earl Long was preparing for his last and most splendid return to the governor's mansion. He thought Miss Lucille still had marqee value and invited her to join his ticket, running for her old office. "He let Miss Grace grab his coattails in 1956 and pulled her back into office, allowing her to win a race that she had no real chance of winning without Earl's support," Bill Dodd later remarked.[104]

At first Grace was hesitant. She was weary of Long and still bitter over remarks he had made about her in the 1951 race. But, finally, she told Hebert, "I made up my mind that I would get along with him. I would work harmoniously with him regardless of my feelings."[105]

Public reaction to Grace's new candidacy delighted her: "The response has been wonderful," she concluded. "Factionalism has not entered into it. It has been the same from every section of the state."[106]

This time she ran a limited campaign. Long's powerful organization made sure it got out the vote for her. "She seemed to recover a lot of her resiliency," recalled son Fred. "She could count her friends on one or two hands after the last election. But she went ahead and tried for political office again. It takes a really strong person to do something like that."[107]

On election day in January of 1956, Miss Lucille was

The twilight. (Courtesy John Dominis/TimesPix)

returned to her old office with nearly 55 percent of the vote. But as she prepared to take control of that office, she knew she was not the woman she was before. "She was a different person that last time, much more tired and weak than before," said Ory Poret. "She never really got back her health."[108]

The spring of 1957 would bring devastating news: her malignant hypertension had greatly advanced to the point where it now seemed certain she could count what was left of her life by months, not years. On May 21, a bright sunny afternoon, Miss Lucille took out her stationary and wrote a letter to her family, warning her husband and son of the darkness to come. "I have made a superhuman fight to get better, to live, but I am afraid that unless something is done . . . I won't be here much longer," she wrote.[109]

After she died, she said, her dresses and business suits were to be donated to charity. "There is no value to any of my clothes, realizing my condition I have purposely deferred getting anything new." The furniture that specifically belonged to her, she added, should be auctioned off. She wished to be buried in Plaquemine, near the grave of her beloved father. And she did not want a ton of flowers decorating her grave. She asked that the proceedings be kept simple.[110]

As the afternoon wore on, Miss Lucille grew tired. But two days later, she took out three large index cards and, in much less steady handwriting, added: "I can hardly realize that my end is almost here." Her husband's "patience, understanding, and efforts to pull me through are more than could ever be expected. I love Fred with all of my heart."[111]

"As for my boy," Grace added, "what a joy he has been to us. I will watch my two sweethearts from above."[112]

Then, as Miss Lucille neared the end of the final card, she added: "My heart is broken, but I pray God to give me courage."[113]

On October 27 she was rushed to the Baton Rouge General Hospital. Although allowed to return home several weeks later, Miss Lucille never regained her strength. On Saturday, December 21, she suffered a series of brain spasms and finally died nearly twenty-four hours later.[114]

It was a gray, overcast week in Baton Rouge. The paper was filled with stories of Christmas.

"I was hoping she could live," Earl Long remarked upon hearing of Miss Lucille's passing. "I was pulling for her."[115]

The next day hundreds of visitors, including Governor Long, the chief justice of the Louisiana Supreme Court, John B. Fournet, and dozens of lawmakers, mayors, assessors, and sheriffs turned out to give Miss Lucille a grand send-off, pushing "elbow-tight into the modest funeral home to hear the last words spoken about a great woman," a reporter for the *Baton Rouge Morning Advocate* said.[116]

In an editorial placed in the middle of its front page, the *St. Bernard Voice* mourned: "Death is a hard master; he would take from us our brightest, our dearest, and our best, but he cannot mar memory—and that of Lucille May Grace shall ever be green."[117]

Hermann Deutsch in the *Item* said he just could not believe that the next time he visited Baton Rouge Miss Lucille would not be there with a "warm greeting." Added the columnist: "I wonder how many hundreds of thousands of others still feel the same way."[118]

James McLean, a long time statehouse reporter, called Grace a "pioneer in the modern political life of Louisiana," a "tall woman of commanding appearance." He added that her speaking voice "could reach the backrows without the aid of a loudspeaker."[119]

Margaret Dixon, in her popular Sunday political column in the *Advocate,* saw Miss Lucille's final months as a "lesson in courage." She was gravely ill, Dixon said of Grace, but "You'd never have suspected it. When you met her she always said she was better. Until the end, she kept her chin up."[120]

Hale and Lindy Boggs sent their condolences.

Nothing was heard from Leander Perez.

"That's because he killed her," Naomi Marshall later asserted. "What he did to her, how he used and exploited her, is what led to her decline. She was just fine before that."[121]

"That is certainly part of the family legend," son Fred would say. "My dad oftentimes told me that Leander Perez had double-crossed my mother or duped her, led her astray, whatever you want to call it. And that it was right after that that she got real sick, and never really got better."[122]

Slowly, with rain in the air, the large funeral party made its way across the Mississippi River to the old St. John's Catholic Church in Plaquemine, bringing Miss Lucille back to the small town that gave her life.

She was buried next to her father in the historic eighteenth-century cemetery near the church in a tree-covered glade.[123]

Months earlier she had asked that a mass be said in her memory "at least four times a year."[124]

But her survivors did better that that. They marked her gravesite with a simple but elegant stone, its etched message recording when she was born and died. Then came these words:

> Courageous in conviction,
> firm in friendship,
> a living embodiment of the ideas of womanhood,
> loved and admired for her wisdom,
> kindly guidance, and generous spirit.
> May we catch the challenge of her life.

CHAPTER TEN

"God Bless His Soul"

The Louisiana countryside surrounding Lucille May Grace's gravesite was a wistful mosaic of broken dreams and forlorn hopes punctuated by violent nights and an elusive, misty promise of the morning after.

In hamlets deep inside the state, places where visitors extolled the country music or Creole tomatoes, men were obscured by the white sheets they wore, warning of a coming mongrel nation as flames from nearby burning crosses cast shadows on their words. In other places, dirty old neighborhoods in dirty old cities near the river's edge, Negro girls, their hair in kinky braids, walked with spindly purpose into the first integrated classrooms in their blocks, braving angry white crowds chanting: "Eight, Six, Four, Two. We don't want no jigaboos."[1]

Louisiana in the 1950s had television, fallout shelters, rock 'n' roll singers, and a suburban sprawl that started near the green levees outside New Orleans and crept westward to dusty cottonpatch towns pinpricking the Texas border.

But Louisiana, however much it danced with modernity, was also a state of habit and history. Coca-Cola, the favorite drink of the South, was also number one in Louisiana. Families in their Sunday finery mourned only the *Confederate* dead on Memorial Day, and signs instructed people who were black to sit in this balcony or that lunchroom everywhere.

Across a canvas dripping in violence and blood, Hale Boggs

and Leander Perez would stage their last great battle. It was over civil rights, but it was never a meeting of equals.

From the start, Perez was resolute, never wavering in his convictions: "The American Negro," he announced, "by virtue of his short sojourn in this country, has taken on a veneer of our way of life. But he is still rooted in the mores of his ancestors in the savage jungle life."[2]

At a lavish ceremony attended by more than one thousand supplicants who showed up bearing silver trays, expensive cigars, and plaques, Perez made his intentions clear: "I am dedicating the rest of my life to the fight to prevent the relaxing of segregation policies."[3]

"Bravo, Mr. Perez!" a fan of the Judge wrote in large letters on a cardboard postcard. "At least some of us are very happy to know that you plug for segregation, and better still, fight hard for it." The correspondent signed off identifying himself only as a "100 percent Caucasian."[4]

There were millions of Caucasians throughout the South and across America in the 1950s whose ethnic ancestry may not have been as pure, but were nonetheless devoted to Perez. In just a matter of months in the mid-1950s, more than 125,000 people in Louisiana alone put their signatures over pledge cards vowing their support of the White Citizens Council, a group headed by Perez that dominated the white Southern response to civil rights thoughout the late 1950s.[5]

Just two months after the death of Earl Long in 1960, New Orleans sought to launch a program of moderate integration. But Perez sped into town to spearhead the local resistance. "Don't wait for your daughters to be raped by these Congolese!" he yelled to a sea of Confederate flags and rebel caps during a rowdy rally at the city's Municipal Auditorium. "Don't wait until these burrheads are forced into your schools!"[6]

Always a man of action, the Judge lifted the crowd with a clarion call: "Do something about it now!"[7]

The following morning some two thousand white teenagers roamed downtown New Orleans, heaving rocks, bottles, and stones as they assaulted dozens of black people. That evening, scores of young Negroes, deciding they had had enough, responded in kind. "For much of its present trouble, Louisiana can thank Leander Perez," judged *Time* magazine.[8] Of single purpose, Perez never wavered. Although he still spoke of the Communist infiltration that would soon destroy America and was wildly supportive of a series of Communist-control laws passed by the state legislature in 1962, it was increasingly integration that preoccupied Perez's time and energy for the remainder of his years.[9]

"I know Negroes," he would tell a dumbfounded William F. Buckley on a nationally broadcast program. "We have a number of Negroes in our community, and I know that basically, fundamentally, they are immoral. Why should I try to deny it?"[10]

Hale Boggs, meanwhile, simply tried to keep track of Perez's movements. When the Judge announced the formation of a third party for the 1960 presidential campaign, it was Boggs who was appointed by John and Robert F. Kennedy to report on Perez's success. When his campaign failed, Perez tried the same thing again for the 1964 election, and this time Boggs recorded his movements for Lyndon B. Johnson.[11]

Excommunicated by the Catholic church for his racial views in 1962, Perez appeared unfazed, promising to start his own religion, which he said would be called "Perezbyterianism." And as Martin Luther King, Jr., and his followers advanced the cause of non-violent protest throughout the South, Perez invited the national press to Plaquemines Parish to see his latest defense in the war: a prison he had built at the old Fort St. Philip, a lonely place surrounded by swamps and infested with snakes and mounds of angry fire ants. He specifically invited King and all the other civil rights activists to come to Plaquemines, offering them a rest of unlimited duration in the dark fort.[12]

"How many people can you incarcerate in here?" a television reporter asked the Judge as he led the way through the fort's shadowy tunnels.[13]

Perez suddenly stopped. "Well, that depends on how many people come to Plaquemines Parish to try and break down our local government and cause trouble," he said, gesturing towards one of the damp cells with his cigar. "If they come in the tens and twenties, we'll take care of them." Thrusting his jaw toward the journalist, Perez added in a louder voice: "If they chose to come in the hundreds, *we'll pack them in just the same.*"[14]

Because of his shameless bellicosity, everyone was fascinated with Perez. *The New York Times* put him on its front page; he was a feature in *Esquire.* Richard Avedon, the noted photographer, came South to snap his portrait.

By contrast, Hale Boggs, as he neared middle age, was a quiet man in a huge, impersonal government. He was, of course, connected; frequently he told the voters back home of his close friendship with presidents John F. Kennedy and Lyndon B. Johnson.

But he lacked the resolve, the certainty, and, for that matter, even the charm of Judge Perez. And as a result, Boggs, for the rest of his life, was never quite able to free himself from a morbid fascination with Leander Perez. In the fall of 1963, as CBS broadcast an hour-long documentary on Perez, Boggs planted himself in front of a television with a small notepad on his lap, jotting down random observations and remarks that Perez himself made on the show.

"Some other notes . . ." Boggs penned to himself near the end of the show, revealing, once again, that he could never quite forget the 1951 election nor the damage Perez had done: "Lucille May Grace," Boggs wrote, perhaps struck by an idea, "—her death."[15]

Why Boggs wrote Miss Lucille's name can only be imagined. She was not mentioned in the documentary, nor did Boggs ever publicly say anything about her again.

The vast majority of the CBS documentary, in fact, was devoted to Perez's response to civil rights. Days after the program aired, Perez received hundreds of letters from viewers across the country who admired his firm stands.

At the same time, few people—least of all his constituents—were sending similar notes to Hale Boggs. And the reason was clear: on the most important issue to face the South since the Civil War, Boggs wavered wildly.

First, he claimed to be a segregationist and even signed the notorious Southern Manifesto, a document endorsed by the vast majority of Boggs' fellow Southern lawmakers pledging an absolute resistance to further integration. But after John F. Kennedy won the Democratic nomination for president in the summer of 1960 and Boggs helped craft the famous JFK/LBJ ticket, he backtracked, refusing to condemn the liberal party platform calling for school integration. In early 1961, he was spectacularly confused as House liberals sought to enlarge the membership of the Judiciary Committee, infamously a cemetery for most civil rights legislation.

Southerners, naturally, were horrified by the proposal: the extra members would, undoubtedly, give the committee a pro-civil rights majority. Publicly, Boggs declared his opposition to the move. Then several days later he said he was undecided. Finally, after basking in Kennedy's glow at his inaugural—Lindy was JFK's inaugural chairman—Boggs stopped answering questions on the matter and quietly voted with the liberals.[16]

Perez's *Plaquemines Gazette* had a name for people who voted the way Boggs did: TRAITORS, the paper headlined on its front page over a photo of Boggs.[17]

Perez vowed revenge. For the duration of the 1960s, he sent money and manpower across congressional lines in an endless effort to finally drive Hale Boggs from office. Never abundantly generous with financial backing, the Judge sometimes gave as little as a couple of hundred dollars to a candidate he liked to as much as the several thousand, even upwards of $20,000, which he gave in 1968 to George Wallace, who was running as a third-party candidate for the presidency. 1972 campaign documents indicate that Perez's survivors gave Wallace at least half that much for his spring presidential primary challenge.[18]

But to worry about the precise dollar amount Perez spent

Hale Boggs in the middle of history. (Courtesy Photofest)

to defeat Boggs misses the point. "He had other ways of getting things done," said Ben Toledano, who managed one campaign against Boggs in the 1960s. "The Judge could connect
people with people. He had a network of friends who would
do his bidding, and that was more important than the
money."[19]

"Don't ask questions," a man with a broken nose and a
forty-year rap sheet would later remark. "All I can say is if we
got a call from the Judge, we did what he told us. If that
meant trying to get rid of Boggs, whom the Judge hated, I can
attest to it—that's what we tried to do."[20]

"Anyone could see what was happening," remembered
Times-Picayune reporter James Gillis, who covered all of
Boggs' congressional campaigns in the 1960s. "Perez was
bringing in his money and men to destroy Boggs. He had
enormous influence in the city and few people would tell him
no. That was something that Hale just had to contend with for
the rest of his life."[21]

"You are being painted as the Devil himself," one supporter
of Boggs told him in 1962 as Perez's efforts were being felt.
Another correspondent noticed a large number of far-right
political organizations forming in New Orleans—nearly all
with ties to Perez—coming together to get Boggs out of office.
"There are so many of these organizations, it is hard to keep
track of them."[22]

For his part, Boggs was rattled. From Washington he later
observed: "It got so that those of us who had the responsibility
of representing our constituencies here were being looked
upon in a good many quarters as almost aliens." It seemed to
him, he said, like some sort of "mad disease," something sinister and nebulous that was seeping into every corner of the city.[23]

Life was only made worse for Boggs in the summer of 1963
when he attended a labor banquet in New Orleans and
watched in astonishment as the audience booed the names of
Martin Luther King, Jr., and John F. Kennedy. Even worse,
when Perez's name was mentioned, the working men

cheered. Once again the subject was civil rights. Boggs, at the
podium, declared: "The sooner all of our people, particularly
our political leaders, recognize that this is a problem largely
moral in its nature, the sooner the answer will be found."[24]

But the tough laborers were hardly impressed. They were
the ones who saw Negroes moving into their neighborhoods
and schools while Boggs' children went to an all-white private
school. And they, too, saw their jobs being given to black workers. Hale Boggs did not speak for them. Leander Perez did.

"I think the hatred some people had for him really began
to wear him down," Laurence Eustis would say of Boggs in the
1960s. "He just couldn't figure out what he was doing wrong
and how he could make people like him again."[25]

And no one seemed to care that by the 1960s in Washington, Hale Boggs had real power, tangible power, the kind of
power that built roads, bridges, and schools and got people
jobs. After Speaker Rayburn died in late 1961, Boggs became
the new Majority Whip, third in line to the speakership. And
his almost daily meetings at first with Kennedy and then President Johnson in the White House suggested an insider's influence unknown to previous New Orleans congressman.

"But who's paying the price?" Perez asked when he one day
decided to discuss Boggs' growing shadow in Washington. If
that influence meant more civil rights and governmental
interference, Perez concluded, then Boggs' connections really
weren't worth much at all.[26]

Not until the summer of 1965 would Boggs make a break.
Kennedy was dead, and Boggs undiplomatically blamed what
he called the haters in New Orleans for creating an atmosphere that encouraged violence against the young president.
Now Johnson was in the White House, and Southerners—
Perez's people—were outraged over the new president's civil
rights measures.

Although Boggs voted against the historic 1964 Civil Rights
Act, the following year he decided to come out for the equally
sweeping Voting Rights Act. "I'm going to vote for it, Cokie,"

Boggs wearily revealed to his daughter a few nights before the House vote. But Cokie, like many Northern white girls educated at east coast schools, was a dedicated liberal and wanted more. She urged her father to also make a speech for the bill.[27]

"That's enough," was all the father would say by way of a reply.[28]

Boggs' congressional district in 1965 was still nearly two-thirds white. Even if every black under the Voting Rights Bill registered and supported him, it would not be enough to offset the presumed angry white opposition, particularly in growing Jefferson Parish, where the Boggs name was now anathema.

All through the spring and summer of that year Louisiana broiled in racial conflict. In the tiny mill town of Bogalusa, an armed black militia threatened to fight force with force if efforts to register blacks to vote were imperiled. That same spring Leander Perez flew to Washington and warned senators that Louisiana would resist any voting rights law. Before a panel of transfixed senators, Perez dismissed Martin Luther King as a "boycott artist," charged that Washington was a town of "queers . . . thousands and thousands of them," and flatly judged that no legislation could compel black people to vote.[29]

"You have to bribe them," he said. "You have to to pay the preachers—now that is the story and that is why we do not try to register them."[30]

Perez then quickly returned to Louisiana to unveil his latest project: a recall of Hale Boggs, as well as the other Louisiana congressmen who voted his way, from Congress. "More can be accomplished against these Communist-directed demonstrations in Bogolusa and the rest of the South by getting rid of the Southern renegades in Congress," Perez explained.[31]

From Washington, some of Boggs' allies fought back. Boggs, however, mostly remained silent.

Only once did he reveal his still-bitter feelings towards Perez when he read a letter from a New Orleans attorney, who said of Perez: "It is about time someone in authority spoke out against this asinine old man."[32]

Boggs was quick to reply: "I couldn't agree with you more."[33]

On July 9 Boggs was driven into Washington by an aide, remarking: "Jimmy, today will change the life of everyone in politics because politics is going to change."[34]

When he strolled onto the House floor, Boggs heard Rep. Joe Waggoner of Plain Dealing, Louisiana, extolling the benefits of the South *as is* for both blacks and whites. The Old Confederacy was doing fine by its people and had no need for a bunch of federal laws telling people how to vote, Waggoner said, satisfied.

Boggs asked for five minutes to respond.

He was not scheduled to speak and reporters instinctively suspected something was up. Boggs walked to the well of the darkened chamber and shortly captivated the gallery audience with an address that many would come to see as the finest in his career.

"I am a part and parcel of it," Boggs said of the South as he began. His great uncle, he noted, served with General Lee, and so did a grandfather. He took a back seat to no one in his love of Dixie. And he yearned to say that all was fine in the South.[35]

"But," Boggs continued, "it is not so."[36]

Now, as Boggs plowed into his text, listeners realized they were not hearing the kind of point-by-point argument normally delivered on the House floor, but something entirely unique, a confession of sorts, an attoning, the accounting of a singular journey.

He talked of the fundamental right to vote, of the franchise that must be enjoyed by every American. And then, in this his finest moment, he could not resist alluding to Leander Perez.

In some precincts in Lousiana, Boggs noted, Negroes were already voting without incident. "But there are other areas of Louisiana; one is directly south of the great cosmopolitan city of New Orleans, where out of about 3,000 Negroes, less than 100 are registered to vote as American citizens."[37]

"Can we say there has been no discrimination?" Boggs thundered. "Can we honestly say that from our hearts?"[38]

He concluded: "I shall support this bill because I believe the fundamental right to vote must be a part of this great experiment in human progress under freedom which is America."[39]

With that, cheers engulfed the House chamber. The presiding officer attempted to gavel the session back to order, but the noise would not stop. The following day, when the Voting Rights Act passed, reporters saw Boggs' remarks as a pivotal turning point, one that inspired at least another two dozen Southern lawmakers to vote the same way.

Several days later, *Times-Picayune* reporter Edgar Poe visited Boggs in his Washington office. Together the two men, who had been friends for decades, chewed over the voting rights measure and the impact it would have on politics. Then, as the interview neared its conclusion, Poe bluntly asked Boggs if the parish he referred to in his speech was in fact Plaquemines Parish, the "stronghold of Leander Perez," as Poe put it.[40]

Yearning for nothing less than the last word, Boggs gave it: "Yes," he replied, and said no more.[41]

II

"If I had to do it over again, I would do so willingly," Perez told a packed group of admirers at the courthouse in Pointe a la Hache as he watched his son Chalin sworn in as president of the commission council—the same council the Judge had dominated since its creation.[42]

Reminding his adoring audience that another son, Leander, Jr., was now also the parish district attorney, Perez, on this bright day in the fall of 1967, added: "I give to you my two sons. Together, I hope to see them carry on the tradition."[43]

He owned and dominated a parish and people; he was the unquestioned master of his own empire. What, for the man who carefully and ruthlessly constructed his own world, brick by brick, was left to accomplish?

The Plaquemines Gazette

THE ONLY NEWSPAPER DEDICATED TO SERVING THE BEST INTERESTS OF PLAQUEMINES PARISH

Vol. 41 No. 37   BELLE CHASSE, LA., FRIDAY, MARCH 28, 1969   PUBLISHED EVERY FRIDAY – $3 YEARLY (b

THOUSANDS MOURN DEATH OF JUDGE PEREZ

Casket Borne By Grandsons And Loyal Friend

Half Century Of Dedicated Service Ends

JUDGE L. H. PEREZ

The thousands of mourners who attended the funeral services and burial of Judge L. H. Perez March 21st were eloquent in their manifestations of grief, love, devotion and admiration, for a man whom they believed to be a true friend, a leader of vision and compassion, a noble statesman, an astute lawyer, a defender of the people's rights, and one of the greatest American patriots this country has known, a man who had the courage and ability to dissent - when principles and his convictions were in jeopardy.

Judge L. H. Perez, revered in Plaquemines as not only the leader but the father of the Parish, died Wednesday evening, March 19 at six o'clock in his Idlewild Ranch home – but only after he had fulfilled his promise to rebuild Plaquemines after it had been devastated by Hurricane Betsy in 1965. He was 77.

He was alone in his study when he breathed his last, when his stout heart stopped causing him to topple from a chair where he was found within a few short minutes by his late wife's doctor, Mrs. Marguerite Perez.

Like his beloved wife, Judge Perez had been told that day by his doctor that he could plan resuming his activities in moderation. He had even stopped off at his New Orleans office. Returning to Idlewild, he enjoyed his dinner – and then it happened.

He had been under treatment following a heart attack January 10th.

Death In Shock

Word of his death shocked his relatives, friends and associates and the countless thousands who looked upon Judge Perez as their protector, their friend.

The following evening, thousands stood in line to pass the silver casket where their silver-haired friend lay. A funeral director of the House of Bultman, New Orleans, said it was the largest funeral he had known of in the city during the past 30 years.

The next day for the services, thousands again came and formed the procession to the Holy Name of Jesus Church where a Requiem Mass was said. The procession - was - over - 200 cars long.

Adding to the tribute of their presence, it appeared that every Catholic in the church during the Mass received Communion flowed into the streets.

In addition to relatives, dignitaries, parishioners and other friends, there were school children who carried a heart-shaped floral arrangement; a group of scouts, and even a cab driver was said to have locked up his cab and attended Mass.

"Hear Us Oh Lord"

The faces of the mourners were riled stricken as Father Peter Dowding of St. Thomas Church in Pointe-a-la-Hache, celebrant, intoned many litanies during the Mass, "Hear us Oh Lord ... answer our prayers for Leander." Father Dowding, sprinkling the casket with holy water, said of Judge Perez, "God has taken him to Himself

(Continued on Page 5)

Priests, Altar Boys Lead Procession To Chapel

Memorial Fund For All Private Schools To Honor Judge Perez

When the announcement of the death of Judge Perez was made, members of the Perez family stated in lieu of flowers, that they preferred donations to go to the independent schools of the Parish in memoriam.

In compliance with this request, and because of the pride Judge Perez felt in the development of the private schools of the Parish, which gives parents a choice for their children, THE PLAQUEMINES GAZETTE offers to publish the names of persons making such donations

to the JUDGE PEREZ MEMORIAL FUND FOR PRIVATE SCHOOLS.

Such names must be accompanied either by a donation to the JUDGE PEREZ MEMORIAL FUND FOR PRIVATE SCHOOLS, mailed to The Plaquemines Gazette, 1901 Belle Chasse Highway North, Belle Chasse, La. 70037, or the names of persons making such donations must be furnished by the schools to The Gazette.

The Independent School System was established and five

school buildings completed within a matter of months and opened for operation November 1966.

The apparently insurmountable problem of financing and building the schools in time for the 1966-67 term, was accomplished through a Citizens Committee working shoulder to shoulder with parents who acquired an association of school builders – janitors – and – fundraisers. Their accomplishments was termed a miracle.

The Final Resting Place Of Judge Perez

This Is Idlewild Where There Was Much Happiness

Plaquemines grieves. (Courtesy the *Plaquemines Gazette*)

Less than two years later, on the cold night of March 19, Perez was resting in the quiet study of his Idlewood Ranch, once more contemplating strategy for yet another court battle over the Tidelands. He held the receiver of a telephone in his hand when suddenly a violent explosion pushed him to the floor, where he grasped briefly for air.

It took a massive heart attack to finally finish the great Leander Henry Perez.

His passing unleashed passions throughout Plaquemines and across the South. Congressmen mourned him and entered their remarks into the *Congressional Record*. On a sunny winter day, George Wallace and a host of Southern governors flew in for his funeral.

More than one thousand people turned out for the Judge's sendoff, a sendoff whose most touching moment for many may have been the procession of silent school children who placed a large, heart-shaped display of red and white carnations on top of the Judge's casket.[44]

"His thousands of friends know that this world is a better place in which to live for Judge Perez having lived in it," Cong. Otto Passman grieved.[45]

As Leander Perez's body was removed to the family mausoleum at Idlewood, shadowed by huge Spanish oaks, Hale Boggs could console himself. He had outlived his greatest foe. In a distinctly morbid appreciation of things, he had won.

But by 1969, Hale Boggs had another enemy with which to contend, an enemy even more deadly than Perez.

The enemy was himself.

Beginning in the late 1960s, Boggs began to drink. He drank sporadically, but wildly. He was, his friends would later say, a sloppy drunk, alternately loud and abusive, or sullen and depressed. "He had sort of lost it," his old friend Walter Cowan, who had known Boggs since boyhood, sadly remarked.[46]

"I don't remember one meeting we went to where Boggs was sober," William Nunguesser, who worked to defeat Boggs in the 1960s, asserted, adding that Boggs aides were frequently dispatched in the morning to "apologize for what he might have said or done the night before."[47]

"Lindy used to keep an eye on him," remembered Floyd Newlin. "My God, she would watch him like a hawk at social functions because she knew it took so little for him to get completely stone-cold drunk." Even the new president, Richard Nixon, was aware of Washington gossip concerning Boggs' drinking. "He's on the sauce, right?" Nixon eagerly interrogated Rep. Gerald Ford one day.[48]

Ford, a long time friend of Hale and Lindy, responded: "I'm afraid that's right."[49]

By the fall of 1972, Boggs was exhausted. He was now the Democratic Majority Leader, and the schedule, he complained, was a form of murder. "This is an absolutely killing job," Boggs remarked. "It just never stops—I never leave my office before eight or nine o'clock." And even when he did, Boggs added, he was usually forced to attend a political or social function of one kind or another, often lasting late into the evening.[50]

He yearned for rest and an end to the current session when he could simply get away from it all.

He had gained at least thirty pounds since the days of the 1951 campaign—reporters thus described his frame as "ample" or "well-fed." His hair was a thick thatch of white crowning a face that was ruddy and full.

Yet, despite his fatigue, Boggs felt compelled to honor a commitment he had made to a fellow Democrat from Alaska to campaign for him in his native state. This was how Majority Leaders someday rise to become Speakers, by delivering hundreds of small favors to grateful members who would never forget. And Boggs wanted nothing more than to be the next Speaker of the House.

"I really do not feel like going," he remarked. But he went anyway.[51]

On a cold gray morning in Alaska, the day after Boggs had wowed an Anchorage crowd with a rousing fund-raising speech, a small white-and-orange Cessna 310 transported him

and three other men, including a pilot who was given to dare-
devil flying displays, into a mountain pass. An eerie whiteness
enveloped them as the plane quite simply disappeared.[52]

Signals from the craft were never heard again.

Over the next month the Coast Guard, the Air Force, and a
host of Alaskan state and local officials energetically fanned
out over a 326,000-mile grid of ice and snow, hoping to find
some sign, even the smallest remnant, of Boggs' plane. After
the most exhaustive effort in Alaskan history, the searchers
gave up. Two months later, at an elaborate memorial mass in
the St. Louis Cathedral in Jackson Square, former President
Lyndon Johnson, vice-presidents Hubert Humphrey and
Spiro Agnew, and a host of senators and representatives
pressed in to pay their final respects to Hale Boggs.[53]

The man who would be governor was gone, his strange
ending eventually becoming the thing that most people would
remember about him.

III

In death Hale Boggs and Leander Perez were inspirational
figures. Roads, bridges, and parks bore Perez's name throughout Plaquemines Parish, where his birthday was also deemed
an official parish holiday, a day that school children often
spent visiting the Judge's handsome bronze likeness in Ollie,
his boyhood home.

Perez's spirit was made real, meanwhile, by the dynasty he
had created. Chalin and Lea divided power in the parish and
seemed, initially, satisfied with the arrangement, convincing
the people of the parish that someone named Perez would be
their leader into eternity.

But the boys soon entered into a quarrel of biblical propor-
tions and voters, tired of their squabbles and emboldened by
a new generation of reformers and black leaders, eventually
turned both men out of office. Sometime in the early 1980s a
milestone in Plaquemines was reached—it was the morning

when there was suddenly no member of the Perez family run-ning Plaquemines Parish.[54]

As Chalin and Lea were forced into private life, their father's name was gradually removed from the same roads, bridges, and parks where his admirers had honored him before.[55]

The era of Leander H. Perez, more than half a century after its beginning and a decade and a half since the Judge's death, was finally nearing its end.

Hale Boggs' legacy, however, proved rather more enduring. In downtown New Orleans, a modern marble white federal courthouse was named in his honor in 1974, followed by a 4,400-foot mountain peak in Alaska two years later. In 1984 a huge, $135-million, twin-towered bridge spanning the Missis-sippi River in St. Charles Parish was given his name.[56]

Boggs, like Perez, also left a dynasty, this one remarkably devoid of implosion. Lindy won her husband's congressional seat in 1973 and served until her retirement in 1990. In the late 1990s, she was appointed as America's first official ambas-sador to the Vatican. Son Tommy, who tried and failed to win a congressional seat in Maryland, became instead a founding member of the Washington consulting firm of Patton, Boggs, and Blow, a firm that would eventually become the most influ-ential of its kind in the city. Oldest daughter Barbara would serve as mayor of Princeton, New Jersey, and was thought to be a top contender for that state's governorship before dying tragically from brain cancer in 1990.[57]

Youngest daughter Cokie became the most famous Boggs of them all. Married to journalist Steven Roberts, she was assigned by both National Public Radio and ABC Television to cover Congress, a subject she came to naturally, she said, recalling the many times her father, taking his young daugh-ter by the hand, brought her to work with him.[58]

Even the shadow Communism cast across Louisiana would live beyond Boggs's and Perez's years on earth. The bloated old Soviet Union may have collapsed of its own volition in 1991, but Louisiana still kept on the books a series of Communist control laws, loudly backed by Perez, into the new century. One law made the distribution of what was called "Communist propaganda" a felony that might result in a fine of $10,000 or a prison sentence of up to six years.[59]

The law would remain a reality nearly forty years after its enactment, when, in the fall of 2000, a federal district judge in New Orleans declared that it interfered with free speech and was thus unconstitutional.[60]

IV

In death, Hale Boggs and Leander Perez had their monuments. Lucille May Grace got nothing at all. Her longtime friend Naomi Marshall frequently petitioned the state legislature to name at least one state building after Miss Lucille, but she never won any takers. Grace's son, Fred Dent, Jr., later pondering the career of his colorful mother, remarked: "I always thought someone should write something about her— a woman before her time, facing the glass ceiling and all." But no one did.[61]

Decades later, when women's groups gathered in Louisiana to celebrate their heritage and history, they usually recited the names of women elected to the legislature and local offices—in 1996 Louisiana would even have its first woman U.S. senator.

But the name of Lucille May Grace nearly always went unmentioned. A woman of mysterious fortitude, she has only been made more elusive and invisible with the passage of time.

V

The year before Hale Boggs' disappearance he was entertaining New Orleans journalist Rosemary James in his Washington office. James thought the congressman looked good and was hopeful he had stopped drinking. Boggs had invited James to Washington after she told him she was writing a lengthy profile of him for *New Orleans Magazine*.

He and Lindy cooked for James and over a period of several days he regaled her with the highlights of his long career: his battle against Huey Long in Louisiana, his rise in Congress under the steady hand of Speaker Rayburn, his friendships with John F. Kennedy and Lyndon B. Johnson, and his slow emergence as a Southern force for civil rights change.[62]

Listening to the congressman talk, James knew she was getting a good story. In his office he sat at an enormous wooden desk decorated with an oversized bottle of tabasco sauce. But inside the desk was even more good stuff: a junk drawer filled with old Mardi Gras doubloons, tickets to Harry Truman's inaugural and the Kentucky Derby, a worn Social Security card, buttons from past campaigns in New Orleans.[63]

But in one separate drawer, tucked away in a dusty envelope, could be found the remnants of the old Perez file Boggs had been maintaining on his greatest foe for nearly twenty years: a handful of newspaper articles from the New Orleans and national press, all revealing some unsavory aspect of life under Perez's Plaquemines rule.[64]

On that day with Rosemary James, Boggs' greatest foe had already been dead for more than two years. But still Boggs kept the inflamatory material snugly tucked inside his desk, safely within easy reach.

"Leander Perez," Boggs revealed to James, "was my greatest enemy. But he is dead now and God bless his soul."[65]

Notes

CHAPTER ONE

1. Helene de la Houssaye, interview by the author, tape recording, New Orleans, La., 13 November 1997.

2. For a brief biographical sketch of Bisso, see Bisso Tugboat Company Incorporated (New Orleans: Rosemary James and Associates, 1991) 2-4; "Funeral Today for Captain Bisso," *Times-Picayune*, 3 July *The Cajuns—Essays on Their History and Culture* (Lafayette: Center for Louisiana Studies, 1983), 174-94.

3. For more information on LeBlanc, see Perry Howard, "The Politics of the Acadian Parishes," 179-80, *The Cajuns—Essays on Their History and Culture* (Lafayette: Center for Louisiana Studies, 1983). Also Floyd Martin Clay, *Coozan Dudley LeBlanc: From Huey Long to Hadacol* (Gretna: Pelican Publishing, 1973).

4. "Boggs Hearing Colorful Drama," *New Orleans Item*, 10 October 1951, p. 3, c. 2.

5. Ory G. Poret, interview by the author, tape recording, New Orleans, La., 9 April 1999.

6. James Graham Cook, *The Segregationists* (New York: Appleton-Century-Crofts, 1962), 195.

7. Rosemary James, interview by the author, tape recording, New Orleans, La., 21 September 1993.

8. Leander H. Perez, interview by Douglas Edwards, 23 June 1962, Special Collections, Howard-Tilton Memorial Library, Tulane University, New Orleans, La.; see also Fred Friendly, "The Priest and the

Politician," "CBS Reports, 18 September 1963."

9. Perez, interview.

10. Rosemary James, "The Majority Leader—A Short History of a Controversial Man," *New Orleans Magazine*, 5, no. 7 (July 1971), 44-46.

11. Joseph C. Myers, Jr., interview by the author, tape recording, New Orleans, La., 24 April 1997.

12. Claire Boggs Morrison, interview by the author, tape recording, Long Beach, Ms., 18 May 1994.

13. Jack Lait and Lee Mortimer, *U.S.A. Confidential* (New York: Crown Publishers, 1952), 79.

14. Lindy Boggs, interview by the author, tape recording, New Orleans, La., 16 March 1992.

15. Bobby Baker and Larry L. King, *Wheeling and Dealing—Confessions of a Capitol Hill Operator* (New York: W. W. Norton and Company, 1978), 149-50. For more information on the Board of Education meetings, see David Brinkley, *Washington Goes to War—the Extraordinary Story of the Transformation of a City and a Nation* (New York: Ballantine Books, 1988) 269-70; Tip O'Neill and William Novak, *Man of the House—The Life and Political Memories of Speaker Tip O'Neill* (New York: Random House, 1987), 127-28; D. B. Hardemann and Donald C. Bacon, *Rayburn—A Biography* (Austin: Texas Monthly Press, Inc., 1987), 303-08.

16. Laurence Eustis, interview by the author, tape recording, New Orleans, La., 23 April 1992.

17. Robert Maloney, interview by the author, tape recording, New Orleans, La., 21 September 1993.

18. Boggs, interview.

19. Ibid.

20. Ibid.

21. Michael L. Kurtz and Morgan D. Peoples, *Earl K. Long—The Saga of Uncle Earl and Louisiana Politics* (Baton Rouge: Louisiana State University Press, 1990), 129.

22. James Gillis, interview by the author, tape recording, New Orleans, La., 24 March 1999.

23. "Grace Contends Boggs Ineligible," *Times-Picayune*, 16 October 1951, p. 1, c. 6; "Boggs Raps 'Perez Smear,'" *New Orleans Item*, 16 October 1951, p. 1, c. 1; "Boggs Brands Charges Filed By Miss Grace as 'False, Low and Vicious,' Cites Record," *Baton Rouge Morning Advocate*, 17 October 1951, p. 1, c.3.

24. "Grace Contends Boggs Ineligible," p. 1, c. 6.

25. "Miss Grace Makes Announcement for Governor's Race," *Baton Rouge Morning Advocate*, 22 April 1951, p. 1, c. 2.

26. "Full Text of Boggs Hearings," *New Orleans Item*, 21 October 1951, p. 18, c. 1.

CHAPTER TWO

1. Richard Hayman, *Tennessee Williams—Everyone Else is an Audience* (New Haven: Yale University Press, 1993), 108.

2. Ibid, 110.

3. Michel Ciment, *Kazan on Kazan* (New York: The Viking Press, 1974) 62; *Elia Kazan, A Life* (New York: Alfred A. Knopf, 1988), 279. For more information on the Kazan-Williams relationship, see their correspondence housed in the Tennessee Williams Collection, the Harry Ransom Humanities Research Center at the University of Texas, Austin.

4. *Kazan, A Life*, 279.

5. Hayman, *Tennessee Williams*, 110, 117; Ciment, *Kazan on Kazan*, 62-72; "Leigh's Desire," by Thomas Griffin, *New Orleans Item*, 31 October 1950, p. 15, c. 1.

6. "Miss Leigh (Scarlett O'Hara) Visits New Orleans for Role in 'Streetcar,'" by Rose Kahn, *New Orleans States*, 27 October 1950, p. 5, c. 1; "Desire Motorman Sees Self on Screen," *New Orleans Item*, 6 November 1951, p. 9, c. 3.

7. *Kazan, A Life*, 387-88; for Kazan's testimoney before HUAC, see Communist Infiltration of Hollywood Motion-Picture Industry—Part VII, House UnAmerican Activities Committee Hearings, 82nd Congress, 2nd Session, 1952 (Washington: Government Printing Office, 1952).

8. David McCullough, *Truman* (New York: Simon & Schuster, 1992), 550-52; Griffin Fariello, *Red Scare—Memories of the American Inquisition* (New York: W. W. Norton and Company, 1995), 36-40.

9. *McCullough*, Truman, 550-52.

10. "Board Plans Ruling Today in Case of Civics Teacher," *Times-Picayune*, 27 August 1948, p. 1, c. 3; "Board Clears Civics Teacher," *New Orleans Item*, 28 August 1948, p. 1, c. 1; "Shift of Civics Teacher Halted," *Times-Picayune*, 28 August 1948, p. 1, c. 2.

11. "They Recall When Bourgeois Taught 'Em," by Thomas Sancton, *New Orleans Item*, 10 January 1951, p. 1, c. 6.

12. "Board Plans Ruling Today in Case of Civics Teacher," *Times-Picayune*, 27 August 1948, p. 1, c. 3.

13. Ibid.

14. Ibid.

15. Ibid.

16. "Shift of Civics Teacher Halted," *Times-Picayune*, p. 1, c. 2.

17. Ibid.

18. Ibid.

19. Rufus Harris to F. Edward Hebert, 28 November 1948, Communism 1947 folder, F. Edward Hebert Collection, Special Collections, Howard-Tilton Memorial Library, Tulane University, New Orleans, La. Many have found that Hebert's mere presence on HUAC makes him a suspicious character, but historian Fawn Brodie, who excoriates Richard Nixon's work on the same committee, called Hebert "intelligent, vigorous, and less bigoted" than most of the rest of the HUAC membership. Fawn Brodie, *Richard Nixon—The Shaping of his Character* (New York: W. W. Norton and Company, 1981), 191.

20. F. Edward Hebert and John McMillan, *Last of the Titans—The Life and Times of Congressman F. Edward Hebert of Louisiana* (Lafayette: Center for Louisiana Studies, 1976), 64.

21. Ibid., 38.

22. "Hebert Sees Wide Net of Spying," by Carter Stevens, *New Orleans Item*, 17 December 1948, p. 2, c. 1; "Hebert Anti-Red Booklets

Coming," *Times-Picayune*, 4 August 1948, p. 28, c. l. For an extended discussion concerning Hebert's contention that the Tulane University faculty was partly composed of Communists, see Hebert to Harris, 21 December 1948 and Hebert to Westbrook Pegler, 5 December 1949, Communism 1947 folder, Hebert Collection.

23. "Hebert Anti-Red Booklets Coming," p. 28, c. 1.

24. "FBI Scans Orleans Reds," *Times-Picayune*, 23 July 1948, p. 24, c. 4.

25. "Reds, Once Ousted, Now Hold Union Whip," by John Collier, *New Orleans Item*, 24 September 1947. For more on the Communist influence in local unions see Adam Fairclough, *Race & Democracy— The Civil Rights Struggle in Louisiana, 1915-1972* (Athens: The University of George Press, 1995), 142-43; James A. Cook and James R. Watson, *Louisiana Labor—From Slavery to 'Right to Work'* (Lanham: University Press of America, 1985), 238-42.

26. "New Orleans Red Barred From U.S.," by John Collier, *New Orleans Item*, 26 July 1948, p. l, c. 5; "108 Reds Defeated by NMU," by John Collier, *New Orleans Item*, 26 July 1948, p.l, c., 5; "NMU Acts to Bar Red Infiltration," *Times-Picayune*, 4 December 1948, p.6, c. 5; "Himmaugh Pleads Guilty to Lie on Loyalty Oath," *New Orleans States*, 25 July 1949, p. l, c. 4.

27. "Himmaugh Pleads Guilty to Lie on Loyalty Oath, " p. l, c. 4.

28. Ibid.

29. "Kurtagh Leaves Kingsley House," *New Orleans States*, 12 April 1949, p. l, c. 1.

30. Ibid.

31. Floyd Newlin, interview by the author, tape recording, New Orleans, La., 21 April 1997.

32. Walter Cowan, interview by the author, tape recording, New Orleans, La., 21 October 1997.

33. Avery Alexander, interview by the author, tape recording, New Orleans, La., 20 June 1996.

34. Fairclough, *Race & Democracy*, 138-39.

35. Ibid.; Investigation of Communist Activities in the New Orleans Area–Hearing before the House UnAmerican Activities Committee,

85th Congress, First Session, February 15, 1957 (Washington: Government Printing Office, 1957), 119-178.

36. "Schools Shine Light on Reds," *New Orleans Item*, 8 May 1948, p. 1, c. 6; "7 Students Tell of Red Propaganda," *New Orleans States*, 7 May 1948, p. l, c. 5; "92 N.O. Students Reveal Red Propaganda," *New Orleans States*, 8 May 1948, p. 1, c. 4; Fairclough, *Race & Democracy*, 143.

37. "Tulane Professor Blames Dismissal On Anti-Red Actions," *New Orleans Item*, 7 December 1949, p. l, c. 1; "An Editorial," *Tulanian 23, No. 3* (January 1950), 2.

38. "Red War Growing Hotter Mrs. Luce Says," by Gerald Taitt, *New Orleans Item*, 17 September 1948, p. 20, c. 1; *The Loyola Wolf 1949*, (New Orleans: American Printing Company, 1949), 152-55; *The Loyola Wolf 1952* (New Orleans: American Printing Company, 1952), 185-88.

39. Taitt, "Red Cold War Growing Hotter, Mrs. Luce Says," p. 20, c. 1.

40. Ibid; *The Loyola Wolf 1949*, 152-55; *The Loyola Wolf 1952*, 185-88.

41. "Decline To Act On Czech Exhibit," *Times-Picayune*, 6 May 1949, p. 12, c. 2; "Public Schools Send Red Propaganda Back," *New Orleans Item*, 27 February 1950, p. 5, c. 3; "Communist Sheet Found Near Camp," *New Orleans Item*, 24 May 1951, p. 1, c. 8.

42. "Cancel Act On Protest Of Legion," *New Orleans Item*, 5 November 1952, p. 33, c. 1; "Cancel Adler's N.O. Opening Here," *New Orleans States*, 5 November 1952, p. 4, c. 2; "Billy Vine Is Smash Hit of New Swan Room Show," by Frances Weller, *New Orleans States*, 7 November 1952, p. 24, c. 5.

43. "Chaplin Film On As Legion Asks Bar," *New Orleans States*, 5 February 1953, p. 5, c. 4; Fariello, *Red Scare*, 260.

44. Hebert to Harris, 12 December 1948, 1947 Communist folder, Hebert Collection.

45. "64 Fined $5 in 'Disturbance Trial,'" *New Orleans States*, 7 February 1949, p. 11, c. 1; "65 Intimidated, Woman Claims," *Times-Picayune*, 9 February 1949, p. 2, c. 1; Hebert to Leander Perez, 8 February 1949, Perez file, Hebert Collection.

46. "64 Fined $5 in 'Disturbance Trial," p. 11, c. l.

47. "Judge Reverses Conviction of 60," *Times-Picayune*, 9 June 1949,

p. 16, c. 3; "Letter from Tulane," *New Orleans States*, 18 June 1949, p. 4, c. 6; Ruffus Harris to Hebert, 1 November 1949, Tulane University file, Hebert Collection.

48. "Culbertson Hits Foreign Policy, "*Times-Picayune*, 16 March 1949, p. 3, c. 6; "Huft To Head State Defense," *New Orleans Item*, 27 February 1950, p. 5, c. 2.

49. "Civil Defense News", No. 1, 2 October 1951, p. 1, c. 1. A complete collection of the newsletter is available at the Special Collections department of the Howard-Tilton Memorial Library at Tulane University. See also "Baton Rouge Trains Citizens For Atom-War Responsibilities," *Louisiana Municipal Review*, 14, no. 5, (August 1951), 15 ; "What Are We Doing About Civil Defense?" *Louisiana Municipal Review* 13, No.1, (September 1950), p. 1, c. 1.

50. "Lafayette To Practice 'Air-Attack,'" *New Orleans Item*, 28 January 1951, p. 19, c. 1; "City Must Be Saturated With First Aid in Event of Atom Bomb Attack, Says Ives," *Baton Rouge Morning Advocate*, 1 March 1951, p. 8-A, c. 1; "Baton Rouge To Be Target For 'A-Bomb,'" *New Orleans States*, 31 March 1951, p. 3, c. 2; "Medical Effects of Atomic Bomb Shown in Army Training Film," by Vincent Randazzo, *Hullabaloo 46, no.23* (13 April 1951), p. 2, c. 1.

51. "490 Students Go Through Paces at Sophie B. Wright," by Elsie Brupbacher, *New Orleans States*, 9 February 1951, p. 1, c. 4.

52. "Over Ground Shelters for N.O. Urged," *New Orleans Item*, 9 January 1951, p. 1, c. 5; "Shelters Below Ground Backed," *Times-Picayune*, 10 January 1951, p. 15, col 5; "N.O. Atom Blast Toll Estimated," *Times-Picayune*, 25 November 1951, p. 3, c. 3; "Orleans Bombing Resistance High," *Times-Picayune*, 12 September 1950, p. 1, c. 7.

53. "Warning Issued to Tulane Grads," *Times-Picayune*, 7 June 1950, p. 16, c. 2; "Archbishop Hits At Intolerance," *New Orleans States*, 5 July 1949, p. 17, c. 2.

54. The Security of America, Appendix to the *Congressional Record* (Washington: Government Printing Office, 1950), A4616-14.

55. Ibid.

56. Leander H. Perez, interview; "'Democracy' in the Deep Delta," by Lester Velie, *Collier's* 109, no. 54 (17 December 1949), 21-44.

CHAPTER THREE

1. Leonard Huber, *Landmarks of New Orleans* (New Orleans: Louisiana Landmarks Society, 1984), 35; *Polk's New Orleans City Directory, 1949* (New Orleans: Polks Publishing Company, 1949), 63.

2. Lester Velie, "Kingfish of the Dixiecrats," *Collier's* 109, no. 54 (24 December l949), 21-44.

3. Ibid.

4. F. Edward Hebert, interview by Glen Jeansonne, 16 July 1972, Archives and Special Collections, Louisiana State University at Shreveport, Shreveport, La.

5. Ben Toledano, interview by the author, tape recording, New Orleans, La., 3 March 1999.

6. William Nunguesser, interview by the author, tape recording, New Orleans, La., 2 July 1996.

7. Toledano, interview.

8. Velie, "Kingfish of the Dixiecrats."

9. Leander Perez, interview by Glen Jeansonne, 27 August 1966, Archives and Special Collections, Louisiana State University at Shreveport.

10. Ibid.

11. Ibid.

12. "Ted Lewis and Act Scores in Blue Room," by Ted Liuzza, *New Orleans Item*, 18 March 1956.

13. Perez, interview by Douglas Edwards.

14. Hebert, interview.

15. Ibid.

16. Perez to Hebert, 3, February 1949, Perez folder, Hebert Collection.

17. Ibid.

18. Perez to Hebert, 30 April 1953; Hebert to Ezra Taft Benson, 6 May 1953; Hebert to Perez, 6 May 1953; True D. Morse to Hebert,

21 May 1953; Hebert to Perez, 22 May 1953; Morse to Hebert, 16 June 1953; Hebert to Morse, 2 July 1953; Morse to Hebert, 6 July 1953; Perez folder, Hebert Collection.

19. Hebert internal office memo by Betty Hartery, 3 September 1953, Perez folder, Hebert Collection.

20. Ibid.

21. Hebert, interview.

22. Hebert to A.N. Goldberg, 3 June 1947. See also Hebert to Ellen Henican, 9 October 1967; Henican to Perez, 5 October 1967; all in Perez folder, Hebert Collection.

23. Hebert, interview.

24. Perez, interview by Edwards.

25. W. H. Harris, *Louisiana—Products, Resources, and Attractions* (New Orleans: New Orleans Democrat Print, 1881), 182-89. See also Harnett T. Kane, *Deep Delta Country* (New York: Duell, Sloan and Pearce, 1944), 200-13; William Springfield, *United States Census, 1920, Plaquemines Parish, Louisiana* (Greenville, South Carolina: Southern Historical Press, 1993); Mary Knill, "Anatomy of an Antebellum Sugar Parish: Plaquemines Parish, 1850-1860," Tulane University master's thesis, 1987, Special Collections, Howard-Tilton Memorial Library.

26. James Conaway, *Judge—The Life and Times of Leander Perez* (New York: Alfred A. Knopf, 1973), 10-11.

27. "Parish News," *Plaquemines Gazette*, 19 May 1934, p.l, c. 5.

28. Cook, *The Segregationists*, 204-05. The encyclopedia, in subsequent editions, also stated: "Mentally, the Negro is inferior to the white . . . we must necessarily suppose that the development of the negro and white proceeds on different lines." *The Encyclopaedia Britannica* (New York: Encyclopaedia Britannica Company, 1911), 344-49.

29. Cook, *The Segregationists*, 205.

30. Velie, "Kingfish of the Dixiecrats."

31. T. Harry Williams, *Huey Long* (New York: Vintage Books, 1981), 369.

32. "John Dymond Dies At Home," *New Orleans Item-Tribune*, 13 November 1932, p.4, c. 11; "John Dymond, Jr., Political, Social

Leader, Succumbs," *Times-Picayune*, 13 November 1932, p. 1, c. 3; "Notice," *Tulane News Bulletin*, 13, Number 3, Fall 1932, p. 36.

33. John Dymond, *The Oyster in Louisiana* (New Orleans: American Press, 1904).

34. Ibid., 12.

35. Glen Jeansonne, *Leander Perez: Boss of the Delta* (Lafayette: Center for Louisiana Studies, 1995), 18-20; "John Dymond Dies At Home," p. 4, c. 11.

36. William Ivy Hair, *The Kingfish and His Realm—The Life and Times of Huey P. Long* (Baton Rouge: Louisiana State University Press, 1991), 11; Williams, *Huey Long*, 131-32; John V. Baiamonte, Jr., *Spirit of Vengeance—Nativism and Louisiana Justice, 1921-1924* (Baton Rouge: Louisiana State University Press, 1986), 120.

37. "Cheers Approve John M. Parker's Declaration: 'The Ring Must Go!'" *Times-Picayune*, 19 September 1919, p. 1, c. 6.

38. "Ouster Hearing Reveals Secret of Defalcation," *Times-Picayune*, 15 May 1924, p. 1, c. 2.

39. "Louisiana Jurist Falls From Boat and is Drowned," *Times-Picayune*, 5 December 1919, p. 1, c. 1.

40. "Two Are Named Judges in Twenty-Ninth District," *Times-Picayune*, 9 December 1919, p. 20, c. 8; "Two Judges Named for Hingle Post In Plaquemines," *New Orleans Item*, 5 December 1919, p. 2, c. 1.

41. "Two Judges Named For Hingle Post In Plaquemines," p. 2, c. 1.

42. "Ouster Hearing Reveals Secret of Defalcation," p. 1, c. 2.

43. Especially in his conversations with others, Hebert used the title "Judge" whenever speaking of Perez. See Hebert to Henican, 9 October 1967, Perez folder, Hebert Collection; Toledano, interview.

44. I base my assessment of Perez's record from a survey of hundreds of his decisions, which were weekly published in the "District Court" column of the *St. Bernard Voice* from 1920 to 1923; A. Sidney Cain, interview by Jeansonne, 19-20 July 1972, Archives and Special Collections, LSU at Shreveport.

45. "Clerk Testifies Judge Perez Had Pistol On Bench," *Times-Picayune*, 28 May 1924, p. 6, c. 1.

46. Ibid.

47. Jeansonne, *Leander Perez*, 25.

48. "Dymond Gives Lie to Perez in Ouster Case," *Times-Picayune*, 12 October 1923, p. 1, c. 3; "Warrant Issued To Arrest Perez In Slander Case," *Times-Picayune*, 12 December 1923, p. 1, c. 3.

49. "Dymond Gives Lie To Perez in Ouster Case," p. 1, c. 3.

50. "Dymond Stands Severe Grilling In Perez Trial," *Times-Picayune*, 11 May 1924, p. 1, c. 2.

51. "Ouster Program Is Political Plot," *Times-Picayune*, 11 October 1923, p. 1, c. 4.

52. "Dymond-Leopold Faction Defeated On Lower Coast," *New Orleans Item*, 17 January 1924, p. 13, c. 5; "Dymond Loses; Says Rum Ring Defeated Him," *New Orleans Item*, 18 January 1924, p. 2, c. 5.

53. "Dymond Stands Severe Grilling In Perez Trial," p. 1, c. 2.

54. "Ouster Program is Poltiical Plot," p. 1, c. 14; "Suit To Impeach Judge Perez Ends In A Love Feast," by David Baldwin, *New Orleans Item*, 18 June 1950, p. 1, c. 5.

55. "Reports Calling Dymond 'Grafter' In Affadavit," *Times-Picayune*, 13 December 1923, p. 4, c. 1.

56. "Ouster Charges Denied By Perez As Trial Begins," *Times-Picayune*, 13 May 1924, p. 1, c. 3.

57. Jeansonne, Leander Perez, 28-29; "Suit To Impeach Judge Perez Ends In A Love Feast," p. 1, c. 5; "Perez Charges Dropped," *New Orleans Item*, 4 June 1924, p. 1, c. 8; "Judge Perez Wins, Ouster Suit Dropped," *New Orleans States*, 4 June 1924, p. 1, c. 8.

58. Jeansonne, *Leander Perez*, 29.

59. Ibid.

60. "Judge Perez Wins; Ouster Suit Dropped," p. 1, c. 8.

61. "Boundless Enthusiasm Grips Long's Headquarters Throughout All Evening," by Thomas Ewing Dabney, *New Orleans Item*, 17 January 1924, p. 6, c. 2.

62. "Votes of Parishes," *New Orleans Item*, 17 January 1924, p. 13, c. 2.

THE BIG LIE

63. Perez, interview by Edwards.

64. Perez, interview by T. Harry Williams, 28 May 1961, the Interview Collection, the Louisiana Lower Mississippi Valley Collections, Hill Memorial Library, Louisiana State University, Baton Rouge, La.

65. Cain, interview; Hair, *The Kingfish and His Realm*, 160; "Vote for Governor," *New Orleans Item*, 20 January 1928, p. 1, c. 7.

66. Williams, Huey Long, 365.

67. Perez, interview by Williams; Velie, "'Democracy' in the Deep Delta," 42.

68. Harvey Peltier, interview by Glen Jeansonne, 18 September 1972, Archives and Special Collections, Louisiana State University at Shreveport; Cain, interview.

69. Cain, interview.

70. Perez, interview by Williams.

71. Cain, interview.

72. "Bribery, Incompetence And Misuse Of Funds Charges Fail," by Hermann B. Deutsch, *New Orleans Item*, 16 May 1929, p. 1, c. 6.

73. Williams, Huey Long, 351-52; "Trial of Gov. Long Opens In Lousiana," *New York Times*, 15 May 1929, p. 12, c.1.

74. "Long Given Decision On Blackmail, 21-28, Most Charges Stand," by Hermann Deutsch, *New Orleans Item*, p. 1, c. 4; Velie, "'Democracy' in the Deep Delta," 42; "Governor Defeats Illegal Charges," *Plaquemines Gazette*, 25 May 1929, p. 1, c. 1; *The Official Journal of the Proceedings of the Senate of the State of Louisiana at the Fifth Extra Session of the Legislature* (Baton Rouge: Ramires-Jones Printing Company, 1929), 252.

75. *Official Journal of the Proceedings of the Senate*, 252.

76. Perez, Williams interview; Cain, Jeansonne interview.

77. "Impeachment of Gov. Long Suddenly Dropped as 15 Louisiana Senators Hold Trial Illegal," *New York Times*, 16 May 1929, p. 1, c. 3; "Long Given Decision on Blackmail," p. 1, c. 4.

78. "Long Given Decision on Blackmail," p. 1, c. 4.

79. Ibid.

80. "Judge Perez Defeats Manship Charge," p. 1, c. 1; "Whopee Party," *Plaquemines Gazette*, 25 May 1929, p. 1, c. 5.

81. "Legislators Are Honor-Guests," *St. Bernard Voice*, 8 June 1929, p. 1, c. 8; "Long Supporters Are Given Dinner," *Times-Picayune*, 3 June 1929, p. 3, c. 3.

82. Perez interview, Williams.

83. "Everybody Votes in the Perez Parish," by David Baldwin, *New Orleans Item*, 13 June 1950, p. 1, c. 1; Conaway, *Judge, 43.*

84. "Everybody Votes in the Perez Parish," p. 1, c. 1.

85. Cain, interview.

86. Ibid.

87. Conaway, Judge, 22-33; "Perez Made Millions From Public Land," by James O'Byrne, *Times-Picayune*, 1 June 1986, p. 1, c. 1; "Parish Rounds Up Last Of Oil Fortune," by Karen Turni, *Times-Picayune*, 8 October 1987, p. 1, c. 1.

88. "Budget Plan Blocked As State 'Revolts,'" by Hermann B. Deutsch, *New Orleans Item*, 7 June 1934, p. 1, c. 6; "Right of Local Self-Government Protected by Judge Perez in Strong Fight Before Legislative Committee," *Plaquemines Gazette*, 19 June 1934, p. 1, c. 4.

89. Perez, Edwards interview.

90. I base the statement that Perez supported Long's Share Our Wealth program on the appearance of pro-SOW columns that appeared in Perez's newspaper, the *Plaquemines Gazette*. See "Share-Our-Wealth Plan By Huey P. Long," *Plaquemines Gazette*, 14 July 1934, p. 1, c. 2; "Dictators," *Plaquemines Gazette*, 27 July 1935, p. 4, c. 3; "Balancing the Budget," *Plaquemines Gazette*, 29 June 1935, p. 4, c. 1.

91. "Noe, Martin Out For 2 Highest Offices, Cause Party Split," by Ralph Wheatley, *New Orleans States*, 19 September 1935, p. 1, c. 7; "Noe Announces For Governor; Martin Seeks Senate Post," *Times-Picayune*, 20 September 1935, p. 1, c. 1; "Long Wanted Leche To Be Governor, He Declined, Noe Says," *Morning Tribune*, 2 October 1935, p. 1. c. 1; "State Administration Ticket Is Endorsed," *St. Bernard Voice*, 5 October 1935, p. 1. c. 1.

92. "Mopping Up Louisiana," by Robert Van Gelder, *New York Times Sunday Magazine*, 15 September 1940, p. 17, c. 1.

93. Memorandum from William A. Friedlander to John E. Tobin, 20 February 1953, containing copy of 1943 Internal Revenue Service investigation of Perez, Perez folder, Boggs Collection. "Lawyer: 1940 Probe Blocked At Every Turn," by James O'Byrne, *Times-Picayune*, 2 June 1986, p. 3, c. 1.

94. Press release dated 9 October 1943 in Governor Sam Jones file, Military Library, Jackson Barracks, New Orleans, La.; see also "Use of Federal Troops at Request of the State" memorandum, 24 July 1943, in same file.

95. "Blaize To Try Peace Gesture," *New Orleans Item*, 8 October 1943, p. 1, c. 4.

96. "Flaming Barrier Delays Troops Near Courthouse," *New Orleans Item*, 9 October 1943, p. 1, c. 7; "Troops Seize Town in Louisiana as District Attorney's Men Flee," *New York Times*, 10 October 1943, p. 1, c. 2.

97. Velie, "Kingfish of the Dixiecrats."

98. "Perez—Tough, Able Political Boss," by David Baldwin, *New Orleans Item*, 14 June 1950, p. 1, c. 1.

99. "Boggs Formally Announces for Governorship," *New Orleans States*, 16 June 1951, no page number given, in June 1951 Gubernatorial campaign folder, Boggs Collection.

100. "Jones Endorses Boggs Candidacy," *Times-Picayune*, 19 June 1951, no page number given, in June 1951 Gubernatorial campaign folder, Boggs Collection.

CHAPTER FOUR

1. Boggs, interview.

2. Ibid.

3. Press release dated 19 July 1940, from July 1951 Gubernatorial campaign folder, Boggs Collection; see also "Jones-Noe Slate

Pledged Backing By Old Regulars," *Times-Picayune*, 18 July 1940, p. l, c. 4.

4. Lindy Boggs, *Washington Through a Purple Veil—Memories of a Southern Woman* (New York: Harcourt, Brace, and Company, 1994), 63-67; Pamela Tyler, *Silk Stockings and Ballot Boxes—Women and Politics in New Orleans, 1920-1963* (Atlanta: Georgia University Press, 1996), 122-30, 141-53.

5. "Lindy Boggs, Heir to the House," by Myra MacPherson, *The Washington Post*, 4 March 1973, p. KL, c. 1; see also Rosemary James, "Lindy Boggs," *New Orleans Magazine* 7, no. 2, 78-103; "Mixture of Charm, Persistence Wins Influence, Affection," by Bruce Alpert, *Times-Picayune*, 19 July 1990, p. l, c. l; "Boggs Offspring Born Into Politics," by Thomas Fitzgerald, *Times-Picayune*, 9 October 1988, p. l, c. l.

6. Frederick Starr, *New Orleans UnMasqued* (New Orleans: Dedeaux Publishing, 1985), 192.

7. Boggs, *Washington Through a Purple Veil*, 28-33.

8. MacPherson, "Heir to the House," p. K1, c. 1.

9. Boggs, interview.

10. MacPherson, "Lindy Boggs, Heir to the House," p. KL, c. 1.

11. James Coleman, interview by the author, tape recording, New Orleans, La., 6 April 1992.

12. Ben C. Toledano, interview by the author, New Orleans, La., 3 March 1999.

13. "Lindy Boggs Quits Congress to Close Ranks with her Two Remarkable Daughters; One Gravely Ill with Cancer," by Garry Clifford, *People*, 13 August 1990, Volume 34, Number 6, 57-61.

14. Lindy Boggs to Hale Boggs, 11 January 1944 and 2 February 1944; in Personal Correspondence folder, Boggs Collection.

15. Lindy Boggs to Hale Boggs, 2 February 1944.

16. Lindy Boggs to Hale Boggs, 11 January 1944.

17. Ibid.

18. Lindy Boggs to Hale Boggs, 17 February 1944.

19. Laurence Eustis, interview.

20. Claire Boggs Morrison, interview; Boggsdale folder, Biloxi Public Library, Biloxi, Mississippi; Boggsdale folder, Mississippi Department of Archives and History, Jackson, Mississippi.

21. "Mississippi Drama Between the Wars, 1870-1916," *The Journal of Mississippi History*, Volume XXVI, Number Three, 301.

22. Uncited obituary notice from the *Biloxi Sun Herald*, circa 16 August 1919, Boggsdale folder, Biloxi Public Library.

23. William Chafe, *Never Stop Running—Allard Lowenstein and the Struggle To Save American Liberalism* (New York: Basic Books, 1983) 156-57; Morrison, interview.

24. Morrison, interview.

25. Personal Correspondence folder, Boggs Collection.

26. Ibid.

27. Morrison, interview.

28. Mary E. Boggs, no date given, but probably late 1980s, interview on file with the Mississippi Oral History Program at the University of Southern Mississippi, Hattiesburg, Ms.

29. Beatrice Cosgrove to Boggs, 29 November 1929, Personal Correspondence folder, Boggs Collection.

30. Copies of Cosgrove's column from the *Times-Picayune* in Personal Correspondence folder, Boggs Collection.

31. Dr. W. A. Dearman to the Registrar of Tulane University, 16 May 1931; B. F. Brown to the Register of Tulane University, 11 May 1931; both in Personal Correspondence folder, Boggs Collection; James, "The Majority Leader," p. 42.

32. "The Depression and N.O.," by John Pope, *Times-Picayune*, 31 October 1979, p. D1, c. 1.

33. Ibid.

34. Douglas L. Smith, *The New Deal in the Urban South* (Baton Rouge: Louisiana State University Press, 1988), 11; see also Roman Heleniak, "Local Reactions to the Great Depression in New Orleans, 1929-33," Louisiana History, 10 (Spring 1969), 294-97.

35. "'Mr. Boggs Goes To Washington,' Is Hope Of Hale and His 'Boss,'" 21 August 1940, copy of article in 1940 Congressional campaign folder, Boggs Collection.

36. Howard K. Smith, interview by the author, tape recording, New Orleans, La., 17 June 1996.

37. Coleman, interview.

38. "The Majority Whip," by Ed Brooks, *Tulanian*, 33, No.3, (March 1962), 8; "Proxies Perform Prexy Politics," *Hullabaloo*, Volume XXVIII, No. 3, 14 October 1932, p. 5, c. 3.

39. "Light Vote Cast In Campus Poll," *Hullabaloo*, Volume XXVIII, Number 5, 28 October 1932, p. 1, c. 2.

40. Ibid.

41. "The Ones Who Are Left," essay in Personal Papers, 1914-1940, Boggs Collection.

42. Ibid.

43. Ibid.

44. Ibid.

45. James, "The Majority Leader," 42.

46. Ken Burns, *Huey Long*, 88 min. (RKB/Florentine Films, 1985).

47. Eustis, interview.

48. Moises Steeg, interview by the author, tape recording, New Orleans, La., 5 May 1992.

49. Coleman, interview.

50. Boggs, interview.

51. Video conference tape discussing the People's League, spring 1992. I am grateful to Moises Steeg for letting me view and quote from the tape.

52. "Mass Protest Is Held," *New Orleans Item*, 10 October 1939, p. 1, c. 7; "Throngs Demand Recall of Byrne, Hearing Set," *New Orleans States*, 10 October 1939, p. 1, c. 1.; The People's League Collection, David R. McGuire, Jr., Memorial Collection, Special Collections, Howard-Tilton Memorial Library; Steeg, interview. An example of how Boss was able

to exploit his limited role in the People's League for larger publicity reasons can be seen in "People's League Head Has Always Been Busy," in the *States*, 28 October 1939 and "'Mr. Boggs Goes To Washington,' Is Hope of Hale and His 'Boss,'" *States*, 21 October 1940; copies of both can be found in the McGuire Collection.

53. Steeg, interview.

54. Boggs, *Washington Through a Purple Veil*, 71-72.

55. Boggs, interview; Eustis, interview. For more on Paul Maloney, see T. Harry Williams' interview with him, 26 July 1957, the Interview Collection, the Louisiana Lower Mississippi Valley Collections; Hill Memorial Library; Paul Maloney entry, *Biographical Directory of the American Congress 1774-1971* (Washington: Government Printing Office, 1971), 1332.

56. Undated speech, most likely written and delivered in late August 1940, in August 1940 Congressional campaign folder, Boggs Collection; see also Jerry Sanson, "Reflections of Reform, Shadows of War, and a Portent of Things to Come: The Louisiana 1940 Congressional Elections," *Louisiana History*, 32 (Fall 1992), 350-51.

57. Undated radio address, circa mid-September 1940, September 1940 Congressional campaign folder, Boggs Collection.

58. Ibid.

59. "Boggs, Hebert Win Congress Contests," *Times-Picayune*, 11 September 1940, p. 1, c. 7; " 2 Congressmen Face Runoffs; Orleans Is Swept By Ticket," *New Orleans States*, 11 September 1940, p. 1, c. 1.

60. Boggs, interview; Boggs, *Washington Through a Purple Veil*, 75-76.

61. *Congressional Record—Proceedings and Debates of the 77th Congress—First Session*, Volume 87, Part 7, August 12, 1941 to October 20, 1941 (Washington: Government Printing Office, 1941), 7039.

62. Robert Maloney, interview by the author, tape recording, New Orleans, La., 7 September 1994; Hebert, *The Last of the Titans*, 164-70.

63. *Report of the Secretary of State, 1942*, Louisiana Secretary of State (Baton Rouge: Ramires Press, 1942), 11; Boggs to Eustis, 16 September 1942; September 1942 Congressional campaign folder, Boggs Collection.

64. Boggs to Eustis, 16 September 1942, September 1942 Congressional campaign folder, Boggs Collection.

65. Boggs to Eustis, 16 September 1942; Boggs to Robert Ainsworth, 31 March 1945; Frank Ellis to Boggs, 31 March 1945; Boggs to Ellis, 7 April 1945; Charlie Popora to Boggs, 10 April 1945; Eustis to Boggs, 19 August 1945; Boggs, *Washington Through a Purple Veil*, 93-100. As early as the week after his 1942 defeat, Boggs was making plans for a comeback, telling Eustis in his 16 September 1942 letter: "Maloney is washed up for good and I have already announced that I will oppose him in 1944."

66. "Vosbein Urges Tax Aid For Elderly," *Times-Picayune*, 29 August 1946, newspaper clip in the August 1946 Congressional campaign folder, Boggs Collection.

67. "Vosbein Attacks Boggs' War Record," *New Orleans States*, 3 September 1946; "Hits Record," *New Orleans Item*, 29 August 1946; newspaper clips in August and September 1946 Congressional campaign folders, Boggs Collection.

68. "Boggs, Knight and Hebert Win; Runoff For Judges," *Times-Picayune*, 11 September 1946, p. 1, c. 8; "Vote Returns Taken Casually," by William Korns, *New Orleans Item*, 11 September 1946, p. 1, c. 5.

69. *Congressional Record—Proceedings and Debates of the 80th Congress*, Volume 93, Part I, January 3, 1947 to February 24, 1947 (Washington: Government Printing Office, 1947), 1047.

70. Arnold A. Rogaw, James Forestal—A Study of Personality, Politics, and Policy (New York: Macmillan Company, 1963), 25-26. Boggs was eloquent in defense of Forestal, noting that "In this Capitol of the United States the most devastating weapons used—more devastating than machine guns or mortars or any other weapons of battle—are the cruel weapons of distorted words, and they were used against this great man in a most unfair, uncharitable, and unthinkable manner." Boggs' address won the attention of President Harry Truman and perhaps warmed HST to Boggs; see Boggs to Truman, 20 October 1949; Truman to Boggs, 27 October 1949; Truman to Boggs, 25 January 1950; and Boggs to Truman, 2 February 1950; in the latter letter Boggs thanks the president for sending his son, Tommy, an autographed card, noting "both Tommy and I

appreciated the autograph. He has, of course, shown it to all of his 'pals' at school. You made a nine-year old quite happy." Hale Boggs, President Truman's Personal Files, 1949 and 1950, Harry S. Truman Presidential Library, Independence, Missouri.

71. "Louisiana Votes Given to Russell," by Edgar Poe, *Times-Picayune*, 15 July 1948, p. l, c. 17. For more on the historic 1948 civil rights battle at that year's Democratic convention, see Hubert H. Humphrey, *The Education of a Public Man—My Life and Politics* (Minneapolis: University of Minnesota Press, 1991), 75-79; and McCullough, *Truman*, 636-44.

72. "Louisiana Delegates Split But Stick by Party Ticket," by Edward Jamieson, *New Orleans States*, p. 2, c. 3.

73. "Louisiana Bars Truman Votes," by Ed M. Clinton, *Times-Picayune*, 11 September 1948, p. l, c. 8; "Presidential Votes Pledged to Thurmond," by Henry Edge, *New Orleans States*, 10 September 1948, p. l, c. 6; "Louisiana Scratches Truman Off Ballot," *Atlanta Constitution*, 11 September 1948, p. 3, c. 4.

74. Boggs to Jacob E. Davis, 14 October 1948, 1948 Presidential Election folder, Boggs Collection. Early in his career, Boggs was a supporter of the white South. "As you know, I am definitely commited against the so called 'Civil Rights Program,'" he told one constituent in 1948. Boggs to R. G. Robinson, 19 November 1948.

75. "Judge Perez Address N.O. Chamber of C," *Plaquemines Gazette*, 4 March 1950, p. l, c. l.

76. D. B. Hardeman and Donald C. Bacon, *Rayburn—A Biography* (Austin: Texas Monthly Press, 1987), 414; James, "The Majority Leader," 46.

77. William F. Dodd, *Peapatch Politics—The Earl Long Era in Louisiana Politics* (Baton Rouge: Claitor's Publishing Division, 1991), 77-94.

78. Ibid.

79. James, "The Majority Leader," 46.

80. Ibid.

81. Hardeman and Bacon, *Rayburn*, 414.

82. "Boss William Green Tries Hand On Governorship," *Plaquemines Gazette*, 17 March 1951, p. l, c. 3.

83. Ibid.

84. "South Will Back Ike, Says Perez," *Plaquemines Gazette*, 25 August 1951, p. 1, c. 3.

CHAPTER FIVE

1. *Telephone Directory—Plaquemine, Louisiana; White Castle, Louisiana; June 1950* (New Orleans: Southern Bell and Telegraph Company, 1950), 14, 16, 24-27. A copy of this book is in the Iberville Parish Library in Plaquemine, Louisiana. Brief but concise descriptions of Plaquemine are found in *Louisiana—A Guide to the State* (New York: Hastings House, 1941), 534-35; Albert Grace, *The Heart of the Sugarbowl—Iberville* (Baton Rouge: Franklin Press, 1946), 104-07; and Macon Fry and Julie Posner, *Cajun Country Guide* (Gretna: Pelican Publishing Company, 1992), 137-42.

2. *Telephone Directory*, 29; *Louisiana Almanac and Fact Book*, 1953-1954, (Gretna: Pelican Publishing Company, 1953), 440.

3. "Local Radio Programs," *Baton Rouge Morning Advocate*, 18 November 1951, p. 8-A, c. 1.

4. "WDSU-TV," *Baton Rouge Morning Advocate*, 18 November 1951, p. 8-A, c. 1.

5. *Telephone Directory*, 34.

6. "Plaquemine Books, Dice Given OK," by Henry Edge, *New Orleans States*, 18 May 1949, p. 5, c. 4.

7. "Plaquemine Proclaims Lucille May Grace Day," *Baton Rouge Morning Advocate*, 17 November 1951, p. 8-A, c. 4.

8. "Fifteen Years A State Official—Lucille May Grace," by Katherine Bourgeois, *Baton Rouge Morning Advocate*, 1 September 1946, p. 2-B, c. 6; "The Private Life of 'Miss Lucille,'" by Patricia Sinclair, *New Orleans Item*, 30 May 1951, p. 15, c. 3. See also "Land Office Chief Always Wins In Landslide," by Edward W. Stagg, *New Orleans Item*, 13 May 1948, p. 10, c. 10.

9. Sinclair, "The Private Life of 'Miss Lucille,'" p. 15, c. 3.

10. "Lucille May Grace Returns As Register of State Lands," by Margaret Dixon, *Baton Rouge Morning Advocate*, 16 May 1948, p. 13, c. 1.

11. "Grace-Long Apparent Coolness Held Surprise," by Edgar Poe, *Times-Picayune*, 4 February 1950, p. 2, c. 1.

12. "Mrs. Grace Talks of Govenor's Race," by E.M. Clinton, *Times-Picayune*, 26 February 1950, section 2, p. 3, c. 6.

13. Ken Gormin to Boggs, 18 January 1951, in Personal Correspondence folder, 1951-1952 Gubernatorial Election, Boggs Collection.

14. Fred Dent, Jr., interview by the author, tape recording, New Orleans, La., 20 October 1997; Dodd, *Peapatch Politics*, 229-30.

15. Uncited clipping, Lucille May Grace Scrapbook. Volume I, February 1929-May 1936, the Lower Louisiana Mississippi Valley Collections, Hill Memorial Library.

16. Naomi Marshall, interview by the author, tape recording, New Orleans, La., 20 October 1997.

17. Ory G. Poret, interview by the author, tape recording, New Orleans, La., 8 April 1999.

18. "Lucille Grace To Stump State Today," *New Orleans States*, 17 November 1951, p. 2, c. 1; "Miss Grace Says Good Government Is Need of State," *Baton Rouge Morning Advocate*, 18 November 1951, p. 7, c. 1.

19. "Miss Grace Says Good Government Is Need of State," p. 7, c. 1.

20. Poret, interview.

21. "Miss Grace Says Good Government Is Need of State," p. 7, c. 1.

22. Ibid.; "Gov. Long Promises $100 Lump Sum Pension Payment If Spaht Elected to Office," *Baton Rouge Morning Advocate*, 6 January 1952, p. 1, c. 2.

23. "Miss Grace Says Good Government Is Need of State," p. 7, c. 1.

24. Ibid.

25. Ibid.

26. "Frederick Jumel Grace," by Desdemona Redlich, uncited clipping in Grace family folder, Iberville Public Library.

27. Ibid.

28. Ibid.

29. Ibid.; "Fred J. Grace Dies Suddenly On Visit Here," *Morning Tribune*, 10 September 1931, p. l, c. l; "Fred J. Grace, 61, In State Office 24 Years, Is Dead," *Times-Picayune*, 10 September 1931, p. l, c. 2.

30. *The Gumbo 1920* (Nashville: Benson Printing, 1920), 31-63.

31. *The American Heritage History of the 1920s and 1930s* (New York: American Heritage Publishing Company, 1970), 38-39; see also "New Faction for Suffrage Formed," *The Daily Reveille*, Volume XXIV, No. 28, 21 May 1920, p. 6, c. 1; "'They Shouldn't Shimmie' If Thou Dost Not Desire Publicity'—Latest Edict," *The Daily Reveille*, Volume XXIV, No. 23, 16 April l920, p. 6, c. 1.

32. "Pink Pierettes Cleverly Acted At Garig Hall," by Helene Robbins, *The Daily Reveille*, Volume XXlll, No. 26, 15 May 1919, p.8, c.1; "'All of a Sudden Peggy,' Opens In S. Central Louisiana," *The Daily Reveille*, Volume XXIV, No.9, 5 December 1919, p.9, c.a; *The Gumbo 1920*, 37.

33. "Thousands At Rites For Grace," *New Orleans Item*, 11 September 1931, p. l, c. 4; "Miss Grace In Father's Post," *Morning Tribune*, 11 September 1931, p. l, c. 6; "Oldest Daughter of Grace Given Land Office Post," *Times-Picayune*, 11 September 1931, p. l, c. 2.

34. Uncited clipping, Lucille May Grace Scrapbook, Volume One, February 1929-May 1936.

35. Bourgeois, "Fifteen Years a State Official—Lucille May Grace," p. 2-B, c. 6; Sinclair, "The Private Life of 'Miss Lucille,'" p. 15, c. 3; "Grace in Old Job," *Baton Rouge Morning Advocate*, 13 May 1956, p. 3-B, c. 1.

36. Hermann B. Deutsch, *The Huey P. Long Murder Case* (New York: Doubleday and Company, 1963), 110-11.

37. "First Woman Candidate to Enter State Primary Is New Appointee," 12 September 1931, 12 September 1931; uncited clipping, Lucille May Grace Scrapbook, Volume One, February 1929-May 1936.

38. Ibid.

39. Sinclair, "The Private Life of 'Miss Lucille,'" p. 15, c.3.

40. *Compilation of Primary Election Returns of the Democratic Party, State of Louisiana* (Baton Rouge: Ramires-Jones Printing, no date given), 1932 ledger, 87.

41. Ibid., 99.

42. Ibid., 122, 176.

43. Ellen Bryan Moore, interview by the author, tape recording, New Orleans, La., 16 April 1999.

44. Compilation of Primary Election Returns, 87.

45. Marshall, interview.

46. Moore, interview.

47. Gillis, interview.

48. Poret, interview.

49. Bourgeois, "Fifteen Years A State Official—Lucille May Grace," p. 2-B, c. 6.

50. Dent, interview.

51. Deutsch, *The Huey Long Murder Case*, 110-13; David Zinman, *The Day Huey Long Was Shot* (Jackson: University Press of Mississippi, 1993), 117, 142.

52. Lucille May Grace to F. Edward Hebert, 20 May 1941, Lucille May Grace folder, Hebert Collection.

53. Sinclair, "The Private Life of 'Miss Lucille,'" p. 15, c. 3.

54. Ibid.

55. Boggs, interview.

56. Dodd, *Peapatch Politics*, 233-34.

57. Grace to Hebert, 10 March 1950, Lucille May Grace folder, Hebert Collection.

58. Ibid.

59. Moore, interview.

60. Poret, interview.

61. Dent, interview.

62. Ory G. Poret, *History of Land Titles in the State of Louisiana* (Baton Rouge: State Land Office, 1972), 25-29; *Louisiana: Its History, People, Government and Economy* (Baton Rouge: Louisiana Legislative Council: 1955), 62-63.

63. Poret, *History of Land Titles in the State of Louisiana*, 31-36.

64. Poret, interview.

65. "North Louisiana," The Oil and Gas Journal, Volume 26, No. 52; 17 May 1928; 181-82.

66. "State Receives Millions," by Lucille May Grace, *Sunday Item-Tribune*, 14 March 1937, p. 5, c. 1; "Tidelands Important to State," by Lucille May Grace, *New Orleans Item*, 3 January 1951, p. 28, c. 6.

67. "Days of Grace," by Hermann Deutsch, *New Orleans Item*, 24 December 1957, p. 7, c. 1.

68. "State Receives Millions," p. 5, c. 1.

69. Ibid.

70. "US Control Over Tidelands Would Cost State Millions," by Ken Gormin, *Times-Picayune*, 23 December 1948, p. 14, c. 3.

71. "Tidelands Important to State," p. 28, c. 6.

72. Ibid.

73. Ibid.

74. "US Control Over Tidelands Would Cost State Millions," p. 14, c. 3.

75. "Miss Grace Hits At Alleged Deal," *Times-Picayune*, 29 May 1951, p. 23, c. 4; "Miss Grace Opposes Constitutional Convention Call," *Plaquemines Gazette*, 19 August 1950, p. 1, c. 1; "Land Office Head Hits Elimination in Constitution," *Baton Rouge Morning Advocate*, 14 February 1950, p. 1, c. 4.

76. "US Control Over Tidelands Would Cost State Millions," p. 14, c. 3.

77. "Miss Grace Raps Boggs Candidacy," *Plaquemines Gazette*, 7 July 1951, p. 1, c. 5.

78. "Miss Grace Says Boggs Trumanite," *Plaquemines Gazette*, 9 June 1951, p. 1, c. 5.

79. Ibid.

80. Dodd, *Peapatch Politics*, 91-92.

81. "Tidelands Funds May Be Problem," *Times-Picayune*, 6 October 1950, p. 8, c. 3.

82. "Perez Opposes Boggs, Gives OK for Miss Grace," *New Orleans States*, 14 September 1951, p. 3, c. 2; "Perez Backs Grace; Ticket Being Formed," *New Orleans Item*, 29 September 1951, p. l, c. 4.

83. For an example of the favorable coverage Grace received, see "Miss Lucille May Grace Formally Announces for Governor of Louisiana," *Plaquemines Gazette*, 28 April l951, p. 1, c. 6; Maurice Gatlin, *The Election of 1952—Louisiana At the Cross Roads* (New Orleans: self-published, 1951) 11-12.

84. Gatlin, *The Election of 1952*, 8-9.

85. "Two Parish Bloc for Miss Grace," *Times-Picayune*, 13 October 1951, p. 31, c. 4; "Dutch Rowley Going Own Way In State Election," *New Orleans States*, 1 October l951, p. l, c. 2; "Rowley-Perez Split In Making Over Candidate," *New Orleans States*, 2 October l951, p. 2, c. 6.

86. "Two Parish Bloc for Miss Grace," p. 31, c. 4.

87. Testimony of Anita Conrad, Lucille May Grace vs. T. Hale Boggs, Nineteenth Judicial District Court, Parish of East Baton Rouge, State of Louisiana, Division C, Number 40,078, October 29, 1951, 10-13.

CHAPTER SIX

1. David W. Reinhard, *The Republican Right Since 1945* (Lexington: University Press of Kentucky, 1983), 65-67.

2. Thomas C. Reeves, *The Life and Times of Joe McCarthy—A Biography* (New York: Stein and Day, 1982), 205-33.

3. Reinhard, *The Republican Right Since 1945*, 62-63.

4. Brodie, Richard Nixon, 232-45.

5. Ibid.

6. Claude Pepper, Pepper: *Eyewitness to a Century* (New York: Harcourt, Brace, Jovanovich, 1987), 195-214.

7. Reeves, *The Life and Times of Joe McCarthy*, 311; Lisle A. Rose, *The Cold War Comes to Main Street—America in 1950* (Wichita: University Press of Kansas, 1999), 275-79.

8. McCullough, *Truman*, 813-14; Merle Miller, *Plain Speaking—An*

Oral Biography of Harry S. Truman (New York: Berkley Publishing Company, 1974), 321-22, 447.

9. Miller, Plain Speaking, 47.

10. "Grace Contends Boggs Ineligible," *Times-Picayune*, 16 October 1951, p. 1, c. 7; "Boggs Brands Charges Filed By Miss Grace as 'False, Low, and Vicious,' Cites Record," *Baton Rouge Morning Advocate*, 17 October 1951, p. 1, c. 3.

11. "The Front Row," by Hale Boggs, *Hullabaloo*, Volume XXXI, No.4, 18 October 1935, p. 1, c. 1.

12. John P. Dyer, *Tulane—The Biography of a University, 1834-1965* (New York: Harper & Row, 1966), 228-29.

13. Ibid.

14. Coleman, interview.

15. William Manchester, *The Glory and the Dream—A Narrative History of America, 1932-1972, Volume One* (New York: Little, Brown, and Company, 1973), 152-53; Eileen Eagan, *Class, Culture, and the Classroom—The Student Peace Movement of the 1930s* (Philadelphia: Temple University Press, 1981), 41, 61-62.

16. "Student Anti-War Meeting," *Hullabaloo*, Volume XXXI, No. 8, 15 November 1935, p. 5, c. 3.

17. "The Front Row," by Hale Boggs, *Hullabaloo*, Volume XXXI, No. 30, 16 April 1936, p. 1, c. 1; "Students Protest in Annual Demonstration," *Hullabaloo*, Volume XXXI, No. 30, 16 April 1936, p. 1, c. 6; "Blair Plans Local Strike Against War," *Hullabaloo*, Volume XXXI, No. 29, 9 April 1936, p. 7, c. 1; Eagan, *Class, Culture, and the Classroom*, 121-35, 186-87.

18. "Students Protest in Annual Demonstration," p. 1, c. 6; "Speakers Battle On Stand While 1500 Students Applaud," *New Orleans States*, 22 April 1936, p. 1, c. 7; "'Arms Maker,' 'General' Defend War at Tulane-Newcomb Rally," *New Orleans Item*, 22 April 1936, p. 1, c. 4.

19. Smith, interview.

20. Ibid.

21. "Students Protest in Annual Demonstration," p. 1, c. 6; "Speakers Battle On Stand While 1500 Students Applaud," p. 1, c. 7.

22. Ibid for both above citations.

23. Ibid.

24. Ibid.

25. Ibid.

26. Maurice Clark, interview by the author, tape recording, New Orleans, La., 22 April 1997.

27. *Soards City Directory, 1938* (New Orleans: Soards Publishing Company, 1938), 1235.

28. Undated pamphlet promoting the New Orleans Socialist Party, Harold Newton Papers, Box One, Folder 245-1-3, Special Collections, Howard-Tilton Memorial Library.

29. "Mass Meeting Demands End of Martial Law," *New Orleans Tribune*, 7 August 1934, p. 1, c. 7; Kupperman, interview.

30. "More Pickets Arrested at 'Red Salute,'" *New Orleans Morning Tribune*, 11 December 1935, p. 3, c. 1; "Mayor Urged to Intervene for Pickets," *New Orleans Morning Tribune*, 12 December 1935, p. 9, c. 4; "Score Arrest of Pickets at 'Red Salute,'" *New Orleans Morning Tribune*, 13 December 1935, p. 3, c. 5.

31. "The Front Row," by Hale Boggs, *Hullabaloo*, Volume XXXI, no. 3, 11 October 1935, p. 1, c. 1.

32. *Jambalaya 1935* (Nashville: Benson Printing Company, 1935), 108.

33. Newlin, interview.

34. Coleman, interview.

35. Ibid.

36. Eustis, interview.

37. Ibid.

38. "The Front Row," by Hale Boggs, Number XXXI, No. 30, 16 April 1936, p. 1, c. 1.

39. Gore Vidal, *Screening History* (Cambridge: Harvard University Press, 1992), 60; Eric Sevareid, *Not So Wild a Dream* (New York: Knopf, 1979), 63.

40. Eagen, Class, Culture, and the Classroom, 95, 115-18, 107, 121-35, 186-87, 170-71, 186-93; Lawrence S. Wittner, *Rebels Against*

War—The American Peace Movement: 1933-1983 (Philadelphia: Temple University Press, 1984), 14, 20; Maurice Isserman, *If I Had a Hammer—The Death of the Old Left and the Birth of the New Left* (New York: Basic Books, 1987), 131-32. For more information on both the League for Industrial Democracy as well as the American Student Union, see the Swarthmore College Peace Collection at Swarthmore College, Swarthmore, Pa., which contains one of the largest collections anywhere of pamphlets, magazines, and other material produced by a variety of leftist organizations in the 1930s. See in particular the *Student Advocate*, the official publication of the American Student Union. Addition information on the ASU at the collection is listed under the League for Industrial Democracy.

41. "The Front Row," by Hale Boggs, *Hullabaloo*, Volume VVVII, No. 12, 11 December 1936, p. 1, c. 1.

42. Cowan, interview. De la Housaye also annually marked the anniversary of the Battle of Liberty Place, a violent response in 1874 among local whites to Reconstruction. See De La Houssaye to New Orleans Mayor Robert Maestri, 8 September 1939 and 20 September 1945. Correspondence file, Robert Maestri Mayoral Papers, Louisiana Collection, New Orleans Public Library.

43. De la Houssaye, interview.

44. Ibid.

45. De La Houssaye to Boggs, 11 September 1951; Boggs to De La Houssaye, 12 September 1951; September 1951 Gubernatorial folder, Boggs Collection.

46. Membership drive letter from the Louisiana Coalition of Patriotic Societies, no date given but most likely the spring of 1937; Lee Papers, Box One, folder 245-1-3, Special Collections, Howard-Tilton Memorial Library.

47. *Lucille May Grace vs. T. Hale Boggs, Et Al*, 151.

48. Ibid.

49. "Burlesque Drive on Reds Held at Tulane," *New Orleans States*, p. 1, c. 7, 17 December 1936; "'Red-Baiters' Are Goaded By Tulane 'Student-Society,'" *Times-Picayune*, 18 December 1936, p. 20, c. 1; see also Moises Steeg to Harold Lee, early April 1937, Folder 245-1-13, Box One, Lee Papers.

50. Adam Fairclough, *Race & Democracy*, 34.

51. "An Open Letter to the People of New Orleans," New Orleans Socialist Party pamphlet and "Statement of Terror Against Farmers Union Leaders in West Feliciana Parish, Louisiana," 2 July 1937, both in Box One, Folder 245-1-5, Lee Papers, Howard-Tilton Memorial Library. See also letter from labor organizer T. J. Darcy to Mayor Maestri protesting the arrest of striking longshoremen by the New Orleans police: "There is not a Communist among our men," Darcy wrote; Darcy to Maestri, 4 November 1936, Labor folder, Maestri Papers.

52. Statement of Lucille Petty-John, 25 June 1938, Box One, Folder 245-1-17, Lee Papers.

53. Statement of Bernard Mintz, 1 August 1938, Box One, Folder 245-1-14, Lee Papers.

54. Ibid.

55. Statement of Lee Rattner, 5 July 1938, Box One, Folder 245-1-13.

56. Clark, interview; "Jessen Rites Today; Sleeping Tablets Held Cause of Death," *Honolulu Star-Bulletin*, 16 May 1952, no page number given, from the library of the *Honolulu Star-Bulletin*, Honolulu, Hawaii.

57. Trudy Wenzel Lash, interview by the author, tape recording, New Orleans, La., 26 April 1997. For more on Lash see "Joseph P. Lash Is Dead'; Reporter and Biographer," by David E. Pitt, *New York Times*, 23 August 1987, p. 40, c.1; Doris Kearns Goodwin, *No Ordinary Time—Franklin and Eleanor Roosevelt: the Home Front in World War II* (New York: Touchstone, 1994), 122-24.

58. Hebert, Jeansonne interview.

59. Ibid.

60. Newlin, interview.

61. *The Federationist*, no date given, but released in October or November of 1951; copy of the paper can be found in the November 1951 Gubernatorial folder, Boggs Collection. There is also a microfilm collection of scattered issues of the paper in the Louisiana Collection of the New Orleans Public Library.

62. "Huey Long's 'Revolution,'" by Alexander Kendrick, *The Nation*, Volume 139, No. 3607, 22 August 1934, 207-09; see also "Future

Veterans Organize Post Here," by Thilo Van, *Hullabaloo*, Volume XXXI, No. 29, 9 April 1936, p. 1, c. 1; "The Front Row," by Hale Boggs, *Hullabaloo*, Volume XXXII, no. 29, 23 April 1937, p. 1, c. 2; "Student Union Sets Goals At First Meeting," *Hullabaloo*, Volume XXXII, No. 12, 1 December 1936, p. 1, c. 6; and "Peace Day Scheduled Thursday," *Hullabaloo*, Volume XXX, No. 30, 16 April 1937, p. 1, c. 5. The New Orleans press also periodically covered Socialist events at Tulane; see in particular "Tulane Planning Socialist Club," *Times-Picayune*, 1 November 1932, p. 19, c. 1; "College Socialists To Conduct School," *Times-Picayune*, 26 March 1933, p. 17, c. 7; "Tulane Club Will Invite Lecturers," *Times-Picayune*, 18 October 1933, p. 12, c. 4.

CHAPTER SEVEN

1. Confidential communication. This source, who years later continued to revere the Judge, fondly remembered a favorite Perez quotation: "Black shoes are for walking on. Blacks pants are for sitting on. And black people are somewhere in between."

2. James, interview.

3. Reese Cleghorn, interview by the author, tape recording, New Orleans, La., 24 March 1999; "The Segs," by Reese Cleghorn, *Esquire*, Volume LXI, No.1, January 1964, 71-133.

4. Cleghorn, interview.

5. "Louisiana Strikes Truman Off Ballot," *The New York Times*, 11 September 1948, p. 1, c. 4; "Dixie Walkout Criticized by Party Leaders," *New Orleans States*, 15 July 1938, p. 13, c. 1; "Louisiana Votes Given to Russell," by Edgar Poe, *Times-Picayune*, 15 July 1948, p. 1, c. 7; "Louisiana Bars Truman Votes," by Ed Clinton, *Times-Picayune*, 11 September 1948, p. 1, c. 8.

6. "Louisiana Votes Given To Russell," p. 1, c. 7.

7. "Dixie Walkout Criticized by Party Leaders," p. 13, c. 1.

8. McCullough, *Truman*, 589.

9. "Louisiana Bars Truman Votes," p. 1, c. 8.

10. Ibid.

11. "Perez Challenges Long on New Constitution," *Plaquemines*

Gazette, 12 August 1950, p. l, c. 8.

12. "Seven Candidates for Governor File; Perez Loses on Constitution," *Baton Rouge Morning Advocate*, 3 October 1951, p. l, c. 4.

13. Ibid.

14. Camille Gravel, interview by the author, tape recording, New Orleans, La., 22 August 1998; "Seven Candidates for Governor File," p. l, c. 4; "Long Wins Electors Fight With Perez," *New Orleans Item*, 3 October 1951, p. 1. c. 7; "Rebuff of Elector Plan May Be Political Issue," by Edward W. Stagg, *New Orleans Item*, 7 October 1951, p. 9, c. 5; "Perez Proposal to Change Electoral Plan Defeated," by E.M. Clinton, *Times-Picayune*, 3 October 1951, p. l, c. 2.

15. "Boggs Blasts Gubernatorial Foes Long, Passman, and Spaht," *New Orleans Item*, 3 October 1951, p. 12, c. 2.

16. "Seven Candidates For Governor File," p. l, c. 4.

17. Ibid.

18. Poret, interview.

19. "Seven Candidates For Governor File," p. l, c. 4; "Louisiana Democratic Primaries Lift Ban on Negroes," *Louisiana Weekly*, 6 October 1951, p. l, c. 5; "Negroes Get Party Vote," *The New York Times*, 3 October 1951, p. 28, c. 3.

20. "K.A. Parker Files Fee For Primary," *Times-Picayune*, 13 October 1951, p. 31, c. 6; "Parker Warmly Received at Political Rally Here," *Louisiana Weekly*, 6 October 1951, p. 3, c. 7.

20. Henry Sevier, Jr., interview by the author, tape recording, New Orleans, La., 26 August 1999.

21. *Lucille May Grace vs. T. Hale Boggs*, 10-14.

22. Henry Sevier, Jr., interview by the author, tape recording, New Orleans, La., 26 August 1999.

23. *Lucille May Grace vs. T. Hale Boggs*, 10-14; "Boggs Files Reply Today On Eligibility," *New Orleans States*, 16 October 1951, p. l, c. 6; see also "Boggs Brands Charges Filed By Mis Grace as 'False, Low, and Vicious," p. l, c. 3; "Boggs Raps 'Perez Smear,'" uncited clipping in the October 1951 Gubernatorial campaign folder, Boggs Collection.

24. *Lucille May Grace vs. T. Hale Boggs*, 10-14. "Boggs Files Reply Today On Eligibility," p. 1, c. 6.

25. "Cites Boggs' Challenge of Candidate in 1950," *New Orleans States*, 17 October 1951, p. 24, c. 4.

26. "Boggs' Statement Attacked By Perez," *New Orleans Item*, 17 October 1951, p. 5, c. 5.

27. "Boggs Advisers Confer on Reply To Miss Grace," *New Orleans States*, 17 October 1951, p. 1, c. 5; "Boggs' Statement Attacked By Perez," p. 5, c. 5.

28. "Boggs' Statement Attacked By Perez," p. 5, c. 5.

29. DeLesseps S. Morrison statement, 16 October 1951; statements of congressmen Sam Rayburn, Robert Doughton, John S. Wood, Sidney Camp, Wilbur Mills, Carl Elliott, and Daniel Reed, 17 October 1951, all in the October 1951 Gubernatorial campaign folder, Boggs Collection; Frank Shelf to Matthew J. Connelly, 19 October 1951, Hale Boggs folder, Truman Presidential Library.

30. Lyndon B. Johnson to Boggs, 17 October 1951, October 1951 Gubernatorial campaign folder, Boggs Collection.

31. Reed to Boggs, 17 October 1951, October 1951 Gubernatorial campaign folder, Boggs Collection.

32. Statement of Monsignor Charles Plauche, Rabbi Julian Feibelman and the Rev. J. D. Grey, October 1951, Gubernatorial campaign folder, Boggs Collection; "Editorial: The Issue: Perez vs. The People," *New Orleans Item*, 18 October 1951, p. 1, c. 1.

33. The number of businesses along Airline Highway had more than doubled in ten years. See *Polk's New Orleans City Directory, 1954-55* (Dallas: R. L. Polk and Company, 1954), 23; *Polk's New Orleans City Directory, 1945-46* (Dallas: R. L. Polk and Company, 1945), 3; *Polk's Greater Baton Rouge Directory, 1947* (Dallas: R. L. Polk and Company, 1947), 611-12; *Polk's Greater Baton Rouge Directory, 1959* (Dallas: R. L. Polk and Company, 1959), 60-61.

34. "Boggs to Stage Fight Today on His Right to Seek Govenor's Post," *Baton Rouge Morning Advocate*, 19 October 1951, p. 1, c. 2.

35. "Let Voters Decide, Says Governor," by Alex Vuillemont, *New Orleans States*, 19 October 1951, p. 1, c. 2.

36. Ibid.

37. "Radio Today!" *Baton Rouge Morning Advocate,* 18 October 1951, p. 23, c. 1.

38. Kupperman, interview.

39. De la Houssaye, interview.

40. Gravel, interview.

41. "Full Text of Boggs Hearing," *New Orleans Item,* 21 October 1951, p. 18, c. 1.

42. "Let Voters Decide," p. 1, c. 6.

43. "Full Text of Boggs Hearing," p. 18, c. 1.

44. Ibid.

45. Ibid.

46. "Committee Dismisses Ineligibility Charge Against Hale Boggs," *Baton Rouge Morning Advocate,* 20 October 1951, p. 1, c. 8; "Attack on Boggs' Eligibility Loses at Stormy Session," by E. M. Clinton, *Times-Picayune,* 20 October 1951, p. 1, c. 4.

47. "Full Text of Boggs Hearing," p. 18, c. 1.

48. Ibid.

49. Ibid.

50. Ibid.

51. Ibid.

52. Ibid.

53. Dodd, *Peapatch Politics, 11-12, 106-08.*

54. "Full Text of Boggs Hearing," p. 18, c. 1.

55. Ibid.

56. Ibid.

57. Ibid.

58. Ibid.

59. Ibid.

60. Ibid.

61. Ibid.

62. Ibid.

63. Kupperman, interview.

64. "Full Text of Boggs Hearing," p. 18, c. 1.

65. Ibid.

66. Ibid.

67. Ibid.

68. Ibid.; De La Houssaye, interview.

69. "Full Text of Boggs Hearing," p. 18, c. 1.

70. "Committee Dismisses Ineligibility Charge Against Hale Boggs," p. 1, c. 8.

71. Ibid.

72. "Full Text of Boggs Hearing," p. 18, c. 1.

73. Ibid.

74. "Committee Dismisses Ineligibility Charge Against Hale Boggs," p. 1, c. 8.

CHAPTER EIGHT

1. "Miss Grace Files Suit In Effort to Disqualify Boggs," by E. M. Clinton, *Times-Picayune*, 21 October 1951, p. 1, c. 1; "Court to Act on Boggs Soon," *New Orleans Item*, 22 October 1951, p. 1. c. 1; "Miss Grace Sues Boggs," *New Orleans Item*, 20 October 1951, p. 1, c. 1.; "Rep. Boggs 'Welcomes' Court Hearing of Case," *New Orleans Item*, 23 October 1951, in October 1951 Gubernatorial campaign folder, Boggs Collection.

2. Political ad for Jess Johnson in the *Baton Rouge Morning Advocate*, 23 September 1951, p. 13-A, c. 1.

3. "Bar Association Picks Johnson as Judgeship Choice," *Baton Rouge Morning Advocate*, 26 September 1951, p. 1, c. 6; political ad for Johnson, *Baton Rouge Morning Advocate*, 29 September 1951, p. 8-A, c. 5.

4. "Hamlet D. May, Jess Johnson in Judgeship Race," *Baton Rouge Morning Advocate*, 21 September 1951, p. 6-A, c. 5.

5. "Johnson Wins District Judge Runoff," *Baton Rouge Morning Advocate*, 17 October 1951, p. 1, c. 7; "Johnson Takes Office as Judge," *Baton Rouge Morning Advocate*, 24 October 1951, p. 1-B, c. 6.

6. Jess Johnson, Jr., interview by the author, tape recording, New Orleans, La., 3 September 1999.

7. Ibid.

8. *Biographies of Louisiana Judges—1965 Edition* (Baton Rouge: Louisiana District Judges Association, 1965), 58-59; "Veteran 19th District Judge Succumbs in Baton Rouge," *Baton Rouge Morning Advocate*, 31 October 1975.

9. "Johnson Takes Office as Judge," p. 1-B, c. 6.

10. *Biographies of Louisiana Judges*, 58-59; for more on the Long-Sanders fisticuffs see "J.Y. and Huey Mix in Fistic Combat," *Times-Picayune*, 16 November 1927, p. 1, c. 6.

11. "Johnson Takes Office as Judge," p. 1-B, c. 6.

12. "Rep. Boggs 'Welcomes' Court Hearing of Case," October 1951 Gubernatorial campaign folder, Boggs Collection.

13. Ibid.

14. Radio transcript, 22 October 1951, October 1951 Gubernatorial campaign folder, Boggs Collection.

15. Ibid.

16. "Governor Says He Wants People To Pass on Boggs," *Baton Rouge Morning Advocate*, 22 October 1951, p. 5, c. 1.

17. Ibid.

18. "Perez Raps Boggs in Statement," *New Orleans Item,* 23 October 1951, in October 1951 Gubernatorial campaign folder, Boggs Collection.

19. "Miss Grace His Opponent Again On 'Trumanism," *New Orleans States*, 26 October 1951.

20. "Long Answers Miss Grace, Denies Boggs 'Hook-Up,'" by James McLean, 27 October 1951, uncited newspaper clip, October 1951

Gubernatorial campaign folder, Boggs Collection.

21. Ibid.

22. Ibid.

23. "Boggs Cites Anti-Commy Legislation," *Baton Rouge State-Times*, 30 October 1951, p. 1, c .1.

24. Ibid.; "Boggs' Chief Counsel Is Hospitalized," *New Orleans States*, 30 October 1951, p. 4, c. 3.

25. Barbara Rathe, interview by the author, tape recording, New Orleans, La., 20 February 1998.

26. Boggs, interview; Boggs, *Washington Through a Purple Veil*, 130.

27. Boggs, *Washington Through a Purple Veil*, 131.

28. Fred C. Dent to Boggs, 28 January 1952, 1952 Gubernatorial folder, Boggs Collection.

29. Poret, interview.

30. Johnson, interview.

31. Ibid.

32. Newlin, interview.

33. Boggs, interview; Boggs, *Washington Through a Purple Veil*, 131-32.

34. Boggs, *Washington Through a Purple Veil*, 131-32.

35. Boggs, interview.

36. *Lucille May Grace vs. T. Hale Boggs*, 31-32.

37. Johnson, interview.

38. *Lucille May Grace vs. T. Hale Boggs*, 31-32.

39. Ibid.

40. Ibid., 28.

41. Ibid., 28-29.

42. Ibid., 29-30.

43. Ibid., 30.

44. Ibid.

45. Ibid.; "Hale Boggs Quizzed On Tulane Days," *Baton Rouge State-Times*, 30 October 1951, p. 1, c. 1; "Parade of Witnesses Deny Boggs Joined Communist Group," *Baton Rouge Morning Advocate*, 30 October 1951, p. 1, c. 6.

46. *Lucille May Grace vs. T. Hale Boggs*, 31-32.

47. Ibid., 37.

48. Ibid., 38.

49. Ibid.

50. "Hale Boggs Quizzed On Tulane Days," p. 1, c. 1.

51. *Lucille May Grace vs. T. Hale Boggs*, 45.

52. Ibid.

53. Ibid., 45-46.

54. Ibid.

55. Ibid.

56. Ibid., 54.

57. Ibid., 55.

58. Ibid., 60.

59. Ibid.

60. Ibid., 61.

61. Ibid.

62. "Army Battalion Joins in Search for Missing Boy," *Baton Rouge Morning Advocate*, 30 October 1951, p. 8-A, c. 1. More than a year later the boy's body was found in a shallow grave near the same country road where his mother was murdered; see "Little Boy's Skeleton To Murder, Suicide," *New Orleans Item*, 16 November 1952, p. 6, c. 5; "Three Men Draw Life Sentences in New Roads Rape," *Baton Rouge Morning Advocate*, 30 October 1951, p. 1, c. 5.

63. "Stargazing," *Baton Rouge Morning Advocate*, 30 October 1951, p. 8-A, c. 1.

64. "Hale Boggs Quizzed On Tulane Days," p. 1, c. 1.

65. *Lucille May Grace vs. T. Hale Boggs*, 169.

66. Spaht, interview.

67. For more on Ivor Trapolin's anti-Communist activities, see Trapolin to Leon R. Maxwell, 24 October 1947; Maxwell to Trapolin, 25 October 1947, the Maxwell Collection, Box 3, Folder 6, Letters, 1944-1946, Special Collections, Howard-Tilton Memorial Library. See also "N.O. lawyer, civic activist Ivor Trapolin dies at 78," *Times-Picayune*, 8 December 1996, p. B-3, c. 2.

68. *Lucille May Grace vs. T. Hale Boggs*, 176.

69. Ibid.

70. Ibid.

71. Ibid., 176-77.

72. Ibid., 177.

73. Ibid., 177-78.

74. Ibid., 178-79.

75. Ibid., 183.

76. Ibid., 194; "Boggs Cites Anti-Commy Legislation," p. 1, c. 1; "Says Boggs Hampered Red Trade," *New Orleans States*, 30 October 1951, p. 1, c. 4.

77. Ibid., 196-97.

78. Ibid., 197.

79. Ibid.

80. Ibid., 197-98.

81. Ibid., 200.

82. Ibid., 209.

83. Ibid., 216-17.

84. Ibid., 232.

85. Ibid.

86. Ibid., 234.

87. "Boggs Decision Scheduled Today," *Times-Picayune*, 1 November 1951, p. 5, c. 1.

88. Ibid.

89. "Court Dismisses Grace Suit to Knock Boggs Out of Race," *Times-Picayune*, 2 November 1951, p. 4, c. 3; "Court of Appeal Dismisses Boggs Suit," *Plaquemines Gazette*, 17 November 1951, p. 1, c. 1; "Dismisses Suit to Bar Boggs," *New Orleans Item*, 2 November 1951, p. 1, c. 4.

90. "Miss Grace Appeals To High Court," *New Orleans Item*, 2 November 1951, p. 1, c. 8; "Court Dismisses Grace Suit to Knock Boggs Out of Race," p. 4, c. 3.

91. "Court Dismisses Grace Suit to Knock Boggs Out of Race," p. 4, c. 3.

92. Ibid., "Appeal to High Court Expected in Boggs Case," *Baton Rouge Morning Advocate*, 2 November 1951, p. 1, c. 2. Despite Perez's high profile role in the case against Boggs, it was Grace who received most of the negative publicity after Judge Johnson's ruling; see in particular "Suit Against Boggs Take to Supreme Court by Miss Grace After Dismissal by Johnson," by Margaret Dixon, *Baton Rouge Morning Advocate*, 4 November 1951, p. 7, c. 1; "Significant Features of Miss Grace's Suit," by Edward W. Stagg, *New Orleans Item*, 4 November 1951, p. 8, c. 2.

93. "Louisiana Side-Show," by Irving Ferman, *New Republic*, Volume 126, No. 3, 21 January 1952, p. 13, c. 1.

CHAPTER NINE

1. Boggs, interview.

2. Ibid.

3. For the history of Lucille May Grace vs. T. Hale Boggs, see summary of briefs filed in the Court of Appeal, First Circuit, Number 3,483, and the Supreme Court of Louisiana, number 40,597. See also *Southern Reporter*, Volume 55, So. 2nd (St. Paul, Minnesota: West Publishing, 1951), 45-51.

4. Transcript of speech, 16 November 1951, in November 1951 Gubernatorial campaign folder, Boggs Collection.

5. Ibid.

6. Ibid.

7. Ibid.

8. Ibid.

9. "Boggs Stresses Progress Goals," *Times-Picayune,* 21 November 1951, p. 12, c. 4.

10. "Platform Cited in Boggs Speech," *Times-Picayune,* 27 November 1951, p. 12, c. 1.

11. Uncited newspaper clipping from the *Times-Picayune,* no date given, but in the November 1951 Gubernatorial campaign folder, Boggs Collection.

12. "Boggs Likened to Alger Hiss in Perez Blast," *New Orleans States,* 15 November 1951, p. 1, c. 2.

13. Edward F. Haas, *DeLesseps S. Morrion and the Image of Reform—New Orleans Politics, 1946-61* (Baton Rouge: Louisiana State University Press, 1974), 184-86; John H. Davis, *Mafia Kingfish—Carlos Marcello and the Assassination of John F. Kennedy* (New York: McGraw-Hill, 1989), 56-57, 58-61.

14. Haas, *DeLesseps S. Morrison,* 187.

15. Mark T. Carleton, *Politics and Punishment—The History of the Louisiana State Penal System* (Baton Rouge: Louisiana State University Press, 1971), 153-54.

16. Liva Baker, *The Second Battle of New Orleans—The Hundred-Year Struggle to Integrate the Schools* (New York: Harper Collins Publishers, 1996), 142-43, 175-76.

17. Clarence John Laughlin, *Ghosts Along the Mississippi—An Essay in the Poetic Interpretation of Louisiana's Plantation Architecture* (New York: Bonanze Books, 1951).

18. Spaht, interview.

19. "Long, Miss Grace Loose Barrages in Talk at Fair," New Orleans States, 8 October 1951, p. 5, c. 1.

20. Ibid., "Louisiana Road Show," *Life,* Volume 31, No.22, 26 November 1951, 87-95.

21. "Russell Long," by Liz Galtney, *Gambit Weekly*, 11 November 1986, p. 15, c. 2.

22. Boggs, interview.

23. "Black Cat, Uncle Earl, Edwin, and the Kingfish—The Wit of Modern Louisiana Politics," by Edward F. Haas, *Louisiana History*, Volume XXIX, No. 3, Summer 1988, 217.

24. Gillis, interview.

25. Boggs, interview.

26. Boggs, *Washington Through a Purple Veil*, 150.

27. Brown, interview.

28. Hebert, *The Last of the Titans*, 270.

29. Richard B. McCaughan, *Socks on a Rooster—Louisiana's Earl K. Long* (Baton Rouge: Claitor's Publishing, 1967), 134-35; Perry H. Howard, *Political Tendencies in Louisiana* (Baton Rouge: Louisiana State University Press, 1971), 282.

30. Boggs, *Washington Through a Purple Veil*, 132; McCaughan, Socks on a Rooster, 134-35; Howard, *Political Tendencies in Louisiana*, 282.

31. Clipping, no headline, *New Orleans Item*, 9 December 1951, December 1951 Gubernatorial campaign folder, Boggs Collection.

32. Ibid.

33. "Says Perez Has Dumped Miss Grace," *New Orleans Item*, 5 December 1951, p. 1, c. 4; "Hint Three Withdrawals In Race for Governorship," *New Orleans States*, 11 November 1951, p. 1, c. 2; "Perez Coy on Formal 'Mac' OK," *New Orleans Item*, 11 January 1952, p. 1, c. 1; "Perez Abandons Support of Miss Grace, to Back McLemore," *Baton Rouge Morning Advocate*, 12 January 1952, p. 1, c. 1.

34. "Perez Abandons Support of Miss Grace, to Back McLemore," p. 1, c. 1.

35. Marshall, interview.

36. Gillis, interview.

37. "Spaht Sees Big Lead in Primary," *Times-Picayune*, 8 Janaury 1952, p. 9, c. 4.

38. "The Louisiana Governor's Race," by Lucille May Grace, *New Orleans Item*, 30 December 1951, p. 26, c. 5.

39. Ibid.

40. Ibid.

41. Poret, interview.

42. "Grace Initerary Is Announced," *New Orleans States*, 9 January 1952, p. 2, c. 6.

43. "Boggs Says He Has Supported Aid to Farmers," *Baton Rouge Morning Advocate*, 5 January 1952, p. 5-A, c. 4; "Absentee Balloting Is Stressed," *Times-Picayune*, 4 January 1952, p. 19, c. 3; "Best Bet to Beat Long—Boggs," *Times-Picayune*, 12 January 1952, p. 9, c. 6; "Has Run on Merits—Spaht," *Times-Picayune*, 14 January 1952, p. 15, c. 6.

44. "Miss Dent Reported Ill," *New Orleans Item*, 13 January 1952, p. 4, c. 4; Dent, interview.

45. Poret, interview.

46. Ibid.

47. "Victory Seen by Boggs and Campaigners," *New Orleans States*, 15 January 1952, p. 2, c. 5.

48. "No Grey Hair For Boggs Or Either His Wife," by Thomas Sancton, *New Orleans Item*, 16 January 1952, p. 35, c. 3; "Boggs Predicts Victory At Rally in Auditorium," *New Orleans Item*, 14 January 1952, p. 7, c. 5.

49. "Parish Vote in Governor's Race," New Orleans States, 17 January 1952, p. 8, c. 2.

50. Ibid.

51. Ibid.

52. Dent, interview.

53. Marshall, interview.

54. "Days of Grace," by Hermann Deutsch, New Orleans Item, 24 December 1957, p. 7, c. 1.

55. Dent, interview.

56. Grace to Hebert, 8 April 1952, Lucille May Grace folder, Hebert Collection.

57. Ibid.

58. Fred C. Dent to Boggs, 28 January 1952, January 1952 Gubernatorial folder, Boggs Collection.

59. Marshall, interview; Grace to Boggs, 27 February 1952, Lucille May Grace folder, Boggs Collection.

60. Grace to Boggs, 27 February 1952, Lucille May Grace folder, Boggs Collection.

61. Ibid.

62. Ibid.

63. Ibid.

64. Ibid.

65. Boggs to Grace, 4 March 1952, Lucille May Grace folder, Boggs Collection.

66. Boggs, interview.

67. Ellen Bryan Moore, 30 April 1952, April 1952 Personal Correspondence folder, Boggs Collection.

68. Moore, interview.

69. James, "The Majority Leader," 46.

70. Boggs, interview.

71. Hale Boggs, interviewed by Charles T. Morrissey, 10 May 1964, Oral History Collection, John F. Kennedy Presidential Library, Boston, Massachusetts.

72. Ibid.

73. Ibid.

74. Boggs, interview.

75. Ibid.

76. Thomas Furlow to Boggs, 9 November 1951 and Furlow to Boggs, 4 November 1952, Leander Perez folder, Boggs Collection.

77. Furlow to Boggs, 9 December 1951.

78. Boggs to Furlow, 22 January 1953. For the run of the often one-sided correspondence between Boggs and Furlow, see Furlow to

Boggs, 1 March 1952, 3 March 1952, 19 March 1952, 26 April 1952, 24 September 1952, 4 October 1952, 4 November 1952, 24 November 1952, 13 January 1953, and 20 January 1953; Boggs to Furlow, 6 March 1952, 28 April 1952, 2 October 1952, 20 October 1952, 18 November 1952, and 22 January 1953; all in the Leander Perez folder, Boggs Collection.

79. Jacob Morrison to Boggs, 23 November 1951, Perez folder, Boggs Collection.

80. Morrison to Boggs, 16 March 1952, Perez folder, Boggs Collection.

81. J. Rayburn Monroe to Boggs, 18 March 1952, Perez folder, Boggs Collection.

82. Ibid.

83. Boggs to Mabel C. Simmons, 9 February 1952; Simmons to Boggs, 6 February 1952; Boggs to Wilfred C. Gilbert, 9 February 1952, Perez folder, Boggs Collection.

84. J. Ben Meyer, Sr., to Boggs, 25 January 1952; see also Meyer to Boggs, 12 January 1952, 3 February 1952, and 12 February 1952, Perez folder, Boggs Collection.

85. Meyer to Boggs, 25 January 1952.

86. Boggs to Jesse H. Donaldson, 28 February 1952; Boggs to James W. Barr, 19 March 1952; Boggs to the Rev. Vincent O'Connell, 6 March 1952; Perez folder, Boggs Collection.

87. Wood statement, 17 October 1951, October 1951 Gubernatorial campaign folder, Boggs Collection.

88. HUAC joint statement, 21 March 1952, copy sent to Boggs; Boggs to Wood, 26 June 1952, Personal Correspondence folder, June 1952, Boggs Collection.

89. Roy H. Cauley to Boggs, 24 January 1952; James M. Donaldson to Boggs, 5 March 1952; Furlow to Boggs, 19 March 1952; Perez folder, Boggs Collection.

90. Boggs to J. Rayburn Monroe and Jacob Morrison, 1 April 1952, Perez folder, Boggs Collection.

91. Ibid.

92. Ibid.

93. James, "The Majority Leader," 46.

94. Tullis to Boggs, 27 March 1952; Boggs to Tullis, 28 March 1952, Perez folder, Boggs Collection.

95. John Bartlow Martin, *Adlai Stevenson and the World—The Life of Adlai E. Stevenson* (New York: Doubleday, 1972), 202. For more on the Boggs-Stevenson relationship, see the Hale Boggs folder in the Adlai E. Stevenson Papers, Seeley C. Mudd Manuscript Library, University Archives, Princeton University, Princeton, New Jersey.

96. William "Fishbait" Miller, *Fishbait—The Memories of the Congressional Doorkeeper* (Englewood, Cliffs, New Jersey: Prentice Hall, 1977), 220. See also "Rep. Hale Boggs Gets a Surprise," by Isabelle Shelton, *Washington Star*, 17 February 1968; "Boggses Toss a Big Party," by Betty Beale, *Washington Star*, 5 May 1967; "St. Fiarca Clears the All Again for Hale and Lindy," by Isabelle Shelton, *Washington Star*, 23 May 1969, all in the Hale Boggs folder, the Washingtoniana Collection, the District of Columbia Public Library.

97. "St. Fiarca Clears the All Again for Hale and Lindy," no page number given, Washingtoniana Collection.

98. "Miss Grace to End 35 Years With State Land Office Today," *Baton Rouge Morning Advocate*, 23 May 1952, p. 16-A, c. 1.

99. Grace to Hebert, 8 April 1952.

100. Grace to Hebert, 3 June 1953.

101. Grace to Hebert, 23 June 1953.

102. Marshall, interview.

103. Grace to Hebert, 23 June 1953.

104. Dodd, *Peapatch Politics*, 233.

105. Grace to Hebert, 25 April 1955.

106. Ibid.

107. Dent, interview.

108. "Three Runoffs May Be Entered," *Times-Picayune*, 19 January

1956, p. 46, c. 4; "Grace in Old Job," *Baton Rouge Morning Advocate*, 13 May 1956, p. 3-B, c. l; Poret, interview.

109. Grace to Fred Dent, Sr., and Jr., 21 May 1957, Lucille May Grace papers, Special Collections, Tulane University.

110. Ibid.

111. Ibid.; 23 May 1957, Grace to the Dents.

112. Ibid.

113. Ibid.

114. "Land Register Dies In Capital," *Times-Picayune*, 23 December 1957, p. 1, c. 2; "Long Illness Claims Life of Lucille Grace," *Baton Rouge Morning Advocate*, 23 December 1957, p. 1, c. 8.

115. "Funeral Services Held Here for Lucille May Grace," by James McLean, *Baton Rouge Morning Advocate*, 24 December 1957, p. 1, c. 2.

116. Ibid.

117. "Lucille May Grace," *St. Bernard Voice*, 17 December 1957, p. 1, c. 3.

118. "Days of Grace," p. 7, c. 1.

119. "Funeral Services Held Here for Lucille May Grace," p. 1, c. 2.

120. "State Property Tax Assessments Are Again Coming in for Criticism," by Margaret Dixon, *Baton Rouge Morning Advocate*, 29 December 1957, p. 5-B, c. l.

121. Marshall, interview.

122. Dent, interview.

123. Grace to the Dents, 23 May 1957.

124. Ibid.

CHAPTER TEN

1. Baker, *The Second Battle of New Orleans*, 394–409; Fairclough, *Race & Democracy*, 244; uncited newspaper clippings in the School Integration 1960 folder, DeLesseps S. Morrison Collection, Louisiana Division, New Orleans Public Library.

2. Conaway, *The Judge*, 104-05.

3. "Perez Honored At Ceremonies," by Jay Hall, *Times-Picayune*, 13 December 1954, p. 1, c. 4; "Desegregation Blasted By DA Perez at Dinner," *New Orleans States*, 13 December 1954, p. 6, c. 5.

4. Unsigned correspondence in the 1955 Correspondence folder of the Leander Perez Collection, Louisiana Division, the New Orleans Public Library. The collection is an uneven but fascinating look into the segregationist forces that came to the fore in the mid-1950s, most of whom had intimate connections to Perez. See also Wilton P. Mouton to Perez, 18 October 1954, Charles Handle to Perez, 15 October 1954, and Melvin John to Perez, 14 October 1954. Typical of the response Perez engendered among his followers for his anti-civil rights stands was the letter from Colvin Todd and Francis Ward of Tallulah, Louisiana, who wrote: "We are greatly relieved knowing that a man of your brilliant legal talent and ability to fight has taken the firm and correct stand in the recent non-segregation issue." Todd and Ward to Perez, 26 May 1954.

5. Citizen's Council folder, Perez Collection; Neil R. McMillan, *The Citizen's Council—Organized Resistance to the Second Reconstruction, 1954-64* (Chicago: University of Illinois Press, 1971), 59-72; Numan V. Bartley, *The Rise of Massive Resistance—Race and Politics in the South During the 1950s* (Baton Rouge: Louisiana State University Press, 1969), 82-107. When Martin Luther King, Jr., visited New Orleans in early 1957, Perez was aghast, remarking: "Can you imagine bringing in that fellow-travelling Negro agitator in here, a rabble rouser who will stir up our Negroes?" prompting the black *Louisiana Weekly* to respond: "Since when do we Negroes belong to Perez or any of his cohorts?" "Who are Perez 'Negroes'?" *Louisiana Weekly*, 16 February 1957, p. 11, c. 1; "Carry on In Christian Way for Civil Rights Urges Rev. King," *Louisiana Weekly*, 9 February 1957, p. 1, c. 2.

6. Fairclough, *Race & Democracy*, 244; Baker, *The Second Battle of New Orleans*, 415.

7. Baker, *The Second Battle of New Orleans*, 415.

8. "The Battle of New Orleans," *Time*, Volume 76, No. 24; 12 December 1960, 20-21.

9. Fairclough, *Race & Democracy*, 202-03.

10. *The Ends of the Earth—Plaquemines Parish, Louisiana* (New Orleans: Louisiana Center for NorthAmerican Media Company, 1982), produced by Louis Alvarez and Andrew Kolker, 60 minutes.

11. "Unpledged Electors of States' Rights Party To Give The South A Chance To Save The Nation," *Plaquemines Gazette*, 30 September 1960, p. 1, c. 1. See also Bennet J. Voorhis to Mayor Morrison, 9 August 1960, and Ronald W. Ewing to Perez, 15 August 1960, on Perez's third-party efforts, 1960 Presidential Election folder, Morrison Collection; Boggs to Robert F. Kennedy, 5 August 1960, Mayor Morrison to John F. Kennedy, 12 August 1960, 1960 Presidential Election folder, Boggs Collection; "Free Electors Drive Begins," *Times-Picayune*, 3 August 1960, p. 4, c. 5.

12. "3 Racists Excommunicated By Louisiana Archbishop," by Claude Sitton, *New York Times*, 17 April 1962; Henry Cibirac, Jr., to Monsignor Charles J. Plauche, 5 July 1962, Plauche memo on "Perezbyterianism," 8 May 1962, both in the Correspondence File, Archbishop John Patrick Cody, 1961-64, No. 23, Catholic Council of Human Relations Collection, Amistat Collection, Tulane University; "Plaquemines Ready for Demonstrators," *Plaquemines Gazette*, 3 April 1964, p. 1, c. 6; "Twisted Dream," by Jim Amoss, *Times-Picayune*, 11 July 1982, Section 7, p. 1, c. 1; *The Ends of the Earth*.

13. *The Ends of the Earth.*

14. Ibid.

15. Boggs notes on Perez TV show, 18 September 1963, Perez folder, 1963 Congressional Box, Boggs Collection; see also "CBS to Explore Clash Between Political Boss Perez, Priest," *Louisiana Weekly*, 14 September 1963, p. 1, c. 5; "What So Ever," by Juanita Sendker, *Plaquemines Gazette*, 4 October 1963, p. 6, c. 1.

16. "House Votes 217-212 To 'Pack" Rules Unit As Rayburn Urges," by Edgar Poe, *Times-Picayune*, 1 February 1961, p. 1, c. 6; Bruce J. Dierenfeld, *Keeper of the Rules—Congressman Howard W. Smith of Virginia* (Charlottesville: University Press of Virginia, 1987), 176-85. In early 1961 Boggs received more than 1,300 letters urging him to vote against expanding the Rules Committee. After his favorable vote, the local response was chilling: "Sorry to see you have become a 'Yes' man for President Kennedy and Sam Rayburn," wrote Julie Schmidt of New Orleans on 1 February 1961 in a typical correspondence.

"Have 925 votes in family 'if' you desire to run again." Schmidt to Boggs, 1 February 1961, Rules Committee folder, Boggs Collection.

17. "Traitors," *Plaquemines Gazette*, 10 February 1961, p. 1, c. 5.

18. "Victory With Plurality Vote For Wallace Is Seen In November Presidential Campaign," *Plaquemines Gazette*, 28 June 1968, p. 1, c. 1; Wallace Donors Led by Perezes," by James R. Polk, *Washington Star*, 10 May 1972, p. A-18, c. 1, in Perez folder, Washingtoniana Collection; see also interview by the author with Stephen Lescher, New Orleans, tape recording, 16 March 1999.

19. Toledano, interview.

20. Confidential communication.

21. Gillis, interview.

22. Kenneth McLeod to Boggs, 17 March 1962; Paul Martin to Boggs, 21 March 1962. The 1962 Democratic Congressional primary in New Orleans also saw the reappearance of the same issue of the *Federationist* from the 1951 gubernatorial campaign, accusing Boggs of being a Communist. "This stuff was originally written by our Plaquemines friend," Boggs told Louisiana labor leader Victor Bussie after seeing a copy of the paper. But this time the tactic appeared to backfire: a group of Loyola students, repelled by the tactics of another era, sent Boggs a petition decrying the paper's charges. Boggs to Bussie, 19 April 1962; Loyola student petition to Boggs, 1 May 1962; both in 1962 Congressional campaign folder, Boggs Collection. As a factor in New Orleans elections, Perez may have been a wash. According to one survey, 23 percent of respondents said they would automatically support anyone Perez backed, while another 26 percent said they would be just as likely to join his opposition. Voter Opinion Study of the Democratic Race for Congress in the Second District of Louisiana, June 4-14, 1962, Belden Associates, 1962 Congressional Campaign folder, Boggs Collection.

23. Boggs, interview by Morrissey.

24. "The Courage Of His Convictions: Hale Boggs and Civil Rights," by Scott E. Balius (Tulane Univesity graduate thesis, 1990), 91-93.

25. Eustis, interview.

26. "Put LBJ To The Test Now Before Election, Urges Judge Perez In A Television Interview," *Plaquemines Gazette*, 21 August 1964, p. 1, c. 1.

27. Balius, "The Courage of His Convictions," 119; "Lindy Boggs Quits Congress To Close Ranks With Her Two Remarkable Daughters, One Gravely Ill With Cancer," 63; *Hale Boggs—The Man, the Mission, and the Mystery*, produced by Lisa Martin (WLAE-TV, New Orleans, 1997), 60 minutes.

28. Hale Boggs.

29. *Voting Rights: Hearings Before The Committee On The Judiciary, United States Senate, Eighty-Ninth Congress, 1st Session, Part I* (Washington: Government Printing Office, 1965), 461, 324.

30. Ibid, 544; see also "Judge Perez Exposes Proposed Civil Rights Bill As Red Pattern," *Plaquemines Gazette*, 2 April 1965, p. 1, c. 1; "The Segregationists' Segregationist," by Mary McGrory, *Washington Star*, 31 March 1965, Perez folder, Washingtoniana Collection.

31. "Leander Perez Won't Speak At Bogalusa Rally on Friday," *Baton Rouge Morning Advocate*, 6 May 1965, p. 8-G, c. 1; "Perez Decides Against Talk at Bogalusa Rally," *State-Times*, 5 May 1965, p. 48, c. 6.

32. Copy of speeches given on 3 June 1965 in Congress from the *Congressional Record*, Charles R. Maloney to Boggs, 25 May 1965; both in the Perez 1965 folder, Boggs Collection.

33. Boggs to Maloney, 28 May 1965, Perez 1965 folder, Boggs Collection.

34. "Hale Boggs and Civil Rights: A Case Study of a Southern Moderate," by Jonathan Doherty (Tulane University graudate thesis, 1983), 64-65.

35. *Congressional Record, 89th Congress, First Session*, 9 July 1965 (Washington: Govenment Printing Office, 1965), 16221-22.

36. Ibid.

37. Ibid.

38. Ibid.

39. Ibid.

40. "Boggs Reveals Favorable Reaction to His Speech," by Edgar Poe, *Times-Picayune*, 20 July 1965, Section 2, p. 2, c. 3.

41. Ibid.

42. "Chalin Perez Takes Over Post of Father With Legacy of Good Government," *Plaquemines Gazette,* 8 December 1967, p. 1, c. 1.

43. Ibid.

44. "Thousands Mourn Death of Judge Perez," *Plaquemines Gazette,* 28 March 1969, p. 1, c. 1; Conaway, *Judge,* 183-88.

45. *Congressional Record, 91st Congress, First Session,* 20 March 1969 (Washington: Government Printing Office, 1969) 7039.

46. Cowan, interview.

47. Nunguesser, interview.

48. Newlin, interview; "On Tape, Nixon Sounds Off On Women, Blacks, Cabinet," by George Lardner, Jr., *Washington Post,* 29 December 1998, p. 3, c. 1. In his study of congressional leadership, scholar Robert L. Peabody noted that when Boggs in early 1971 fought to become the next Majority Leader, many of his colleagues wondered, as one remarked, whether he possessed "sufficient emotional stability to undertake the job." Speaking on the guarantee of anonymity, another member told Peabody: "My normal inclination would have been to support Boggs, but his performance the last year or two—drinking or some sort of carrying on—convinced me he shouldn't be Majority Leader," *Peabody, Leadership in Congress—Stability, Succession, and Change* (Boston: Little, Brown and Company, 1976), 157-58. In a lengthy examination of the Majority Leader battle, writer Larry L. King noted that at times Boggs "might appear wild or foolish: he had a high appreciation for good whiskey, and even the best brands sometimes loosen tongues or inhibitions," "The Road to Leadership," by Larry L. King, *Harper's,* Volume 242, No. 1453 (June 1971), 42. See also "Boggs Accused of 'Scene' at Dinner," by Clark Hoyt, *Memphis Commercial Appeal,* 22 May 1971, p. 24, c. 1.

49. "On Tape, Nixon Sounds Off On Women, Blacks, Cabinet," p. 3, c. 1.

50. *Citizens Look at Congress, Ralph Nader Congressional Project,* entry on Hale Boggs written by Molly Shryer (Washington: Grossman Publishers, 1972), 1.

51. Memorial Services, Hale Boggs, Late a Representative from Louisiana (Washington: Government Printing Office, 1973), 21.

52. "Alaskans Search, Pray," by Alan Campbell, *Anchorage Daily Times*, 17 October 1972, p. 1, c. 7; "Doubts Plane Equipped," *Anchorage Daily Times*, 3 November 1972, p. 1, c. 4; "Report on Hale Boggs Downed Plane Disclosed," by Glenn R. Simpson, *Roll Call*, 3 August 1992, p. 3, c. 1; Federal Bureau of Investigation internal memoes on Boggs' disappearance, 17 October 1972 to 20 December 1972, serial numbers 11 5368-1 to 115368-12, a copy of the FBI material in the author's posssession.

53. "Family, Friends Say Farewell to Boggs," by Allan Katz, *New Orleans States-Item*, 6 January 1973, p. 1, c. 1; "Nation's Leaders Honor Hale Boggs," *Times-Picayune*, 5 January 1973, p. 20, c. 1; "Agnew, Mrs. Nixon and Johnsons Attend a Mass for Boggs," *New York Times*, 5 Janaury 1973, p. 12, c. 1.

54. "Attacks Against Perez Empire in Louisiana," by Douglas Martin, *New York Times*, 11 May 1981, p. 15, c. 3; "Freedom Flourishes After Judge Perez," by James O'Byrne, *Times-Picayune*, 11 March 1984, p. 25, c. 1; "Louisiana Family Fights the Country It Once Ruled," *New York Times*, 11 November 1984, p. 65, c. 1; "New Day Dawns in Plaquemines," by Michael Perlstein, *Times-Picayune*, 12 December 1987, p. 1, c. 2; "Perez Park's Ruin Reflects Judge's Fall," by Michael Perlstein, *Times-Picayune*, 20 November 1988, p. B-1, c. 5; "Contra Non Valentem: The Family of the Late Leander Perez Cannot Hide Behind the Passage of Time," by Joyce Cossich, *Loyola Law Review*, Volume XXXIII, No. 3, Fall 1988, 1099-1120.

55. "Perez Park's Ruin Reflects Judge's Fall," p. B-1, c. 5.

56. "Boggs Building Bill Is Approved," *Times-Picayune*, 30 December 1973, p. 2, c. 3; "Alaskan Peak Will Bear Name of Rep. Hale Boggs," by Edgar Poe, *Times-Picayune*, 22 July 1976, p. 22, c. 1; "Hale Boggs Memorialized For 'A Life Lived So Well,'" by Francis X. Clines, *New York Times*, 20 May 1981, p. 16, c. 1.

57. Clifford, "Lindy Boggs Quits Congress To Close Ranks With Her Two Remarkable Daughters, One Gravely Ill With Cancer," 63; "King of the Hill," by Carl Bernstein, *Vanity Fair*, No. 451, March 1998, 174-88.

58. "Capitalizing Cokie," by Mark Lorando, *TV Focus*, 11 April 1993, p. 7, c. 1.

59. Fairclough, *Race & Democracy*, 324-25; "Repeal That anti-Red law, please," by Jack Welsh, Times-Picayune, 5 January 2000, p. B-7, c. 1.

60. "Judge Agrees With ACLU's Challenge on Communist Law," by Susan Finch, *Times-Picayune*, 7 October 2000, p. 4, c. 1.

61. Marshall, interview; Dent, interview.

62. James, "The Majority Leader," 46. Only three years before Boggs made his comments to Rosemary James he called Perez "entirely evil" in an interview with author Robert Sherill, and cast doubts on the role Perez played saving Huey Long during the famous 1929 impeachment hearings. "It's a lie, a myth," Boggs contended, contrary to available evidence, prompting Sherill to write: "Of course, Hale Boggs hates Perez." Sherill would later contend that Perez's Communist charges against Boggs "knocked Boggs out of the runoff (he ran a strong third) and very likely out of the governorship; Boggs has always felt so, at least, and most of the evidence seems to support his wistfulness." Sherill, *Gothic Politics in the Deep South* (New York: Grossman Publishers, 1968), 33, 12, 25.

63. Desk drawer contents folder, Boggs Collection.

64. Perez folder, Boggs Collection.

65. James, "The Majority Leader," 46.

Index

277